A History of
British Costume

Henry VII.
From an original portrait in the Sutherland Clarendon, vide page 219.

A History of
British Costume

From Ancient Times to the Eighteenth Century

J. R. Planché

SENATE

A History of British Costume

First published by Charles Knight in 1834

This edition published in 2001 by Senate,
an imprint of Senate Press Limited,
133 High Street, Teddington,
Middlesex TW11 8HH, United Kingdom

ISBN 1 85958 550 7

Printed and bound in Guernsey by
The Guernsey Press Co Ltd

CONTENTS.

CHAPTER I.

		Page
INTRODUCTION	. . . .	xi
List of Authorities quoted	. . . . .	xiv
Ancient British Period	. . . . . .	1
Roman-British Period, A. D. 78—400	. . . .	14

CHAPTER II.

Anglo-Saxon Period, A. D. 450—1016 16

CHAPTER III.

Anglo-Danish Period, A. D. 1016—1041 41

CHAPTER IV.

Reigns of Edward the Confessor and Harold II., A. D. 1042—
1066 50

CHAPTER V.

Reign of William the Conqueror, A. D. 1066—1087 . . 53

CHAPTER VI.

Reigns of William II., Henry I., and Stephen, A. D. 1087—
1154 66

CHAPTER VII.

Reigns of Henry II., Richard I., and John, A. D. 1154—1216 78

CHAPTER VIII.

Reign of Henry III., A. D. 1216—1272 92

CHAPTER IX.

Reigns of Edward I. and II.; Edward I., A. D. 1272—1307 103
——————————————— Edward II., A. D. 1307—1327 120

CHAPTER X.

Reign of Edward III., A. D. 1327—1377 . . . 127

CHAPTER XI.

Reign of Richard II., A. D. 1377—1399 149

CHAPTER XII.

Reigns of Henry IV. and V.; Henry IV. A. D. 1399—1411 170
——————————————— Henry V. A. D. 1411—1422 181

CHAPTER XIII.

Page

Reigns of Henry VI. and Edward IV.; Henry VI., A. D.
1420—1461 190
——————————————————— Edward IV., A. D.
1461—1483 199

CHAPTER XIV.

Reigns of Edward V. and Richard III., A. D. 1483—1485 . 211

CHAPTER XV.

Reign of Henry VII., A. D. 1485—1509 219

CHAPTER XVI.

Reigns of Henry VIII., Edward VI., and Mary; Henry VIII.
A. D. 1509—1547 233
——— Edward VI., A. D. 1547—1553, and Mary, A. D.
1553—1558 251

CHAPTER XVII.

Reign of Elizabeth, A.D. 1558—1603 255

CHAPTER XVIII.

Reign of James I., A. D. 1603—1625 274

CHAPTER XIX.

Reign of Charles I. and Commonwealth, A. D. 1625—1660 282

CHAPTER XX.

Reign of Charles II., A. D. 1660—1685 294

CHAPTER XXI.

Reigns of James II. and William and Mary, A.D. 1685—1702 303

CHAPTER XXII.

Costume of the Eighteenth Century, from the Accession of
Anne to the present Period 310
Reign of Queen Anne, A. D. 1702—1714 . . 310 & 318
——— George I., A. D. 1714—1727 . . . 311 & 321
——— George II., A. D. 1727—1760 . . . 312 & 321
——— George III., 1760 . . . . . 313 & 322

CHAPTER XXIII.

National Costume of Scotland 332

CHAPTER XXIV.

National Costume of Ireland 352

ILLUSTRATIONS.

No.		Page
1.	PORTRAIT of Henry VII.	facing Title
2.	Ancient British weapons of bone and flint	1
3.	British weapons of bronze, in their earliest and improved states	3
4.	Bronze coating of an ancient British shield.	5
5.	Ornaments and patterns of the ancient Britons	10
6.	Bas-relief found at Autun	12
7.	Druidical ornaments	13
8.	Metal coating of an ancient Roman-British shield	15
9.	Anglo-Saxon weapons and ornaments	16
10.	Civil costume of the Anglo-Saxons	22
11.	Jewel of Alfred, found at Athelney	26
12.	The military habits of the Anglo-Saxons	28
13.	Anglo-Saxon mantle, caps, and weapons	33
14.	Anglo-Saxon females	34
15.	St. Dunstan	39
16.	Abbot Elfnoth, and St. Augustine, Archbishop of Canterbury	ib.
17.	Canute and his queen Algyfe	41
18.	Seal of Edward the Confessor	50
19.	Harold II.	51
20.	William I. and attendants	53
21.	William I. and two Normans	57
22.	Helmets, hauberks, a sword, and a gonfanon	ib.
23.	Sicilian bronzes and Norman shields	60
24.	Anglo-Norman ladies	63
25.	A bishop of the close of the 11th century	64
26.	Royal habits of the commencement of the 12th century	66
27.	Habits of the commencement of the 12th century	67
28.	William Rufus; Richard, Constable of Chester; Milo Fitzwalter, Constable of England; Statue of St. Michael	71
29.	Female costume of the reigns of Rufus and Henry I.	75
30.	Arms of the family of De Hastings	76
31.	Effigies of Henry II. and his queen Eleanor; Richard I. and his queen Berengaria; and of King John	79
32.	Seal of Henry II.	83
33.	Seals of Richard I.	84
34.	Effigies of Geoffrey de Magnaville, Earl of Essex, and of William Longespee, Earl of Salisbury	86

No.	Page
35. Mitres from the tomb of King John 91
36. Effigy of Henry III. 92
37. Effigy, surrounded by helmets, &c. of the reign of Henry III. 97
38. Effigy of Aveline, Countess of Lancaster, and two female heads of the 13th century 99
39. Red hat of the cardinals 102
40. Regal costume of the reign of Edward I. . . . 103
41. Costume of the close of the 13th century . . . 105
42. Civil costume of the reign of Edward I. . . . 106
43. Edward Crouchback, Earl of Lancaster; Brass, in Gorleston Church, Suffolk 107
44. Military costume, temp. Edward I. 109
45. Ditto 110
46. Ditto 111
47. Ditto 112
48. Female of the reign of Edward I. 115
49. Female head-dresses, temp. Edward I. . . . 116
50. Coronation of Edward I. 119
51. Effigy of Edward II. 121
52. Military costume of the reign of Edward II. . . 122
53. Female costume of the reign of Edward II. . . 124
54. Ditto. 125
55. Effigy of Edward III. and of his second son, William of Hatfield 127
56. Female costume of the reign of Edward III. . . 132
57. Charles le Bon, Count of Flanders 134
58. Effigy of Sir Oliver Ingham and a visored bascinet . 135
59. Edward III. and the Black Prince 137
60. Tilting helmet and gauntlets of Edward the Black Prince 139
61. Helmet of John, King of Bohemia, and another from seals in Olivarius Vredius 141
62. Civil costume of the reign of Richard II. . . . 150
63. Military costume, temp. Richard II. 158
64. Visored bascinet of the time of Richard II. . . 160
65. Helmets of the time of Richard II. on two female figures ib.
66. Female costume, close of the 14th century . . 164-5
67. Parliament assembled for the deposition of Richard II. 168
68. Effigy of Henry IV., and his queen, Joan of Navarre . 170
69. Crown of Henry IV. and collar of Esses round the neck of the Queen 171
70. Female head-dress of the reign of Henry IV. . . 177
71. Military costume of the reign of Henry V. . . 183
72. Tilting helmet of the commencement of the 15th century 184
73. Tilting helmet and shield . . . . . ib.

No.   Page
74. Helmet of Louis, Duc de Bourbon   .   .   . 185
75. Bascinet of the reign of Henry V. 186
76. Female costume of the reign of Henry V.   .   . 188
77. Horned head-dress of the 15th century   .   .   . 189
78. John Talbot, Earl of Shrewsbury, presenting a book
    to Henry VI. and his queen Margaret   .   .   . 190
79. Civil costume of the reign of Henry VI. .   .   . 191
80. Salades, a bill, and a dagger   .   .   . 194
81. Hand-cannon ; hand-gun and battle-axe united   .   . 196
82. Female costume of the reign of Henry VI.   .   . 198
83. Lord Rivers, and Caxton, his printer, presenting a book
    to Edward IV. and his family   199
84. Civil costume of the reign of Edward IV.   .   . 201
85. Collar of suns and roses   203
86. Casquetel of the reign of Edward IV.   .   .   . 204
87. Female costume of the reign of Edward IV.   .   206-7
88. Sir Thomas Peyton   216
89. Effigy of Lady Peyton   217
90. Female costume of the reign of Richard III.   .   . 218
91. Civil costume of the reign of Henry VII.   .   . 220
92. Costume of the reign of Henry VII.   .   .   . 222
93. Fluted suit of armour of the reign of Henry VII.   . 224
94. Female costume of the reign of Henry VII.   .   . 227
95. Mourning habits of the 16th century   .   .   . 230
96. Henry VIII. from his great seal   .   .   . 241
97. Suit of puffed and ribbed armour, temp. Henry VIII.   242
98. Military costume, temp. Henry VIII.   .   .   . 244
99. General costume of the reigns of Edward VI. and
    Queen Mary   251
100. Powder-flask of the reign of Mary   .   .   . 253
101. Wheel-lock dag, wheel-lock pistol, and pocket wheel-
    lock pistol   254
102. Early costume of Queen Elizabeth   .   .   . 255
103. English lady of quality, 1577 ; English lady of quality,
    1588 263
104. Costume of the reign of Elizabeth, about 1588 .   . 269
105. Morions of the reign of Elizabeth ; the costume from the
    last of the series, temp. 1590   271
106. Fire-arms, musket-rest, and bandoliers, temp. Elizabeth 272
107. Henry, Prince of Wales   278
108. Morion, bourginot, swine's feather, linstock, and butt
    of a pistol   279
109. Helmets or head-pieces of the time of Charles I. and
    Cromwell   286
110. Gentlewoman, citizen's wife, countrywoman   .   . 289

No.   Page

111. English lady of quality, A.D. 1640 293
112. Charles II. and his queen 294
113. Charles II. and a courtier 297
114. Costume of Charles II.'s reign 298
115. Gorget and steel skull-cap 300
116. Bayonets of the earliest form 301
117. Portraits of William III. 303
118. William III. 304
119. Improved bayonets of the reign of William III. . 306
120. Costume of Queen Mary 308
121. Gentlemen of the reigns of Queen Anne, George I. and II. 310
122. Ladies of the reign of George II. 321
123. Costume of the reign of George III. . . . 325
124. Scotch brooch of silver 332
125. Prince Charles Edward Stuart 340
126. Scotch bonnets 342
127. Highland target, dirk, Jedburgh axe, Lochabar axe . 346
128. An Andrea Ferrara, with its original hilt . . . 350
129. Highland fire-lock tack; battle-axes of the Edinburgh and Aberdeen town-guards 351
130. Ancient Irish weapons and ornaments . . . 353
131. Irish costume of the 12th century 355
132. MacMorough, king of Leinster, and his toparchs . 361
133. Irish of the reign of Elizabeth 369
134. Archer, a Jesuit; O'More, an Irish chief . . . 371
135. Wild Irish man and woman; civil Irish man and woman 373
136. Irish gentleman and woman 374

INTRODUCTION.

THE true spirit of the times is in nothing more perceptible than in the tone given to our most trifling amusements. Information of some description must be blended with every recreation to render it truly acceptable to the public. The most beautiful fictions are disregarded unless in some measure founded upon fact. Pure invention has been declared by Byron to be but the talent of a liar, and the novels of Sir Walter Scott owe their popularity as much to the learning as to the genius displayed in their pages or the mystery which so long surrounded the writer*. The days have gone by when archæological pursuits were little more than the harmless but valueless recreations of the aged and the idle. The research, intelligence, and industry of modern authors and artists have opened a treasure-chamber to the rising generation. The spirit of critical inquiry has separated the gold from the dross, and antiquities are now considered valuable only in proportion to their illustration of history or their importance to art.

The taste for a correct conception of the arms and habits of our ancestors has of late years rapidly diffused itself throughout Europe. The historian, the poet, the novelist, the painter, and the actor, have discovered in attention to costume a new spring of information, and a fresh source of effect. Its study, embellished by picture and enlivened by anecdote, soon becomes interesting even to the young and careless reader; and at the same time that it sheds light upon manners and rectifies dates, stamps

* At the same time we must observe, that his descriptions of ancient costume are not always to be relied upon. The armour of Richard Cœur de Lion in " Ivanhoe " is of the sixteenth rather than of the twelfth century.

the various events and eras in the most natural and vivid colours indelibly on the memory.

Of those who affect to ridicule the description of a doublet, or to deny the possibility of assigning the introduction of any particular habit to any particular period (and some have done so in print who should have known better), we would only inquire what criticism they would pass upon the painter who should represent Julius Cæsar in a frock-coat, cocked hat, and Wellington trousers : nor will we admit this to be an extreme case, for how lately have the heroes and sages of Greece and Rome strutted upon the stage in flowing perukes and gold-laced waistcoats.

" What shook the stage and made the people stare ?
   Cato's long wig, flowered gown, and lacker'd chair."

And is the representing Paris in a Roman dress, as was done by West, the President of the Royal Academy, to be considered a more venial offence, because it is more picturesque and less capable of detection by the general spectator ?—The Roman dress is more picturesque than the habits of the present day, certainly ; but not more so than the Phrygian, the proper costume of the person represented. And is it pardonable in a man of genius and information to perpetuate errors upon the ground that they may pass undiscovered by the million ? Does not the historical painter voluntarily offer himself to the public as an illustrator of habits and manners, and is he wantonly to abuse the faith accorded to him ? But an artist, say the cavillers, must not sacrifice effect to the minutiæ of detail. The extravagant dresses of some periods would detract from the expression of the figure, which is the higher object of the painter's ambition. Such and such colours are wanted for peculiar purposes, and these might be the very tints prohibited by the critical antiquary. To these and twenty other similar objections the plain answer is, that the exertion of one-third part of the study and ingenuity exercised in the invention of conventional dresses to satisfy the painter's fancy would enable him to be perfectly correct and at the same time equally effective—often, indeed, more effective, from the mere necessity of introducing some hues and forms which otherwise had never entered into his imagination.

The assertion so coolly hazarded by some writers, that chronological accuracy is unattainable in these matters will be refuted, we trust, by every page of this work ; its principal object being to prove the direct contrary, and establish the credence which may be given to the authorities therein consulted, and lighten the labours of the student by directing him at once to those cotemporary records and monuments which may serve him as tests of the authenticity of later compilers.

Careless translation has done much to deceive, and the neglect of original and cotemporary authors for the more familiarly written and easily obtained works of their successors, has added to the confusion. It is extraordinary to observe the implicit confidence with which the most egregious mistakes have been copied by one writer after another, apparently without the propriety having once occurred to them of referring to the original authorities.

A want of methodical or strict chronological arrangement, has also contributed to the perplexity of the students ; and the works of the indefatigable Strutt have, from this latter defect, misled perhaps more than they have enlightened. To condense and sift the mass of materials he had collected, has been, perhaps, the most laborious portion of our task. Some of his plates contain the costume of two centuries jumbled together, and the references to them in the text are scattered over the volumes in the most bewildering manner. This material defect is remedied, we trust, in our publication; and it is scarcely necessary to point out the advantage of finding every information respecting the dress or armour of a particular reign contained within the few pages allotted to it.

The bulk of all the best works on ancient costume or armour, and their consequent expense, have been formidable obstacles to the artist, and must surely render a pocket volume, comprising every necessary reference and information, a desirable companion; and although we by no means pretend to infallibility, we trust that our jealousy of all questionable documents, and the rigid test to which we have subjected, and by which we have shaken the evidence of many hitherto undoubted, have preserved us from gross misrepresentations, at the same time that they have enabled us to correct some material errors, and explain several obscure passages in our more costly and voluminous precursors.

The following is a list of the works on general costume, or containing notices of British dress, which may be consulted with advantage by the artist, with our own, for a commentary.

Habitus Præcipuorum Populorum, tam Virorum quam Fæminarum, singulari arte depicti. By John Weigel, cutter in wood. 1 vol. fol. Nuremberg, 1577.

Habitus Variarum Orbis Gentium. By J. J. Boissard, 1581.

Habiti Antichi e Moderni di diverse Parti del Mondo. By Cæsar Vecellio. 8vo. Venice, 1590.

Sacri Romani Imperii Ornatus, item Germanorum diversarumque Gentium Peculiares Vestitus; quibus accedunt Ecclesiasticorum Habitus Varii. By Caspar Rutz, 1588.

Diversarum Gentium Armatura Equestris, 1617.

Ornatus Muliebris Anglicanus. By Wencelaus Hollar. 4to. London, 1640.

A Collection of the Dresses of different Nations, ancient and modern. 2 vols. 4to. Published by Thomas Jefferys. London, 1757.

Horda Angel Cynan. By Joseph Strutt. 3 vols. 4to. London, 1774—76.

Dress and Habits of the People of England. By ditto. 2 vols. 4to. London, 1796—99.

Regal and Ecclesiastical Antiquities. By ditto. 1 vol. 4to. London, 1773—93.,

Selections of the Ancient Costume of Great Britain and Ireland. By Charles Hamilton Smith, Esq. 1 vol. fol. London, 1814.

Costume of the Original Inhabitants of the British Islands. By S. R. Meyrick, LL.D. & F.S.A.; and C.H. Smith, Esq. 1 vol. fol. London, 1821.

A Critical Enquiry into Ancient Arms and Armour. By S. R. Meyrick, LL.D., &c. 3 vols. fol. London.

Encyclopædia of Antiquities. By the Rev. T. D. Fosbrooke, M.A. F.S.A. 2 vols. 4to. London, 1825.

Illustrations of British History. 2 vols. 12mo. By Richard Thomson. Published in Constable's Miscellany, Edinburgh, 1828.

Engraved Illustrations of Antient Armour from the Collection at Goodrich Court. By Joseph Skelton, F.S.A. With the descriptions of Dr. Meyrick. 2 vols. 4to. London and Oxford, 1830.

The Monumental Effigies of Great Britain. By Charles Alfred Stothard, F.S.A. Fol. London, 1833.

Walker's History of the Irish Bards. 2 vols. 8vo.

Logan's History of the Gael. 2 vols. 8vo.

To preclude the necessity of long references we here subjoin a list of the principal authorities quoted in this work. Some of them being in manuscript, many of rare occurrence, many not contained even in public libraries, except in some voluminous collection of historians, so that the inquirer may lose much time in seeking for them, unless he knows the exact work in which they are to be found, we have sought to make our catalogue more complete by providing against this difficulty in all cases where it seemed likely to occur. It will not, of course, be supposed that the editions or collections here indicated are the *only* ones in which the writers named are to be found.

List of the principal Ancient Authors and Works quoted or referred to in this Volume.

Herodotus.
Plutarch's Lives.
Cæsar's Commentaries.
Diodorus Siculus.
Polybius.
Strabo.
Pomponius Mela: Geography.
Tacitus: Life of Agricola; Manners of the Germans.
Pliny's Natural History.
Solinus: Polyhistor.
Dion Cassius.
Herodian.
Livy.
Ovid.
Martial.

The Welsh Triads
Taliesin: Poems
Llywarch Hên:
   Elegies
Anuerin: The Go-
   dodins
} Vide Archæologia Britannica, Oxford, 1707; Davies' Celtic Researches, London, 1804: Myvyrian, Archæology of Wales, 2 vols. London, 1801; Dissertatio de Bardis, &c. 8vo. 1764; Owen's Cambrian Biography, London, 8vo. 1803; and Treatise on the Genuineness of the Poems of Anuerin, Taliesin, Llywarch Hên, &c.; with Specimens by Mr. Sharon Turner.

Eginhart: Life of Charlemagne. Vet. Script. Germ. Reub. Han. 1619.
Monk of St. Gall.
History of the Lombards. Printed by Muratori in his Scriptores Italici, vol. i.
Paulus Deaconus.

Theganus: Life of Louis le Debonaire.

Bede.

Adhelm, Bishop of Sherborne. M.S. Brit. Mus. Royal, 15 et 16.

William of Poitou: Gesta Gulielmi Ducis. Printed in Duchesne's Historia Normanorum Scriptores Antiqui. Folio. Paris, 1601.

William of Malmsbury: De Gestis Regum Anglorum. Printed in Sir H. Savil's Collection, entitled Scriptores post Bedam. Frankfort, folio, 1601.

Agathias: History. Printed at Leyden, 1594; and Paris, 1658.

Gregory of Tours: History of the Franks.

Anglo-Saxon Poems of Judith and Beowulf.

Aimion: History of France. Printed in Duchesne's Historiæ Normanorum Scriptores Antiquis. Folio. Paris, 1619.

Encomium of Emma, in Duchesne.

Alcuin: Lib. de Offic. Divin. Folio. Paris, 1617.

Adam of Bremen: Ecclesiastical History. Rer. Germ. Linden. Frankfort, 1630. Langcheck's Collection of Writers on Danish Affairs. 5 vols. folio. Copenhagen, 1772—92.

Arnold of Lubeck. Ibid.

Bartholinus: On the Contempt of Death.

Forfæus: History of Norway.

Asser: Life of Alfred. Printed by Camden in his collection, entitled Anglica, Normanoricum, Hibernica, Cambrica a scriptoribus, a veteribus scripta. Folio. Frankfort, 1603.

John Wallingford: Printed in Gale's Historicæ Britannicæ et Anglicanæ Scriptores. 2 vols. folio. Oxford, 1689—91.

Ingulph: History of Croyland Abbey, and English History, in Savil's Scriptores.

Glaber Rodolphus.

Florence of Worcester: Chronicle. Printed in 4to. London, 1592.

Ordericus Vitalis: Ecclesiastical History.

Wace: Roman de Ron. Printed by M. Pluquet. Rouen, 827.

Henry of Huntingdon: Histories. Printed in Savil's Scriptores.

Johannes de Janua.

Anna Comnena: Alexiad.

Matthew Paris: Historia Major Angliæ; Vita Abbatum; Chronica, &c. 2 vols. folio. Paris, 1641.

John de Meun } Romance of the Rose; various MS.
William de Lorris } in the Mus. Brit.

Gervase of Dover } Printed in Sir John Twysden's His-
John of Brompton } toriæ Anglicanæ Scriptores Decem. Folio. London, 1652.

Dowglas, Monk of Glastonbury: Harleian MS.

Pierce Ploughman: Vision.

Chaucer.

Æneas Sylvius: History of Bohemia.

Froissart.

Henry Knyghton. Printed in Sir R. Twysden's Scriptores.

Monk of Evesham. Printed by Hearne. 8vo. Oxford, 1729.

Thomas of Walshingham: Historia Brevis. Printed in Camden's Collection.

Harding's Chronicle. Printed by Grafton. London, 1543.

Gower.

Occleve.

Monstrelet: Chronicles.

St. Remy. Printed by Sir N. H. Nicholas in his History of the Battle of Agincourt. 12mo. London, 1827.

Elmham. Printed by Hearne. 8vo. Oxford, 1727.

Lydgate: Poems; various MSS. in Mus. Brit.

Philip de Commines: Memoirs.

Monk of Croyland.

Paradin: Histoire de Lyons.

Argentre: Histoire de Bretagne.

Skelton: Poems; Harl. MS. 7333.

Barclay: Ship of Fools of the World. Printed by Pynson. London, 1508.

Hall: Union of the Families of York and Lancaster. Folio. London, 1548—50.

Holinshed: Chronicles. 2 vols. folio, 1577.

John Stow: Chronicle. 4to. 1580—98. Continued by Edmund Howe. Folio. 1615.

John Speed: Theatre of Great Britain (folio, London, 1611); and History of Great Britain. 2 vols. large folio. 1611.

Stubbs: Anatomy of Abuses.

Bulwer: Pedigree of the English Gallant.

Militarie Instructions for the Cavalrie. Cambridge, 1632.

Randal Holmes: Notes on Dress; Harleian MS., written about 1660.

Spectator; Rambler; Adventurer; Gray's Inn Journal; London Journal, &c.

SCOTLAND.

Porphyry.

Ammianus Marcellinus.

Claudian.

Tacitus.

Herodian.

Dion Cassius and Xiphilin.

Isidore.

Gildas. Printed in Bertram's Scriptores. 8vo. 1757.

Matthew Paris.

Winton: Chronicles.

Fordun: Chronicles.

Froissart: Chronicles.

John Lesley: History of Scotland. 4to. 1578.

George Buchannan: History of Scotland; in his works, 2 vols. folio. Edinburgh, 1714.

John Major: History of Scotland.

David Lyndsay of Piscottie: History of Scotland, from 1437 to 1542.

Heron.

IRELAND.

Giraldus Cambrensis, translated by Sir R. Hoare: History of the Conquest of Ireland and Topographia Hibernica, edited by Camden. 1602.

Henry Christall: cited by Froissart in his Chronicles.

Monstrelet: Chronicles.

Spenser.

Stanihurst: in Holinshed's Chronicles.

Camden: History of Elizabeth.
Derricke: Poems.
Morryson.
Speed.

To these may be added the documents printed or cited in Rymer's Fœdera; Wilkins's Concilia; Johnson's Canons; Dugdale's Monasticon and History of St. Paul's; The Archæologia; The Antiquarian Repertory; Camden's Remains; Ashmole's History of the Order of the Garter; Illustrations of Northern Antiquities; Montfaucon's Monarchie Française; Turner's History of the Anglo-Saxons; Williment's Regal Heraldry; Sandford's Genealogical History; Collectanea de Rebus Hibernicis; Keating's History of Ireland; Ledwicke's Antiquities of Ireland; King's Munimenta Antiqua Pennant's Works; Lord Somers' Tracts, &c.

J. R. PLANCHÉ.

HISTORY
OF
BRITISH COSTUME.

CHAPTER I.

ANCIENT BRITISH PERIOD.

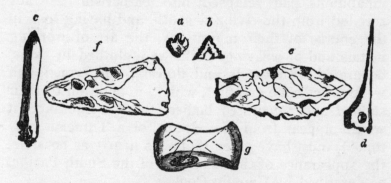

Ancient British weapons of bone and flint.

Fig. *a*, arrow-head of flint, in the Meyrick collection; *b*, another, engraved in Archæologia, vol. xv. pl. 2; *c, d*, lance-heads of bone, from a barrow on Upton Lovel Downs, Wiltshire, engraved in same plate; *e*, spear-head of stone, in the Meyrick collection; *f*, battle-axe head of black stone, in ditto; *g*, another, found in a barrow in Devonshire, and now in the same collection.

RESPECTING the original colonists of Britain—the more adventurous members of the two great nomadic tribes, the Cimmerii or Cimbrians and the Celtæ or Celts, who wandered from the shores of the Thracian Bosphorus to the northern coasts of Europe, and passed, some from Gaul across the channel, others through "the Hazy" or German Ocean to these

islands—a few slight and scattered notices by the
Greek and Latin writers, and an occasional passage
in the Welsh Triads, form the meagre total of our
information [1]. Mere speculations, however ingenious,
it would be foreign to the plan of this work to enter-
tain : however interesting, or even convincing, to
the student of antiquity, they are too shadowy to
be grasped and retained by the unlearned reader.
From the positive evidence, however, of such weapons and ornaments as have been from time to
time discovered in this country, and acknowledged
as neither of Roman nor Saxon workmanship, we
are, with the aid of the scanty testimony before-
mentioned, authorized to presume that its earliest
inhabitants had relapsed into barbarism, as they
receded from the civilized south, and having lost, in
the course of their migrations, the art of working
metals and of weaving cloth, were clothed in skins,
decorated with beads and flowers, and armed with
weapons of bone and flint, which, in addition to their
stained and punctured bodies (the remembrance, it
would appear from Herodotus, of a Thracian custom [2]), must have given them, as nearly as possible,
the appearance of the Islanders of the South Pacific,
as described by Captain Cook.

And with similar policy to that practised by our
famous navigator, did the Tyrian traders apparently
teach the British savages to manufacture swords,
spear-blades, and arrow-heads, from a composition

---

[1] Herodotus, book iv.; Plutarch in Mario ; Welsh Triads, 4
and 5.

[2] Herodotus, v. 6. "To have punctures on their skin is with
them a mark of nobility, to be without these is a testimony of mean
descent." Isidorus describes the British method of tatooing in
these words : "They squeeze the juice of certain herbs into figures
made on their bodies with the points of needles." Orig. lib. xix.
c. 23. It seems to have been done in infancy, as Pliny tells us
the British wives and nurses did it. Nat. Hist. lib. xxii. c. 2.

of brass (or rather of copper) and tin, by first presenting them with models of their own rude weapons in this mixed metal, and then gradually inducing them to adopt the improvements, and emulate the skill of their friendly visitors.

The lance, for instance, formed of a long bone, ground to a point (vide figures *c* and *d* at head of chapter), and inserted into a split at the end of an oaken shaft, where it was secured by wooden pegs, was first succeeded by a metal blade, similarly shaped and fastened (vide fig. *a* in the following engraving) ;

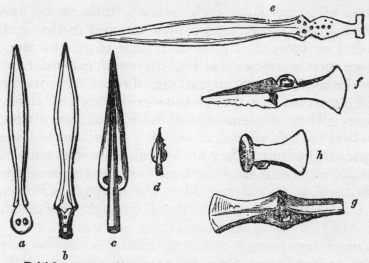

British weapons of bronze in their earliest and improved states.

Fig. *a*, earliest specimen of spear-blade ; *b*, the llaonawr, or blade-weapon, found in the New Forest, Glamorganshire ; *c*, the spear-head, improved with a socket for the shaft, found in Ireland ; *d*, head of hunting spear dug up in Hertfordshire ; *e*, a sword found at Fulbourn, all in the Meyrick collection ; *f*, battle-axe head, of the earliest form, engraved in Archæologia, vol. ix. pl. 3 ; *g*, another, engraved in Archæologia, vol. xiv. ; *h*, another, improved, in the Meyrick collection.

but shortly afterwards, the shaft, instead of receiving the blade, was fitted into a socket in a workmanlike manner, and finally the blade itself assumed a classical form. The arrow and the hatchet, or battle-axe, underwent the same gradual transformation and improve

ment, as may be seen by a comparison of the brazen
weapons here engraved with those of bone and flint
at the head of the chapter. The greater part of the
originals are preserved in the armoury at Goodrich
Court, Herefordshire.

For the sword they were probably indebted to
the Phœnicians, or perhaps to the Gauls, who also
wore them of brass, and of a similar form. The hilt
was cased on each side with horn, whence the British
adage: "A gavas y carn gavas y llavyn." "He
who has the horn has the blade[3]."

The flat circular shields too of the Britons, which
were of wicker (like their quivers, their boats, and
their idols[4]), were soon either imitated in the same
metal or covered with a thin plate of it, and then,
from their sonorous quality, they were called tarians
or clashers[5]. The metal coatings of two of these shields
are preserved in a perfect state in the Meyrick collection. They are ornamented with concentric circles,
between which are raised as many little knobs as the
space will admit. They are rather more than two feet
in diameter, with a hollow boss in the centre to admit
the hand, as they were held at arm's length in action.
"On comparing it with the Highland target," Sir
Samuel Meyrick remarks, "we shall find that, although the Roman mode of putting it on the arm
has been adopted by those mountaineers, the boss,

[3] Meyrick, Engraved Illustrations of Ancient Arms and Armour,
vol. i., text to plate 47.
[4] The ingenuity of the Britons in this species of manufacture
was much admired by the Romans, who, when they introduced
into Italy the British *bascawd* (basket-work), adopted also its
name, terming it *bascauda*. The British name for a quiver is
cawell saethan, i. e. a basket-work case for arrows. The ancient
British wicker boat, called *curwgll* or coracle, formed of osier
twigs, covered with hide, is still in use upon the Wye and other
rivers both of Wales and Ireland.
[5] Archæologia, vol. xxiii. p. 94; Herodian and Xiphilin.

rendered useless, is still retained, and the little knobs imitated with brass nails[6]."

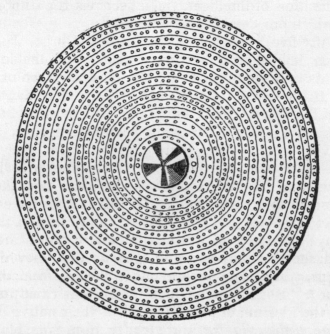

Bronze coating of an ancient British shield, in the Meyrick collection, found at Rhydygorse in Cardiganshire.

Several brazen swords and spear-blades, found in the bed of the Thames near Kingston, have been engraved for a frontispiece to Mr. Jesse's interesting work, entitled ' Gleanings of Natural History ;' but they are there erroneously called Roman. Whoever will take the trouble to compare them with the numberless acknowledged British weapons in various English collections, and with many similar relics found in Ireland, where the Romans never set foot, will scarcely need the additional argument, that the Romans, at the period of the invasion of Britain, used weapons of steel only, to convince themselves of the Celtic origin of those curious military antiquities,

[6] Archæologia, vol. xxiii. p. 95.

But let us hasten to the period when the light of history begins to dawn upon us, and the personal observation of intelligent men becomes the authority on which our descriptions are based.

Fifty-five years before the birth of Christ, Julius Cæsar landed on these shores, and found the inhabitants of Cantium (Kent) the most civilized of all the Britons, and differing but little in their manners from the Gauls[7], from whom they had most probably acquired the arts of dressing, spinning, dyeing, and weaving wool, as they there practised them after the Gaulish fashion, and possessed, in common with their continental kindred, some valuable secrets in them, unknown to other nations. Of this fact we have the direct evidence of Diodorus Siculus, Strabo, and Pliny; the latter of whom enumerates several herbs used for this purpose, and tells us that they dyed purple, scarlet, and several other colours, from these alone[8]. But the herb which the Britons chiefly used was the glastum or woad (called in their native language, *y glâs*, *glas lys*, and *glacilys*, from *glâs*, blue[9]), with which they stained and punctured their bodies, in order, says Cæsar, to make themselves look dreadful in battle[10]. His words are, however, " Omnes vero se Britanni *vitro* inficiunt, quod cœruleum efficit colorem, atque hoc horribiliori sunt in pugnâ adspectu." Now the word *vitro* is disputed, and " nitro," " luteo," " ultro," " glauco," and " guasto,"

[7] De Bell. Gal. lib. v. 14. Strabo says, " the Britons, in their manners, partly resemble the Gauls." Tacitus says, " they are near and like the Gauls;" and Pomponius Mela tells us, " the Britons fought armed, after the Gaulish manner."

[8] Hist. Nat. lib. xvi. c. 18; lib. xxii. c. 26.

[9] Meyrick, Costume of the Original Inhabitants of the British Isles, folio, London, 1821.

[10] De Bell. Gal. lib. v. Herodian says the Britons who resisted Severus painted the figures of all kinds of animals on their bodies, lib. iii. p. 83; and Martial has the words " Cœruleis Britannis," lib. ix. c. 32.

have been alternately suggested as the correct
reading. Pliny says they used "glastum" (i. e. woad),
but Ovid uses the singular expression "*Viridesque
Britannos.*" Amorum. Eleg. 16. And *glas*, in Celtic,
signifies *green* as well as blue. It is applied to the
sea, and to express, poetically, the sea, as *glasmhaigh*,
a *green plain. Crann ghlas* is a *green tree.* It enters
into combination also with a variety of words in the
Celtic expressive of grass, *greens for food, salad, sea
wrack*, and also means *pale, wan, poor*, and even in
colour *greyish. Each glas* is a *grey* horse. The dress
of the fairies is always spoken of as *glas*, Anglice,
green and *shining:* and no doubt it is the origin of our
word *glass*, which has been applied to the composition so called in consequence of its presenting indifferently the hues and lustrous appearance alluded to.
A man could not dye his body with glass, but the
obvious derivation of that word from the Celtic renders the *vitro* of Cæsar a still more curious expression.
The word "cœruleum" may also be translated *green,
wan*, or *pale*, like the Celtic *glas*, and the skin washed
lightly over with blue or grey would present a green-
ish and ghastly appearance. And here it may be
remarked, that from the fact of the Romans, on their
first invasion of the island, beholding the inhabitants
only when, according to a common Celtic custom[11]
(a custom partially followed by the Scotch Highlanders to the days of the battle of Killicrankie), they
had flung off their garments to rush into action, arose
the vulgar error that the Britons lived continually
"*in puris naturalibus;*" whereas, we have the testimony of Cæsar himself to the fact, that even the

[11] Livy says, that at the battle of Cannæ there were Gauls who
fought naked from the waist upwards (xxii. 46) ; and Polybius
tells us, that some Belgic Gauls fought entirely naked, but it was
only on the day of battle that they thus stripped themselves. Lib.
ii. c. 6.

least civilized, "those within the country," went clad
in skins; whilst the southern or Belgic Britons were
like the Gauls, and therefore not only completely but
splendidly attired, as may be proved from various unquestionable authorities.

Of the several kinds of cloth manufactured in Gaul,
one, according to Pliny[12] and Diodorus Siculus[13],
was composed of fine wool, dyed of several different
colours, which being spun into yarn, was woven
either in stripes or in chequers, and of this the Gauls
and Britons made their lighter or summer garments.
Here we have the undoubted origin of the Scotch
plaid or tartan, which is called "the garb of old
Gaul" to this day; and indeed, with the exception
of the plumed bonnet and the tasselled sporan or
purse, a Highland chief in his full costume, with
tunic, plaid, dirk, and target, affords as good an
illustration of the appearance of an ancient Briton
of distinction as can well be imagined.

Diodorus, describing the Belgic Gauls, says, they
wore dyed tunics, beflowered with all manner of
colours (χιτῶσι βαπτοῖς χρώμασι παντοδαποῖς διηνθισ-
μένοις). With these they wore close trousers, which
they called *bracæ*[14]; these trousers, an article of
apparel by which all barbaric nations seem to have
been distinguished from the Romans, being made by
the Gauls and Britons of their chequered cloth, called
breach and *brycan*, and by the Irish, *breacan*[15]. Over

---

[12] Hist. Nat. lib. viii. c. 48.   [13] Lib. v. c. 30.
[14] Ibid.   Martial has the line,
    "Like the old bracchæ of a needy Briton." Epig. xi.

[15] *Breac*, in Celtic, signifies anything speckled, spotted, striped,
or, indeed, party-coloured.   The brindled ox was, therefore,
called *brych* by the Britons.   *Breac* is the Celtic name for a
trout, from its speckled skin.   *Baran breac*, literally spotted food,
is the name for a Christmas cake, or bread with plums in it.
Breac is also applied to a person pitted with the small-pox, or to
one whose skin is freckled.   The termination *an*, in compound

the tunic both the Gauls and the Britons wore the
sagum, a short cloak so called by the Romans, from
the Celtic word *saic*, which, according to Varro, signified a skin or hide ; such having been the materials
which the invention of cloth had superseded. The
British *sagum* was of one uniform colour, generally
either blue or black [16]. The predominating colour
in the chequered tunic and *bracæ* was red. The hair
was turned back upon the crown of the head, and fell
down in long and bushy curls behind [17]. If covered
at all, it was by the *cappan* or cap, from the British
cab, a hut, which it resembled in its conical shape ;
the houses of the Britons being made with wattles
stuck in the ground, and fastened together at top.
"It is somewhat singular," remarks the learned author
to whose indefatigable research we are indebted for
the first general collection of ancient British authorities, "that the form of this ancient pointed cap is to
this day exhibited in what the Welsh children call the
cappan cyrnicyll, the horn-like cap, made of rushes
tied at top, and twisted into a band at bottom [18]."

Men of rank amongst the Gauls and Britons, according to Cæsar and Diodorus, shaved the chin, but
wore immense tangled mustaches. Strabo describes
those of the inhabitants of Cornwall and the Scilly
Isles as hanging down upon their breasts like wings.
These latter people, he says, wore long black garments like tunics, and carried staves in their hands,
so that, when walking, they looked like furies in a
tragedy, though really a quiet and inoffensive
people [19].

words, signifies " in ;" so that *breachan* or *brychan* is literally " in
spots," or " in chequers :" *an* is also used in Gaelic as a diminutive ; and *breachan* might, therefore, signify " *little* spots,"
" *small* chequers," or " *narrow* stripes."

[16] Diodorus Siculus, lib. v. c. 33.
[17] Ibid. lib. v. ; and Cæsar De Bell. Gal. lib. v.
[18] Meyrick, Costume of the Orig. Inhab. ut supra.
[19] Lib. iii.

The ornaments of the Britons, like those of the Gauls, consisted of rings, bracelets, armlets, a collar or necklace of twisted wires of gold or silver, called *torch* or *dorch* in British, and peculiarly a symbol of rank and command. The ancient Lord of Yale was called Llewellyn am Dorchog, or Llewellyn with the Torques. The one here represented is of brass, and was found on the Quantoc Hills. So fond, indeed, were the Britons of ornaments of this kind, that those who could not procure them of the precious metals wore torques of iron, " of which they were not a little vain [20]." The ring, according to Pliny, was worn on the middle finger [21].

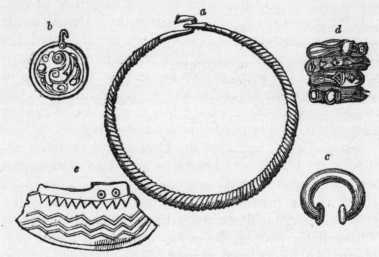

Ornaments and patterns of the ancient Britons.

Fig. *a*, a torque of brass found on the Quantoc Hills, and engraved in the Archæologia, vol. xiv. ; *b*, an ornament of brass; *c*, a bracelet; *d*, an annular ornament of bronze for fastening the mantle, Archæologia, vol. xxii. pl. 25, but therein called a bracelet; *e*, a piece of British earthenware, Archæologia, vol. xxi. Appendix.

[20] Herodian, lib. iii. c. 47.   [21] Hist. Nat. lib. xxxiii. c. 6.

THE DRESS OF THE BRITISH FEMALES

may be ascertained from Dion Cassius's account of the appearance of Boadicea, Queen of the Iceni. Her light hair fell down her shoulders. She wore a torque of gold, a tunic of several colours, all in folds, and over it, fastened by a *fibula* or brooch, a robe of coarse stuff[22].

THE COMMONALTY

and the less civilized tribes that inhabited the interior, as we have already stated on the authority of Cæsar, went simply clad in skins[23]. The hide of the brindled or spotted ox was generally preferred, but some wore the *ysgyn*, which was the name for the skin of any wild beast, but more particularly the bear; while others assumed the sheepskin cloak, according as they were herdsmen, hunters, or shepherds[24]. That, in the absence of more valuable fastenings, the cloak was secured, as amongst the ancient Germans, by a thorn, we have tolerable evidence in the fact of this primitive brooch being still used in Wales.

There remains another class to be considered—

THE PRIESTHOOD.

It was divided into three orders. The Druids, the Bards, and the Ovates. The dress of the druidical or sacerdotal order was white, the emblem of holiness and peculiarly of truth. The Welsh bard Taliesin calls it " the proud white garment which separated the elders from the youth[25]."

The bards wore a one-coloured robe of sky-blue, being emblematical of peace; thus another bard[26], in

---

[22] Xiphilin. Abridg. of Dion Cassius.
[23] De Bell. Gal. lib. v. c. 10.   [24] Meyrick, Orig. Inhab.
[25] Owen's Elegies of Llywarch Hên.
[26] Cynddelw. Owen's Elegies of Llywarch Hên

his Ode on the death of Cadwallon, calls them
"wearers of long blue robes."

The ovate or *Ovydd*, professing astronomy, medi-
cine, &c. wore green, the symbol of learning, as
being the colour of the clothing of nature. Taliesin
makes an ovate say, "with my robe of bright green,
possessing a place in the assembly [27]." The disciples
of the orders wore variegated dresses of the three
colours, blue, green, and white [28].

The arch-druid or high-priest wore an oaken garland, surmounted sometimes by a tiara of gold. A
bas-relief, found at Autun, represents two Druids in
long tunics and mantles; one crowned with an oaken

Bas-relief found at Autun, engraved in Montfaucon.

[27] Mic. Dimbych. Owen's Elegies.
[28] Or blue, green, and red. A disciple, about to be admitted
a graduate, is called by the bards "a dog with spots of red, blue,
and green." Meyrick, Orig. Inhab.

garland, and bearing a sceptre; the other with a crescent in his hand, one of the sacred symbols. They are both engraved below, with a crescent of gold, a druidical hook for tearing down the mistletoe, and three other articles, supposed druidical, all of gold, and found in various parts of Ireland [29].

The mantle of one of the Druids, it will be observed, is fastened on the shoulders by a portion of it being drawn through a ring, and instances of this fashion are met with frequently in Anglo-Saxon illuminations. We believe it has never occurred to any previous writer on this subject, that the annular ornaments resembling bracelets (vide fig. *d*), so constantly discovered both here and on the Continent, and presumed to be merely votive, from the circumstance of their being too small to wear on the arm or the wrist, may have been used in this manner as a sort of brooch by the Gaulish and Teutonic tribes.

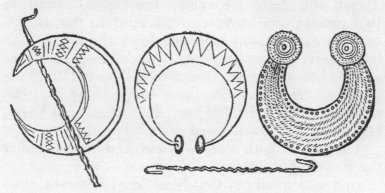

Druidical ornaments, vide note.

[29] Collectanea de Rebus Hibernicis, vol. iv.; Archæologia, vol. iv.; Meyrick's Orig. Inhab. passim; King's Munimenta Antiqua, &c. The centre ornament is supposed to be a tiara for the arch-druid, and that to the right a golden collar or breast-plate. The wreathed rod of gold, with a hook at each end, is probably a small torque flattened out.

ROMAN-BRITISH PERIOD, A. D. 78—400.

Julius Agricola, being appointed to the command
in Britain A. D. 78, succeeded in perfectly establishing
the Roman dominion, and introducing the Roman
manners and language; and, before the close of
the first century, the ancient British habit began to
be disesteemed by the chiefs, and regarded as a
badge of barbarism. " The sons of the British chieftains," says Tacitus, " began to affect our dress[30]."
The *braccæ* were abandoned by the southern and
eastern Britons, and the Roman tunic, reaching to
the knee, with the cloak or mantle, still however
called the *sagum*, became the general habit of the
better classes.

The change in the female garb was little, if any;
as it had originally been similar to that of the Roman
women. The coins of Carausius and the columns of
Trajan and Antonine exhibit the Celtic females in
two tunics; the lower one reaching to the ancles,
and the upper about half-way down the thigh, with
loose sleeves, extending only to the elbows, like those
of the German women described by Tacitus [31]. This
upper garment was sometimes confined by a girdle,
and was called in British *gwn*, the *gunacum* of Varro,
and the origin of our word *gown* [32].

The hair of both sexes was cut and dressed after
the Roman fashion.

In the armoury at Goodrich Court is a most interesting relic of this period. It is the metal coating
of a shield, such as the Britons fabricated after they
had been induced to imitate the Roman fashions.
It is modelled upon the *scutum*, and was called, in
consequence, *ysgwyd*, pronounced *esgooyd*. It appears originally to have been gilt, a practice con-

[30] Iu Vit. Agric.　　　[31] De Morib. German. c. 17.
[32] Meyrick, Orig. Inhab.

tinued for a long time by the descendants of the Britons, and is adorned on the *umbo* or boss with the common red cornelian of the country. " It is impossible," remarks its proprietor, " to contemplate the artistic portions without feeling convinced that there is a mixture of British ornaments with such resemblances to the elegant designs on Roman work as would be produced by a people in a state of less civilization [33]." This unique specimen was found, with several broken swords and spear-heads of bronze, in the bed of the river Witham, in Lincolnshire.

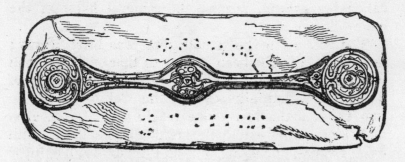

Metal coating of an ancient Roman-British shield, found in the bed of the river Witham, and now in the Meyrick collection.

[33] Archæologia, vol. xxiii.

Chapter II.

ANGLO-SAXON PERIOD, A.D. 450—1016.

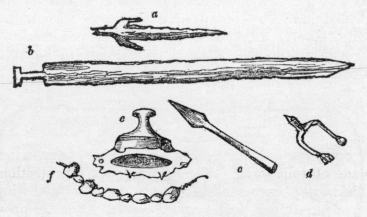

Anglo-Saxon weapons and ornaments.

Fig. *a*, a dagger; *b*, a sword; *c*, the head of a spear; *d*, a spur, from Strutt's Horda Angel Cynan; *e*, the iron boss of a shield from a barrow in Lincolnshire, and now in the Meyrick collection; *f*, a row of amber beads found in a tumulus on Chatham Lines.

FOR upwards of three centuries Britain was the seat of Roman civilization and luxury. The Saxons made descents upon it at the close of the fourth century, and were repulsed by Theodosius and the natives. Abandoned by its conquerors and instructors, divided into numberless petty sovereignties, harassed by barbarians from without, and ravaged by a frightful pestilence within, the handful of strangers who landed by accident or invitation in 449, became first the subsidiaries of its principal chiefs, and ultimately masters of the greater part of the island. In seven years from their arrival at Ebbsfleet in the Isle of Thanet, the province of Cantium became the Saxon

kingdom of Kent, under one of the leaders of that
wandering band; and Anuerin, a Welsh bard who
flourished early in the sixth century, and fought in
person against the invaders, gives us the following
account of the

MILITARY HABITS OF THE PAGAN SAXONS,

in his famous poem called the Gododin, which
procured for him amongst his countrymen the title
of "King of the Bards." There were present at the
battle of Cattraeth "three hundred warriors arrayed
in gilded armour, three loricated bands with three
commanders wearing golden torques." They were
armed with "daggers," "white sheathed piercers,"
and "wore four-pointed (square) helmets." Some
of them carried spears and shields, the latter being
made of split wood. Their leader had a projecting
shield, was harnessed in "scaly mail," armed with
"a slaughtering pike," and wore (as a mantle probably) the skin of a beast. His long hair flowed
down his shoulders, and was adorned, when he was
unarmed, with a wreath of amber beads; round his
neck he wore a golden torques[1]. The scaly mail of
which Anuerin speaks was the well-known armour
of the Sarmatian and Gothic tribes, from whence
the Romans derived their *lorica squamata*[2]. *Mael*
was indeed but the British word for iron. The tunic
covered with rings, to which the word mail was afterwards applied by the Norman French, was literally
called by the Saxons *gehrynged byrn*, ringed armour.
The British word *lluryg* in like manner, or the

[1] Gododin, by Anuerin, passim.
[2] The Sarmatians made theirs of thin slices of horses' hoofs,
cut in the shape of scales or feathers, and sewn in rows upon an
under garment of coarse linen. Pausanias saw and inspected one
of them that was preserved in the temple of Esculapius at Athens.
Lib. i. p. 50.

Roman *lorica*, from which it was derived, was used
generally for defensive body armour, and it is only
by a welcome adjective, as in this instance the word
"scaly," that we discover the peculiar sort of armour
alluded to. It is the want of attention to the true
meaning of words in the original authors, and a careless trust in translations, that have caused the very
obscurity and apparent discrepancy of which writers
on antiquarian subjects so frequently complain.

The square or four-pointed helmet was worn as
late as the ninth century in France, by the guards of
Lothaire and Charles the Bald, and square crowns
are frequently seen in the Anglo-Saxon illuminations[3].
Amber beads are continually found in Saxon tumuli.
The row engraved at the head of this chapter (fig. *f*)
was found in a tumulus on Chatham Lines. The
iron *umbo* or boss of an Anglo-Saxon shield above it
(fig. *e*) was found in a barrow in Lincolnshire, and
is now in the Meyrick collection.

In a MS. in the Cotton collection, marked Claudius, B. 4, we find one of the earliest specimens of
the ringed byrn, borrowed from the Phrygians, which
was formed of rings sewn flat upon a leathern tunic.
The wearer is a royal personage, crowned and armed
with the long, broad, straight iron sword, found in
Saxon tumuli, and the projecting or convex shield.
He is attended by a page or soldier, in a plain tunic
with sleeves, and a cap completely Phrygian in form,
bearing also a shield of the same fashion as his sovereign, who is in fact intended to represent no less a
person than Abraham fighting against the five kings
to rescue his brother Lot, and who wears a crown as
an emblem of superiority and chief command (vide

[3] An indication of the square helmet is discernible in an Anglo-
Saxon MS. of the eleventh century in the Harleian collection,
but the figures are so small and so rudely drawn with a pen that
no reliance can be placed upon the details.

figs. *a* and *b*, page 28). To the invariable practice, however, of the early illuminators, of pourtraying every personage habited according to the fashion of the artists' own time, we are deeply indebted. Had they indulged their fancy in the invention of costumes, instead of faithfully copying that which they daily saw, our task would have been almost impracticable ; for it is seldom, if ever, that the most minute description can convey to the mind an object as successfully as the rudest drawing, and the impression received by the eye is as lasting as it is vivid.

As we are now entering upon the period when illuminated MSS. become our principal guides, it is necessary to notice an error into which Mr. Strutt has fallen, and consequently led those who have implicitly confided in him. We allude to his own belief in the dates affixed to the MSS. in the printed catalogues at the British Museum. Where the MS. is itself without date, or from its subject does not admit of allusions to persons or events cotemporary with its execution, there is much difficulty in ascertaining its age, with any thing approaching to precision, in these early times, when there are no monumental effigies by which we can put its illuminations to the test of comparison.

The MS. just quoted, containing the figure of Abraham, is stated by Strutt to be of the eighth century; and another, marked Junius XI., in the Bodleian Museum at Oxford, from which he has taken the third figure in his fifth plate in the work on ' Habits and Dresses,' is also said to be of the same period. The latter is now generally acknowledged to be as late as the close of the tenth, perhaps the commencement of the eleventh century, and the former is certainly not much its senior. Again, the very first figure of his first plate, subscribed ' Rustics of the *Eighth* Century,' is taken, according to his own reference, from a Harleian MS. marked 603, which in that very reference is said to be of the tenth century; and two warriors are afterwards given from it in their true chronological order. The MS. is, we should say, even later than that. The kite-shaped shield and the gonfanon occur in it; and in the last illumination in the volume is a figure of Goliath, armed precisely like the warriors in the Bayeux tapestry [4]. These circumstances, with other internal evidence, would induce us to date it about the reign of Harold II., and an illumination, representing Harold crowned and enthroned, is engraved in Montfaucon's ' Monarchie Française,' the style of which perfectly corresponds with that of the miniatures in the Harleian MS.

The earliest illuminated Saxon MSS. in the British Museum, on the dates of which we can depend, are, a splendid copy of the Gospels, written by Eadfrid, Bishop of Durham, and illuminated by Ethelwold his successor, about the year 720, and a book of grants by King Edgar to the Abbey of Winchester, written in letters of gold, A. D. 966. The first of these contains representations of the four Evangelists, copied, it is probable, from some of the paintings brought over by the early missionaries, and affording us therefore no information on the subject of Anglo-Saxon costume. The latter is embellished with a figure of the monarch (vide fig. *a* in the following engraving), and presents us therefore with the regal, and we may add, noble costume of the first half of the tenth century. For the remainder of the Anglo-Saxon era we have authorities enough; but we have digressed, and must return.

Some change must have taken place in the apparel of the Anglo-Saxons after their conversion to Christianity at the beginning of the seventh century,

[4] Vide chap. v.

for at a council held at the close of the eighth, it was said, " you put on your garments in the manner of pagans whom your fathers expelled from the world ; an astonishing thing that you imitate those whose life you always hated[5]." The acknowledgment, however, of this return to their ancient habits authorizes us to consider Anuerin's description as applicable to their dress in the eighth as in the sixth century ; and indeed, from an inspection of numerous Anglo-Saxon MSS. illuminated during the tenth century, and the testimony of various writers of the sixth, we are led to conclude that little alteration in dress took place amongst the new masters of Britain for nearly four hundred years. And, strange as this may seem, we have strong collateral evidence in support of this belief in the unvarying costume of the Franks during nearly as long a period[6]. Of the same oriental origin, they seem to have adhered to their national dress with the same oriental tenacity ; and though they may not, like the Persians, have handed down the identical clothes from father to son as long as they could hang together, the form of their garments appears to have been rigidly preserved and the material unaltered.

The general

CIVIL COSTUME OF THE ANGLO-SAXONS, FROM THE
EIGHTH TO THE TENTH CENTURY,

consisted then of a linen shirt [7], a tunic of linen or woollen, according to the season, descending to the

---

[5] Concil. Calchut; Spelman, Concil. p. 300.

[6] Vide Montfaucon's Monarchie Française. The Frankish dress was, as nearly as possible, the Anglo-Saxon ; and Eginhart's elaborate description of Charlemagne's is a most valuable authority for the costume of this period.

[7] Charlemagne's shirt is expressly said to have been of linen, " Cammissium lineam." Eginhartus de Vita Caroli Magni.

Civil costume of the Anglo-Saxons.

Fig. *a*, King Edgar, from his Book of Grants to the Abbey of Winchester, A. D. 966; Cotton MSS. marked Vespasianus, A. VIII.; *b*, a figure in regal costume, from the splendid Benedictional of St. Æthelwold, in the possession of his Grace the Duke of Devonshire; *c*, noble Saxon youth, from Cotton MS. Claudius, B. iv.

knee, and having long close sleeves, but which set in wrinkles or rather rolls from the elbow to the wrist [8]. It was made like the shirt, and open at the neck to put on in the same manner. It was sometimes open at the sides, and confined by a belt or girdle round the waist. Its Saxon name was *roc* or *rooc*, and it was either plain or ornamented round the collar,

[8] In some instances these rolls are so regular as to present the appearance of a succession of bracelets, and when painted yellow they probably are intended so to do, as Malmsbury tells us the English at the time of the conquest were in the habit of *loading* their arms with them (brachia *onerati*); but it is also evident that generally the marks are merely indicative of a long sleeve wrinkled up, and confined by a single bracelet at the wrist, by removing which, perhaps, the sleeve was pulled out of its folds and drawn over the hand as a substitute for gloves, a custom of which we have hereafter historical notice.

wrists, and borders, according to the rank of the wearer[9]. Over this was worn a short cloak (*mentil*) like the Roman pallium or Gaulish sagum, fastened sometimes on the breast, sometimes on one or both shoulders with brooches or fibulæ. It appears that when once fastened it might be removed or assumed by merely slipping the head through; as in an illumination of the tenth century representing David fighting with a lion, he is supposed to have thrown his mantle on the ground, and it is seen lying still buckled in the form represented in our engraving, page 33.

Drawers reaching half way down the thigh, and stockings meeting them, occur in most Saxon illuminations, and are alluded to by writers under the names of *brech* and *hose*[10] Scin hose and leather hose are also mentioned, and may mean a species of buskin or short boot now and then met with, or literally leathern stockings.

Over these stockings they wore bands of cloth, linen, or leather, commencing at the ancle and terminating a little below the knee either in close rolls like the hay-bands of a modern ostler, or crossing each other sandal-wise, as they are worn to this day by the people of the Abruzzi and the Apennines, and in some parts of Russia and Spain. They are called in Saxon *scanc-beorg*, literally shank or leg-

---

[9] Charlemagne's was bordered with silk, " Tunicam quæ limbo serico ambiebatur." Eginhart. Paulus Diaconus, describing the dress of the Lombards, says, their vestments were loose and flowing, and consisted, like those of the Anglo-Saxons, chiefly of linen, ornamented with broad borders, woven or embroidered with various colours. De Gestis Longobardorum, lib. iv. c. 23.

[10] The femoralia or drawers of Charlemagne were of linen. Eginhart. The monk of St. Gall speaks of *tibialia vel coxalia* (stockings or drawers) of linen of one colour, but ornamented with precious workmanship, lib. i. c. 36. By the following note, we shall perceive he meant long drawers, or hose and drawers in one, like the Gaulish bracæ.

guard, and latinized *fasciolæ crurum*. In the
ancient canons the monks are commanded to
wear them of linen, to distinguish them from the
laity, who wore woollen[11]. Those of fig. *b*, in the
last engraving, are of gold in the original.

In some illuminations a sort of half-stocking or
sock, most likely the Saxon *socca*, is worn over the
hose instead of the bandages. It is generally bordered at the top, and reminds one of the Scotch
stocking, which probably, from the red cross gartering
imitated upon it, is a relic of the ancient Saxon or
Danish dress.

The Saxon shoe (*sceo* or *scoh*) is generally painted
black, with an opening down the instep, and secured
by a thong [12]. Labourers are generally represented
barelegged, but seldom barefooted [13].

The above articles composed the dress of all classes
from the monarch to the hind. The bretwald or
king, the ealderman, and the thegn were distinguished by the ornaments and richness, not the form,
of their apparel; except perhaps upon state occasions,
when the nobler classes wore the tunic longer and the
mantle more ample : but the same articles of dress
appear to have been common to Anglo-Saxons of all
conditions.

---

[11] Du Cange, in voce Fasciola. The Monk of St. Gall says
that over the stockings or drawers they (the Franks) wore long
fillets, bound crosswise in such a manner as to keep them properly upon the legs. These were worn as late as the sixteenth
century in France by the butchers, and called *les lingettes*.
Archæologia, vol. xxiv. p. 37.

[12] The terms *slype-sceo* and *unhege-sceo* seem to imply slippers
or shoes, in contradistinction to the boots or buskins sometimes
met with. The buskins of Louis le Debonaire, the son of Charlemagne, were of gold stuff or gilt, *ocreas aureas*. Theganus, in
Vita ejus. The shoes and buskins of Anglo-Saxon princes or
high ecclesiastical dignitaries are generally represented of gold.

[13] For caps and gloves, see pages 33, 34, and 36.

Towards the tenth century the national dress certainly became more magnificent; silk, which was known as early as the eighth century, but from its cost must have been exceedingly rare, was afterwards much worn by the higher classes. Bede mentions silken palls of incomparable workmanship[14], and his own remains were enclosed in silk, as were also those of Dunstan and other distinguished personages[15]. Adhelm, Bishop of Sherborne, who wrote in the seventh century, speaks of "the admirable art" exhibited in the weaving and embroidery of the English females even at that early period[16], and that reputation increased to such a degree as to cause the name of *Anglicum opus* to be given on the Continent to all rare work of that description[17]. A variety of colours appears to have been much admired. Red, blue, and green are most common in the illuminations. The hose are generally red or blue.

Their ornaments consisted of gold and silver chains and crosses, bracelets of gold, silver, or ivory, golden and jewelled belts, strings of amber or other beads, rings, brooches, buckles, &c. elaborately wrought. The metal articles were sometimes beautifully enamelled[18]. A jewel of gold, enamelled like a bulla or amulet, to hang round the neck, circumscribed "Ælfred me haet gewercan" (Alfred ordered me to be made), was found in the Isle of Athelney, whither that monarch retired on the invasion of Godrun. It is now in the Ashmolean Museum, and is engraved

[14] Bede, p. 297.   [15] Anglia Sacra, vol. ii.   [16] De Virginitate.
[17] Guli. Pictavensis, p. 211 ; Gesta Gulielmi Ducis, apud Duchene.
[18] " Charlemagne on state occasions wore a jewelled diadem; a tunic interwoven with gold ; a mantle fastened with a brooch of gold ; his shoes were adorned with gems ; his belt was of gold or silver ; and the hilt of his sword composed of gold and precious stones." Eginhart. Vide also Adhelm, William of Malmsbury, Dugdale, Hickes, &c. for notices of Saxon jewelry and ornaments.

here (from a print in the possession of Sir Henry
Ellis). No doubt is entertained of its authenticity.

That most widely diffused perhaps of all barbaric
customs—the practice of tatooing or puncturing the
skin, declared by the oldest historian extant to have
existed amongst the Scythians and Thracians, and
still at this day considered a badge of courage or
nobility amongst the savages of the South Pacific,
was not unknown to or unadmired by the Saxons.
Whether it was a national one originally, or adopted
in imitation of the Britons, we have no mode of
ascertaining; but that they practised it in the eighth
century is proved by a law having been passed against
it, A. D. 785 [19]. Yet as late as the Norman Conquest
we find included in the list of prevailing English
vices that of puncturing designs upon the skin[20], by
which it appears that fashion was as usual too strong
for the legislature.

[19] Wilkins's Concilia, tom. i.
[20] Malmsbury, De Gestis Regum Angliæ, lib. iii.

Long hair was the distinguishing characteristic of
the Teutonic tribes [21]. It was a mark of the highest
rank amongst the Franks, none of whom, but the
first nobility and princes of the blood, were permitted
to wear it in flowing ringlets [22], an express law com-
manding the people to cut their hair close round the
middle of the forehead [23]. The beard was also held
by them in the greatest reverence, and to touch it
stood in lieu of a solemn oath [24]. Amongst the
Anglo-Saxons the law made no invidious distinctions;
but the clergy preached for centuries against the sin-
fulness of long hair, which seems most perversely
to have grown the faster for the prohibition. In the
illuminations it appears not ungracefully worn, being
parted on the forehead, and suffered to fall naturally
down the shoulders : the beard is ample, and generally forked, and the character of the face immediately
designates the age wherein the early portraits of
Christ, which have been reverently copied to the present day, were originally fabricated [25].

It is a curious circumstance that the hair and beard
in the majority of Anglo-Saxon MSS. are painted
blue. In representations of old men this might be
considered only to indicate grey hair ; but even the
flowing locks of Eve are painted blue in one MS.
and the heads of youth and age exhibit the same
cerulean tint. Strutt says, " I have no doubt in my
own mind that arts of some kind were practised at

[21] Tacitus, De Morib. Germ.
[22] Agathias, lib. i.; Gregory of Tours, lib. vi.
[23] Ad frontem mediam circumtonsos. Jus Capillitii.
[24] Aimoin, lib. i. cap. 4.
[25] The Anglo-Saxon dress, both male and female, has indeed
been handed down to us by the painters of scriptural subjects,
who took of course for their models the effigies of the Apostles
and Saints as designed by the monks in the early ages of Christianity. Compare for instance the usual representations of the
Virgin Mary, with the female figures, page 34, or any others in
the Saxon or early Norman MSS.

this period to adorn the hair, but whether it was done by tinging or dyeing it with liquids prepared for that purpose, according to the ancient eastern custom, or by powders of different hues cast into it, agreeable to the modern practice, I shall not presume to determine [26]." We may add, that, if it *were* a fashion, we trust there is no chance of its revival, though we will not affirm that a generation whose fathers still

The military habits of the Anglo-Saxons.
Figs. *a* and *b*, from Claudius, b. iv.; *c*, from Harleian MS. 603; *d.* from Benedictional of St. Ethelwold.

[26] Dress and Habits of the People of England, vol. i. p. 77. The hair being painted sometimes *green* and *orange* is in favour of his argument, but such instances are very rare, and may have arisen from the idleness of the illuminator, who daubed it, perhaps, with the nearest colour at hand. The custom of washing the hair with a lixivium made of chalk, in order to render it redder, was practised by the Gauls, and the Arabs dye their beards with henna, after the example set them by their prophet Mahmood and his successor Abu-Bekr; but so singular a fashion as staining the hair blue or green could scarcely have escaped the monkish censors, who are so severe upon the minutest follies of their time, had it existed to such an extent as the illuminations would seem to imply. It occurs also in MSS. of the time of Edward I.

wear powder are justified in condemning in their remoter ancestors the use of powder-blue.

THE MILITARY HABIT

differed in no very great degree from the civil, in the earlier Anglo-Saxon times.

The Saxons were all soldiers, as their successors the Danes were all sailors. The addition of a sword or a spear, a shield, and sometimes, but not invariably, a helmet, was only wanting to make them as ready for the fray as for the feast. We should rather say the shield only had to be assumed, for the spear or the sword was the usual companion of a peaceful walk, and to go unarmed was enjoined in the ancient canons as a severe penance [27]. The short linen tunic was preferred to all other vestments, as the one in which they could most freely wield their weapons [28], and the only addition to it appears to have been a border of metal to the collar, which acted as a pectoral, and is most probably alluded to under the name of *broest-beden* or *broest-beorg*, breast-defence or breast-guard.

But though this remained, during the whole Anglo-Saxon era, their general habit in war as well as in peace, they were not unacquainted with defensive body armour, as we have already proved on the evidence of Anuerin; and the enigma of Adhelm, Bishop of Sherborne, who died in 709, proves that as early as the eighth century they were familiar with the *byrne*, or tunic of rings, derived from the Phrygians, and latinized indiscriminately with other armour *lorica*.

" I was produced," runs the enigma, " in the cold bowels of the dewy earth, and not made from the

---

[27] Canones dati sub Edgaro.
[28] Alcuinus, lib. de Offic. Divin. Alcuin wrote in the eighth century.

rough fleeces of wool; no woofs drew me, nor at
my birth did the tremulous threads resound; the
yellow down of silkworms formed me not; I passed
not through the shuttle, neither was I stricken with
the wool-comb; yet, strange to say, in common
discourse I am called a garment: I fear not the
darts taken from the long quivers[29]."

The ringed byrne is not, however, of frequent
appearance in the Anglo-Saxon illuminations, but
in the poems of the tenth century we hear of " the
shining iron rings," the " battle-mail by hard hands
well locked," the " mailed host of weaponed men,"
and "the grey vestments of war." It is probable,
therefore, that it did not become general till the continual descents of the heavily-armed Danes compelled
the Saxons to assume defences equal to those of their
enemies.

Coverings for the head are exceedingly rare in
paintings representing peaceful occupations, but in
battles we perceive the Phrygian-shaped cap before-
mentioned apparently made of leather, and sometimes
bound and bordered with metal. The " leather
helme" is continually mentioned by Saxon writers,
as is also the *fellen hœt*, the felt or woollen hat, which
is the same sort of cap made of those materials; as
the term *camb on hœtte*, or *camb on helme*, is clearly
explained by the serrated outline occasionally forming
the comb or crest of these Phrygian-looking head-
pieces[30]. A cap or helmet, completely conical and
without ornament, occurs in some MSS. and appears
from its shape the immediate predecessor of the nasal
helmet of the eleventh century.

The Anglo-Saxon shields were oval and convex,

[29] Aldhelmi Ænigmatum, headed " De Lorica." MS. Royal,
marked 15, A. 16.

[30] *Hœtt* signifies merely a covering for the head, and indicates
no such particular form as our modern associations are likely to
conjure up for it. The word used by the Latin writers of the
time is *pileus*.

with a peculiarly-shaped iron umbo or boss. They were gilt or painted in circles, but the ground was generally white, and they were held at arm's length in action like those of the Britons. Some of them were large enough to cover nearly the whole figure, but we not only see, but also read of "little shields" and " lesser shields," as well as of "the targan" or target[31]. The body of the shield was made of leather, and the rim as well as the boss was of iron, either painted or gilt.

Their weapons were all formed of iron, and consisted of long broad swords double-edged, daggers, javelins, and long spears, some of which were barbed and others broad and leaf-shaped. They had also axes with long handles which they called bills, and which continued in use almost to our time, and the double-axe or *bipennis* (*twy-bill*). Tradition has attributed to the Saxons a curved sword and dagger[32], called the long *seax* and the hand *seax*, from the use of which it has been supposed they derived their name; while, however, there is evidence of the existence of a Scythic tribe, called Sacassani and Saxones, as early as the days of Cyrus, there is little reason to seek further for the origin of the national name[33]. Our business is with the national weapon. The command of the Saxon leader previous to the celebrated massacre of the Britons at the festal board, as related by Nennius, " *Nimed eure seaxes*"—"Take your *seaxes*," they having concealed them about their persons, would go far to prove them short swords or daggers, but for one unfortunate circumstance : there is no positive proof of the massacre itself! The venerable Bede tells us that Edwin, King of Northumbria,

[31] Will of Ethelstan, son of Ethelred II. dated 1015.

[32] A short curved sword without a hilt is placed in the hands of the Dacians in the combats sculptured on the Trajan column.

[33] Vide Turner's Hist. Ang. Saxons, vol. i. p. 115, where this subject is admirably discussed.

narrowly escaped an assassin sent by Cwichelm, King
of Wessex, A. D. 625, who entered the unsuspecting
monarch's presence armed with a poisoned two-edged
seax ; and, while pretending to deliver a message
from his sovereign, made a blow at Edwin, who was
off his guard and defenceless. Lilla, an attendant
thegn, saw the king's danger, but had no shield. With
a noble devotion he flung himself between the assassin
and his intended victim, and received the weapon in
his own body. The thrust was given with such good
will that the *seax* went through the loyal thegn, and
slightly wounded Edwin. The assassin was cut to
pieces by the attendants, but not before he had
stabbed another knight with the weapon he had
withdrawn from the body of Lilla. The *twi eced
seax* of the venerable Bede has been translated " a
dagger" by Mr. Sharon Turner, and " a sword "
by Mr. Palgrave[34]. It may have been either, and
must have been used for cutting as well as thrusting,
from the expression two-edged ; but whether crooked
or straight does not appear from this story. If a
dagger, it must however have been a tolerably long
one to have gone through one man's body and
wounded another. The Saxon swords, in all the
illuminations we have inspected, are long, broad,
and straight, as we have already described them ;
and therefore, if a crooked weapon, the *seax* must
have been abandoned before the tenth century [35].

[34] Hist. of Eng. vol. i. p. 63.
[35] Major Hamilton Smith, in his Ancient Costume of England,
prints it as a compound " *se-ax*," and calls it a battle-axe ; and
Sir S. Meyrick derives it from *sais*, which in the low Saxon dia-
lect still signifies a scythe. (Costume Orig. Inhab. p. 50.) It
is not improbable that it was that primitive weapon. Of its frightful service in battle the gallant but ill-fated Poles have lately given
their oppressors a terrible proof. A staff so headed, with curved
lateral blades, is engraved on the opposite page, from a Harleian
MS. of the eleventh century, marked 603.

Robert Wace, the Norman poet, of whom more hereafter, mentions the gisarme as an exceedingly destructive weapon used by the Saxons at the battle of Hastings; but by the gisarme he evidently means the byl, to which he gives a Norman name.

Spurs appear in the Saxon illuminations. They have no rowels, but a simple point like a goad, and were therefore called *pryck* spurs, and the goad itself the *spur speare* (vide fig. *d*, p. 16). They were fastened with leathers, nearly as at present.

Anglo-Saxon mantle, caps, and weapons.
Harleian MS. 603; Cotton, Junius, xi.; Claudius, b. iv., &c.

Anglo-Saxon Females.
Fig, *a*, Etheldrytha, a princess of East Anglia, from the Benedictional of St. Ethelwold.

THE ANGLO-SAXON FEMALES

of all ranks wore long loose garments reaching to the ground, distinguished in various documents by the names of the tunic, the *gunna* or gown, the *cyrtle* or kirtle, and the mantle. The first and last articles describe themselves; but the terms gown and kirtle have caused much disputation from the capricious application of them to different parts of dress. The British gown, latinized *gaunacum* by Varro, we have already seen was a short tunic with sleeves reaching only to the elbows, and worn over the long tunic. And that the Saxon gunna was sometimes short, we have the authority of a Bishop of Winchester, who sends as a present " a short gunna sewed in our manner[36]." Now there is also

[36] 16 Mag. Bib. p. 82.   A gown is also mentioned made of otter's skin, which shows it to have been an exterior garment, p. 88.

authority sufficient to prove that a similar description of vestment was called a kirtle[37]. No short tunics are, however, visible in Saxon illuminations, and we must therefore presume the gunna or gown generally means the long full robe, with loose sleeves, worn over the tunic; and the kirtle, an *inner* garment, at this period, as we find it mentioned in the will of Wynflœda among "other *linen* web," and in one place described as *white*. The sleeves of the tunic, reaching in close rolls to the wrist, like those of the men, are generally confined there by a bracelet, or terminate with a rich border, and the mantle hangs down before and behind, covering the whole figure, except when looped up by the lifted arms, when it forms a point or festoon in front like the ancient chasuble of the priesthood[38]. The head-dress of all classes is a veil or long piece of linen or silk wrapped round the head and neck. This part of their attire is exceedingly unbecoming in the illuminations, in a great measure probably from want of skill in the artist; for no doubt it was capable of as graceful an arrangement as the Spanish mantilla. The Saxon name for it appears to have been *heafodes rœgel* (head-rail), or *wœfles*, derived from the verb *wœfan*, to cover; but this head-gear was seldom worn except when abroad, as the hair itself was cherished and ornamented with as much attention as in modern times. The wife described by Adhelm, Bishop of Sherborne,

---

[37] The very name implies a short garment. In the Icelandic song of Thrym we have the line "a maiden kirtle hung to his knees." In the MS. copy of Pierce Ploughman's Creed (Harleian, 2376), the priests are said to have "cut their cotes and made them into curtells" (the printed edition reads *courte pies*); and in a romance called the Chevalier Assigne (MS. Cotton. Caligula, A. 2) a child inquires, "What heavy kyrtell is this with holes so thycke?" and he is told it is "*an hauberke*" (i. e. coat of mail), which seldom reached even to the knee.

[38] Vide page 39.

who wrote in the eighth century, is particularly mentioned as having her twisted locks delicately curled
by the iron of those adorning her[39]; and in the
Anglo-Saxon poem of ' Judith,' the heroine is called
" the maid of the Creator, with twisted locks[40]." As
we find it amongst the Franks and Normans platted
in long tails, it may have been similarly worn by the
Anglo-Saxons; but with the exception of the figure
of Eve, who is represented in most illuminated MSS.
with her hair dishevelled and hanging about her
almost to her knees, we have met with no female
entirely divested of her head-rail.

Golden head-bands, half circles of gold, neck-bands,
and bracelets, are continually mentioned in Anglo-
Saxon wills and inventories. The head-band was
sometimes worn over the veil or head-cloth. Amongst
other female ornaments, we read of earrings, golden
vermiculated necklaces, a neck cross and a golden
fly beautifully ornamented with precious stones[41].

Hose or socca were most probably worn by females
as well as by men, but the gown or tunic invariably
conceals them. As much of the shoes as is visible is
generally painted black. In shape they appear similar to those of the men.

Gloves do not appear to have been worn by either
sex before the eleventh century[42]. In some instances
the loose sleeves of the gown supply their place by
being brought over the hand; in others the mantle is
made to answer the same purpose; but one of the

---

[39] De Virginitate, p. 307.   [40] Frag. Judith, edit. Thwaite.
[41] Dugdale's Monasticon, p. 240-263, and Strutt and Turner,
passim.
[42] At the close of the tenth, or beginning of the eleventh century, five pair of gloves made a considerable part of the duty paid
to Ethelred II. by a society of German merchants for the protection of their trade. Leges Ethelredi, apud Brompton; and quoted
with great propriety by Mr. Strutt in proof of their excessive rarity.
Dress and Habits, vol. i. p. 49.

female figures copied for the heading of this section
has something very like a glove upon the left hand.
It has a thumb but no separate fingers, and is painted
blue in the miniature, which is of the close of the
tenth century : a curious pair of similar mufflers, for
we can scarcely call them by any other name, occurs
in a MS. about a century later. Vide page 63 [43].

Cloth, silk, and linen were of course the principal
materials of which their dresses were made; and red,
blue, and green seem to have been the prevailing
colours with both sexes. Very little white is observed
in female apparel. The head-dress is always coloured. Indications of embroidery are visible in
some illuminations. The patterns are generally
rings, flowers, and sprigs. The standing figure in
page 34 represents Etheldrytha, a princess of East-
Anglia, and is copied from the Duke of Devonshire's
splendid Benedictional of the tenth century. The
dress is sumptuous, consisting of an embroidered
scarlet mantle over a tunic or gown of gold tissue,
or cloth of gold. The veil and shoes are also of the
latter costly material, and yet she is represented as a
sainted abbess. The conventual dress indeed of the
Anglo-Saxon era differed in nowise from the general
female habit, and Bishop Adhelm intimates that the
dress of royal Anglo-Saxon nuns in his time was
frequently gorgeous.

[43] These figures seem to have escaped Mr. Strutt's notice,
though he has inspected both MSS. and drawn much from the
latter.

THE CLERGY

were also undistinguishable from the laity except
by the tonsure[44], or when actually officiating at the
altar; and their inclination to the pomps and vanities
of the world is obvious from the order promulgated
in 785, forbidding them to wear the tinctured colours
of India, or precious garments[45]; and Boniface, the
Anglo-Saxon missionary, in his letter to the Archbishop of Canterbury, inveighs against the luxuries
of dress, and declares those garments that are
adorned with very broad studs and images of worms
announce the coming of Anti-Christ[46].

In the same spirit, at the Council of Cloveshoe,
the nuns were exhorted to pass their time rather in
reading books and singing hymns than in wearing
and working garments of empty pride in diversified
colours[47]. The official ecclesiastical habits will be
best understood by a glance at the engravings. The
mitre it will be perceived formed as yet no part of
the episcopal costume. Its first appearance in the
Latin church was about the middle of the eleventh
century[48].

[44] And this they endeavoured to hide by letting the hair grow
so as to fall over it, notwithstanding their thunders against the
laity; for an article interdicting the practice appears in Johnson's
Canons sub anno 960, c. 47. Beards were forbidden only to
the inferior clergy by the ancient ecclesiastical laws, and "dans
un concile tenu à Limoges en 1031, on declara qu'un prêtre
pouvait se raser ou garder la barbe à volonté." Lenoir, Monu-
mens François.

[45] Spelm. Concil. p. 294.   [46] Ibid. p. 241.

[47] Ibid. p. 256.

[48] Some difficulty exists in detailing the episcopal dress; but
the principal articles were the alb or white under tunic; the
dalmatica, an upper robe; the stole, an embroidered band or
scarf going round the neck, the two ends hanging down before;
the chasuble, which covered the whole person, except when lifted
up by the arms, and afterwards opened at the sides and cut in
front so as to preserve its original pointed appearance when

St. Dunstan.   Royal MS. 10, A. 13.

Abbot Elfnoth, and St. Augustin, Archbishop of Canterbury, Harleian MS.
2908.

the arms were raised ; and the pallium or pall, an ornamental
collar or scarf which a metropolitan or archbishop was in-
vested with, or received from the Pope on his nomination to
the see.   Gregory the Great bestowed the pallium on St. Augustin, first Archbishop of Canterbury, and he wears it embroidered
with crosses over the chasuble in the engraving above.   It may
be as well to remark at the same time that the crosier or cross
was carried by the archbishop, and the pastoral staff, made like the
shepherd's crook, and improperly called the crosier, by the
bishop.   Vide Bacon's New Atalantis.

The preceding figures are those of St. Dunstan, the famous or infamous Benedictine, in the habit of his order, from a drawing said to be by his own hand ; and Abbot Elfnoth (who died A. D. 980), presenting his book of prayers to St. Augustin, the founder of his monastery at Canterbury, from the frontispiece of the book itself, preserved in the Harleian collection of MSS., B.M. marked 2908.

MOURNING HABILIMENTS

are not discoverable in Anglo-Saxon illuminations. Representations of burials continually occur, but the mourners or attendants are not clothed in any particular fashion or colour. " Widow's garments" are mentioned in Saxon records, according to Strutt, but no account is given of their distinguishing character[49].

[49] Vide Strutt's Dress and Habits, vol. i. cap. 5.

Chapter III.

ANGLO-DANISH PERIOD, A.D. 1016—1041.

Canute and his queen Alfgyfe, from a MS. Register of Hyde Abbey, formerly in the possession of Thomas Astle, Esq., and engraved in the first
volume of Strutt's Horda Angel Cynan. Being excessively rude in the
original, they have been put into better drawing.

For the costume of the Danes, from the time of their
first descent upon the English coast to the establishment of their dominion in the island by Canute the
Great, we have but little authority on which we can
depend[1], but that little enables us to ascertain, that in

[1] The illuminations prefixed to a copy of the Gospels supposed
to have appertained to Canute, and preserved in the Cotton Library

many respects it resembled that of their Scythian kindred the Anglo-Saxons. Indeed, Mr. Strutt shrewdly enough remarks, that the silence of the Anglo-Saxon writers on the subject, while they are particularly diffuse in the description of the dress of their own countrymen, is corroborative of such similarity. It would appear, however, from various passages in the Welsh chronicles and the old Danish ballads, that the favourite if not the general colour of the ancient Danish dress was black[2]. Caradoc of Llancarvan repeatedly calls them " the black Danes." The chronicles continually allude to them by the name of the "black army." In the Danish ballad of ' Child Dyring' he is represented as riding even to a bridal feast in " black sendell[3]," and black, bordered with red, is still common amongst the northern peasantry. Black amongst the Pagan Danes had certainly no funeral associations connected with it. We have already noticed the absence of black in representations of Saxon burials, but it is well known that the Danes never mourned for the death of even their nearest or dearest relations[4]; and this sombre hue may have been their national colour, their standard being a raven[5]. Arnold of Lubeck describes the whole

(marked Caligula, A. 7), do not belong to the MS., and were probably executed about the time of Rufus. Mr. Astle's reliquary, which is said to represent the murder of Theodore, Abbot of Croyland, by the Danes in 890, is, we strongly suspect, of the age of Henry II.

[2] The Danes being undoubtedly of Scythic origin, it is a curious circumstance that we should find Herodotus mentioning a nation bordering on Scythia who wore no other clothing than black, and whom he therefore calls the Melanchloenians.

[3] Silk. Danish Kœmpe-Vizer. Illustrations of Northern Antiquities, 4to. Edin.

[4] Adam of Bremen distinctly mentions this fact. He flourished about 1127, and may be called, says Mr. Sharon Turner, the Strabo of the Baltic. Hist. Eng. vol. i. p. 30, note.

[5] See account of the celebrated Ræfan, worked by Ubo's three

nation as originally wearing the garments of sailors, as befitted men who lived by piracy and inhabited the sea; but that, in process of time, they became wearers of scarlet, purple, and fine linen [6]. It is probable, therefore, that on their conversion to Christianity they cast their "'nighted colour off," and on their establishment in England endeavoured to outshine the Saxons; for we are told that " the Danes were effeminately gay in their dress, combed their hair once a day, bathed once a week, and often changed their attire : by these means they pleased the eyes of the women, and frequently seduced the wives and daughters of the nobility [7]."

A Saxon MS. Register of Hyde Abbey, written during the reign of Canute, contains his portrait and that of his queen Alfgyfe. (Vide engraving at the head of this chapter.) The king is in a tunic and mantle, the latter ornamented with cords or ribands, and tassels. He wears shoes, and stockings reaching nearly to the knees, with embroidered tops. The dress is perfectly Saxon. In June, 1766, some workmen repairing Winchester Cathedral discovered a monument, wherein was contained the body of Canute. It was remarkably fresh, had a wreath or circlet round the head, and several other ornaments, such as gold and silver bands. On his finger was a ring, in which was set a remarkably fine stone ; and in one of his hands was a silver penny [8].

The materials of which their habits were composed must have been very splendid. The coronation mantle of Harold Harefoot, given to the Abbey of Croyland, was of silk, embroidered with flowers of gold [9].

sisters in one noontide, and taken by Odon, Earl of Devonshire, in the time of Alfred. Asserius in Vita Alfr.

[6] Chap. 5, ver. 11.   [7] John Wallingford, apud Gale.

[8] Archæologia, vol. iii. p. 890.

[9] Ingulphus, Hist. Abb. Croyl.

The vestment which Canute presented to the same abbey was of silk, embroidered with golden eagles [10]; and the rich pall, which he ordered to be laid over the tomb of Edmund Ironside, was embroidered with " the likeness of golden apples, and ornamented with pearls [11]."

Bracelets of massive gold, and some of them curiously wrought, were worn by all persons of rank, and always buried with them[12]. The Pagan Danes had, indeed, a sacred ornament of this kind kept upon the altar of their gods, or worn round the arm of the priest, and by which their most solemn vows were made; their common oaths being, " by the shoulder of their horse," or " by the edge of their sword." Alfred, having gained an advantage over the Danes, caused them to swear by their holy bracelet, which they had never done before to the king of any nation[13].

Of their pride in their long hair, and the care they took of it, we have several instances recorded. Harold Harfagre, i. e. Fair-locks, who derived his name from the length and beauty of his hair, which is said to have flowed in thick ringlets to his girdle, and to have been like golden or silken threads, made a vow to his mistress to neglect his precious curls till he had completed the conquest of Norway for her love [14]; and a young Danish warrior, going to be beheaded, begged of his executioner that his hair might not be touched by a slave, or stained with his blood[15]. In the Anglo-Saxon poem on Beowolf, mention is made of

> " The long-haired one, illustrious in battle,
> The bright lord of the Danes."

[10] Ingulphus, Hist. Abb. Croyl.   [11] Scala Chron.
[12] Bartholinus ; Johannes Tinmuth.
[13] Asserius in Vit. Alfred, and Ethelwerd, Hist. lib. iv. cap. 3.
[14] Torfœus, Hist. Nor. tom. ii. lib. 1.
[15] Jomswikinga Saga in Bartholinus de Caus. Contempt. Mort. lib. i. c. 5.

On their arrival in England we still find them atten-
tive to these flowing locks, combing them once a day ;
but a few years afterwards the fashion of cropping was
imported from France, as we shall see in the next
chapter, and the portrait of Canute seems to have
been drawn after that change took place. The
Knyghtlinga Saga describes Canute's hair as profuse.

THE ARMOUR OF THE ANGLO-DANES

was similar to that of the Anglo-Saxons of the tenth
century. By the laws of Gula, said to have been
established by Hacon the Good, who died in 963, we
find that any possessor of 600 marks, besides his
clothes, was required to furnish himself with a red
shield of two boards in thickness, a spear, and an axe
or a sword. He who was worth twelve marks, in
addition to the above, was ordered to procure a steel
cap (stàl hufu) ; whilst he who was richer by eighteen
marks was obliged to have a double red shield, a helmet, a coat of mail (brynin), or a *panzar*, that is to
say a tunic of quilted linen or cloth (which hereafter
we shall find worn by the Normans under the name
of a gambeson), and all usual military weapons [16]. In
the history of this same king, who was called " Adel-
stein's Fostra," from having been educated at the
court of our English Athelstan, we read that the king
put on a tunic of mail (brynio) girded round him, his
sword called quern-bit (i. e. millstone-biter), and set
on his head his gilded helmet. He took a spear in
his hand, and hung his shield by his side [17]. So also,
in the description of the battle of Sticklastad, where
King Olaf of Norway, called the Saint, was slain,
A.D. 1030, the monarch is said to have worn a golden

[16] Thorstens Vikings-sons Saga, with Reenhielm's notes, 12mo,
Lips. 1680, cap. 10, p. 78.
[17] Heimskringla, i, 155, edit. Schöning.

helmet, a white shield, a golden hilted and exceedingly sharp sword, and a tunic of ringed mail, " hringa
brynio [18]," the " ringed byrne" of the Saxons. The
Danish helmet, like the Saxon, had the nasal, which
in Scandinavian is called nef-biorg [19].

The Danish shields were of two sorts, circular and
lunated ; the latter rising in the centre of the inner
curve, and therefore exactly resembling the Phrygian
or Amazonian pelta[20]. That they were generally
painted red we learn from the laws of Gula before
quoted ; and Giraldus de Barri, who was an eye-
witness of the transactions of the Northmen in Ireland in the next century, says, " the Irish carry red
shields in imitation of the Danes." Persons of distinction, however, ornamented theirs very highly with
gilding and various colours[21] ; and though regular

[18] Ibid. ii. 352.

[19] Saga Magn. Burf, c. 11.

[20] Strutt, Horda Angel Cynan. The shield engraved there is
from an Anglo-Saxon MS. marked Tiberius, C. 6, in the Cotton
collection. It was not peculiar to the Danes, but carried, apparently, by all who fought with the battle-axe. The expression
" moony shields" occurs in the Lodbroka-quida, but it may mean
orbicular. That the Scythians pursued the Cimmerians into Asia
Minor, six or seven hundred years before Christ, is asserted by
Herodotus and Strabo ; and the tribes that afterwards migrated
with Odin towards the Baltic might have adopted, from their con-
sanguinei, the Phrygian shield as well as the Phrygian cap and
tunic of rings. In the Royal Museum at Copenhagen is an ancient
group of figures cut out of the tooth of the walrus, in which
appears a king on horseback, holding a crescent-shaped shield.
Archæologia, vol. xxiv.

[21] Sir F. Madden has collected all the known authorities on the
subject in an interesting paper in the Archæologia, vol. xxiv. He
remarks " the usual pigments were white and red." The white
shield was the distinction of the ancient Cimbri. Vide Plutarch
in Mario, Val. Max. lib. ii. c. 6. The Goths of all descriptions seem
to have borne them originally white, and ornamented them by degrees with gold and colours. In the poetical Edda Gunnar, one
of the Reguli of Germany is made to say, " my helmet and white
shield come from the Hall of Kiars" (a Gaulish chief who lived

armorial bearings are not acknowledged earlier than
the middle of the twelfth century, fanciful devices and
personal insignia were used by the Romans and the
Gauls, and crosses were gilt and painted on the white
Norwegian shields at the commencement of the
eleventh, according to a MS. quoted by Sperlingius,
describing an expedition of King Olaf the Saint, who
also ordered his soldiers to chalk a cross upon their
helmets. In Sæmund's poetical Edda, mention is
made of a red shield with a golden border, and the
encomiast of Queen Emma, in describing Canute's
armament, speaks of the glittering effulgence of the
shields suspended on the sides of the ships [22].

Of the splendour sometimes exhibited in the military accoutrements of this period, we have another
instance in the attempt of Earl Goodwin to appease
the anger of Hardicanute. He presented that prince
with a magnificent vessel, on board of which were
eighty soldiers, armed in coats of gilded mail, their
shields embossed with gold, and their helmets richly
gilt. Each of them had two golden bracelets on
either arm, weighing sixteen ounces. The hilts of
their swords were also of the same precious metal,
and every man had a Danish axe on his left shoulder,
and a spear in his right hand [23].

The spear, the sword, the bow, and particularly the
double-bladed axe, were their offensive weapons.
They were famous for the use of the latter. The
Welsh bard Gruffyd ab Merredydd speaks of

in the sixth century). The Anglo-Saxon shields in the illuminations are generally white, with red or blue borders and circles
painted on them, but we find no crosses depicted on them before
the eleventh century—a fact which bears out Sperlingius in his conjecture that they were introduced (in the north at least) by St.
Olaf, as above-mentioned.

[22] Encom. Emmæ. Ap. Du Chesne, p. 168.

[23] Florence of Worcester, 403; MS. Chron.; Cotton, Tiberius,
B. i. and iv.

> "A destructive heavy fleet
> Of the men of Lochlyn (Denmark)
> With their keen-edged axes."

"At Scarpa-Skeria," says the dying king, Ragnar Lodbroch, " cruelly hacked the trenchant battle-axe." " To shoot well with the bow" was also a necessary qualification of a Danish warrior. The Saxons had totally neglected archery.

We have little or no authority for the

ANGLO-DANISH FEMALE COSTUME,

but can scarcely doubt its similarity to the general habit of the sex in the north of Europe at this period. Canute's queen wears the tunic, the mantle, the veil, and either the diadem or the half-bend ; but she was the widow of Ethelred, and daughter of Richard, third Duke of Normandy. The mantle, like that of the king, has cords or ribands, with tasselled ends attached to it. In the poem on Beowolf, the following lines appear respecting the Queen of Denmark :—

> "Waltheow came forth,
> The queen of Hrothgar,
> Mindful of her descent,
> Circled with gold.
>   *   *   *   *   *
> She the queen, circled with bracelets."

And again—

> " Encircled with gold she went,
> The queen of the free-like people,
> To sit by her lord."

In the Danish ballad of Ingefred and Gerdrune [24], mention is made of Ingefred's golden girdle, and she takes a gold ring from her arm to give to the physician.

[24] Kempe Viser, p. 662.

It is scarcely necessary to remark, on closing this chapter, that though the monarch, and many of his nobles, warriors, and domestics, were Danes, the people were still Anglo-Saxons ; and if any difference in dress did exist between the two nations, the Danes were as likely to adopt the fashions of their new country, as the English were to assume those of their new rulers.

CHAPTER IV.

REIGNS OF EDWARD THE CONFESSOR & HAROLD II., A.D. 1042—1066.

Seal of Edward the Confessor.

THE short interval between the Danish and Norman conquests, during which the crown of England reverted to the Saxon line, furnishes us with only two anecdotes of costume worth recording. The first is the general complaint of William of Malmsbury, that in the time of the Confessor the English had transformed themselves into Frenchmen and Normans, adopting not only their strange manner of speech and behaviour, but also the ridiculous and fantastic fashions of their habits, wearing shorter tunics, and clipping their hair and shaving their beards, leaving, however, the upper lip still unshorn[1].   They were also guilty of puncturing their skins, and loading their arms with golden bracelets[2].   The second respects a change ordered by Harold in

Harold II. from the Bayeux tapestry.

THE MILITARY HABIT

which led to his decisive successes in Wales.   The heavy armour of the Saxons (for the weight of the tunic, covered with iron rings, was considerable) rendered them unable to pursue the Welsh to their

[1] Hist. Reg. Ang. lib. iii.

[2] In the reign of James II. the chest containing the body of King Edward the Confessor was opened, and under the shoulder bone of the Monarch was found a crucifix of pure gold, richly enamelled, and suspended to a golden chain twenty-four inches in length, which, passing round the neck, was fastened by a locket of massy gold, adorned with four large red stones.   The skull, which was entire, had on it a band or diadem of gold, one inch in breadth, surrounding the temples, and in the dust lay several pieces of gold, coloured silk, and linen.   Archæologia, vol. iii. p. 890.   Introduction to Gough's Sepulchral Monuments.

recesses. Harold observed this impediment, and commanded them to use armour made of leather only, and lighter weapons[3]. This leathern armour we find to have consisted in overlapping flaps, generally stained of different colours, and cut into the shape of scales or leaves. It is called corium by some of the writers in the succeeding century, and corietum in the Norman laws. It was most probably copied from the Normans, for in the Bayeux tapestry we perceive it worn by Guy, Count of Ponthieu, and Odo, Bishop of Bayeux, the brother of William the Conqueror, and it continued in use in England as late as the thirteenth century.

[3] Ingulphus, p. 68.

CHAPTER V.

REIGN OF WILLIAM THE CONQUEROR, A.D. 1066—1087.

William I. and Attendants, from the Bayeux tapestry.

THE best pictorial authority for the habits of our Norman ancestors, at the time of their conquest of England, exists in that curious relic the Bayeux tapestry [1], which, if not worked by the Conqueror's wife Matilda, as currently reported, is certainly not a

[1] Preserved at Bayeux in Normandy. It is 212 feet long, and rudely worked in coloured worsteds like a *sampler*.

great deal later than that memorable event, and fully entitled to our confidence as a faithful representation of the habits, armour, and weapons of William and his followers.

The Saxons, as we have already observed, had, during the reign of Edward the Confessor, affected the fashions of the Norman French; and the similarity of their habits to those of their invaders is the first object of remark on examining their performance: while a singular attention to such little points of distinction, as we have the evidence of cotemporary historians to prove did exist between the two nations, gives additional weight and interest to its testimony.

Offsets of the same great barbaric stock, a species of family resemblance had always existed between the Saxons, the Danes, and the Normans; but the residence of the latter in France, and their expeditions to the Mediterranean, had materially improved their character and manners; and while the Danes continued pirates, and the Saxons, " originally the fiercest nation of the predatory North[2]," had sunk into a slothful and unwarlike people, the Normans became distinguished throughout Europe for their military skill, their love of glory, their encouragement of literature, the splendour and propriety of their habiliments, the cleanliness of their persons, and the courtesy of their demeanour.

The degenerate and sensual Saxons imitated the fashions of their neighbours, but were incapable of copying their virtues, and we therefore find the general

CIVIL COSTUME OF THE NORMANS

consisting, like the Anglo-Saxon, of the short tunic, the cloak, the drawers, with long stockings or panta-

[2] Sharon Turner.

loons with feet to them, called by the Normans "Chaussés," by which term we beg our readers to observe they will be henceforth designated throughout the work, as the use of modern names for ancient habits or weapons creates considerable confusion in dates as well as ideas. Shoes and leg-bandages are worn as before[3]. Short boots are also common towards the close of the reign[4]; and a flat round cap, like a Scotch bonnet, and another, which appears little more than a coif, are the general head coverings of unarmed persons. In

STATE DRESSES

the tunic reaches to the ancle, and the mantle is ample and flowing to correspond. The crown of the monarch is scarcely distinguishable upon his seal, but appears to resemble that of the Confessor. Wace, in his 'Roman de Rou[5],' describes William as lacing and untying his cloak repeatedly in his agitation and anger, on the news being brought him of Harold's accession to the throne of England; and cords and tassels are now seen attached to the mantles of distinguished personages. We have observed them already in the drawing of Canute.

The Normans not only shaved the face *entirely*, in

[3] Duke William's, in the Bayeux tapestry, are tied in front with tasselled ends hanging down like those of the royal figure in St. Ethelwold's Benedictional, engraved p. 22.

[4] Robert, Duke of Normandy, the eldest son of the Conqueror, who died in 1134, was called "Curta Ocrea," or short boots, either from his setting the fashion, or for retaining it perhaps when abandoned by the beaux of the day.

[5] A poem on Rollo, or Rou, and the other Dukes of Normandy. Robert Wace died in 1184. He was born in Jersey, and educated in Caen, and wrote his account of the battle of Hastings from the information of persons who lived at the time: "as I heard it told my father. I well remember it; I was then a varlet," are his words.

contradistinction to the Anglo-Saxons, who left, at
any rate, the upper lip unshorn, but before the time
of the Conquest had adopted the Aquitanian fashion
of shaving the back of the head also, which occasioned the spies of Harold to report that they had
seen no soldiers, but an army of priests[6]. This
anecdote has been quoted by all the historians, as
proving only the absence of beard and moustache
amongst the Normans, as they say it was considered
indecent in priests to wear them ; but clerical personages are, notwithstanding, continually represented
at this period with *both*, and the absence of them,
therefore, would not have borne out the reports of
the spies, but for the other singularity, which is distinctly represented in the Bayeux tapestry, and one
of the strongest proofs of its authenticity. William
and his Normans are therein distinguished by the
backs of their heads being closely shaven, so as really
to give them a monkish appearance, while the Saxons
are represented with hair as usually worn, and
moustaches, as described by William of Malmsbury,
and a few with comely beards [7].

[6] William of Malmsbury, lib. iii. p. 56 ; Roman de Rou. Wace's
words are *tout rez et tondu*. Literally "all shaven and shorn."

[7] That the nobles of Aquitaine had been distinguished by this
extraordinary practice for many years previous to the Conquest,
we find from the following circumstance. Robert, King of France,
who came to the throne in 997, married Constance, Princess of
Poitou. Many of her relations and countrymen followed her to Paris ;
and Glaber Rodolphus describes them, at that time, as full of the
most conceited levity; their manners and dress equally fantastic,
their arms and trappings without taste ; *bare from the middle* of
their heads, their beards shaven like minstrels, their boots and shoes
most unbecoming, &c. &c. He stigmatizes them also, in another
place, for their short garments, and says, their abominable
example infected all the nation of the Francs and Burgundians
till then " honestissima," and drew it into a conformity with their
own wickedness and baseness. Hist. p. 39; Turner's England,
book viii. chap. 3, note.

William I. and two Normans, from the Bayeux tapestry, illustrating the Norman fashion of shaving the back of the head.

Notwithstanding, however, that the Norman rage for cropping and shaving had obtained amongst the English, the old fashion of wearing the hair long and flowing was never entirely abandoned; and the courtiers of the Regent of France, on William's return to Normandy, three months after his coronation, attended by some of his new subjects, were astonished at the beauty of the long-haired English, and their rich gold embroidered dresses [8].

Helmets, hauberks, a sword, and a gonfanon, from the Bayeux tapestry.

[8] William of Poitou, p. 211; Florence of Worcester, p. 431; Ordericus Vitalis, lib. viii.

THE MILITARY HABIT

of this period presents us with several novelties. The
first is the capuchon or cowl [9] to the tunic covered
with rings, which perhaps was worn by the Danes,
but does not appear in Saxon illuminations. Over
this is placed the conical helmet, with its nasal, and,
in some instances, with a neck-piece behind, an
oriental characteristic. Both Normans and Saxons
are represented in the ringed tunic, which descends
below the knee, and being cut up a little way before
and behind for convenience in riding, appears, from
the rudeness of the representation, as though it terminated in short trousers [10]. The Norman name for
this military vestment was *Hauberk*, latinized *Hal-
bercum*, which is commonly derived from *Halsberg*,
a protection for the throat [11]; and as we now bid
adieu to the Saxon era, we shall henceforth gladly

[9] The word " cowl" is used in preference to "hood," as, in the
fourteenth century, " the hood," so called, becomes a very peculiar
feature, and bears no resemblance whatever: o the cowl, with
which it might be confounded, although it was probably invented
from a peculiar fashion of wearing the latter. Vide p. 121. We wish
to keep the ideas perfectly distinct of the cowl or capuchon, and
the hood or chaperon, though the words are frequently used one for
the other by the old writers.

[10] That it does not do so is proved, not only by the appearance
of the tunic alone, as carried by the Normans to the ships (Vide
engraving in p. 57), but by the evident impossibility of getting into
a garment so made. Amongst the·last incidents in the tapestry,
we find one of the victors stripping a dead warrior of his armour,
which he is pulling over his head *inverted*, an act incompatible
with any other form than that of a simple shirt or tunic; and
William himself is stated to have inverted his coat of mail by
mistake when preparing for the battle of Hastings. Guil. Pict.
201 ; and Taylor's Anon. Hist. p. 192.

[11] It is not improbable that the addition of the cowl obtained for
it this particular name, as before that addition it certainly did not
protect the throat. In the laws of William the Conqueror we
find it spelt " Halbers." "viii Chivalz selez e enfrenez, iiii
Halbers e iiii Hammes (Heaumes, Helmets) e iiii Escuz e iiii
Launces e iiii Espes." Leges Gulielmi I. cap. xxii.

use an appellation as familiar to the hot-pressed pages
of modern romance as to the worm-eaten chronicle of
the eleventh century.   Besides the hauberk of rings,
there are some marked with transverse lines, so as to
give the idea of their being either quilted or stitched
in chequers, or covered with small lozenge-shaped
pieces of steel instead of rings, a species of defence
known about this period by the name of mascled
armour, from its resemblance to the meshes of a
net[12].   In some instances the hauberks are composed of rings and mascles mixed ; in others the
body is covered with rings, and the sleeves dia-
monded.   There were other descriptions of armour
in use about this time, which the embroiderers may
have intended to represent, viz. the trelliced, the
rustred, the banded, &c. varieties of mail alluded to
by cotemporary writers[13], but almost impossible to
be distinguished from each other in the half-obliterated
seal or rudely woven tapestry.   Our own opinion
leans to the idea that the garments so chequered are
meant for the quilted panzar or gambeson, known
to the Danes and Northmen, as we have already
remarked, and which we shall have occasion to describe more fully anon.   One of the warriors has the
collar of his hauberk drawn up over his chin and
fastened to the nasal.   By illuminations of the next
century, we find this a common practice, till it was
superseded by the introduction of the vizor.   On the
breast of several knights is a square pectoral[14], either
quilted or covered with rings, as an additional defence,
and some wear chaussés of similar materials.   The
pectorals and the sleeves and skirts of the hauberks

[12] Johannes de Janua says the word is derived from the Latin
macula.
[13] Vide Meyrick's letter on the body armour anciently worn in
England.   Archæologia, vol. xix.
[14] The "breast-beden" of the Saxons,

have yellow borders ; whether of metal for defence,
or of gilt leather, or lace for ornament, we have no
authority for deciding.

The shields of the Normans are nearly of the
shape of a boy's kite, and are supposed to have been
assumed by them in imitation of the Sicilians, as, fifty
years before the Conquest of England, Melo, the
chief of Bari, furnished them with arms, and, twelve
years afterwards, they conquered Apulia[15]. On comparing also the shields in the Bayeux tapestry with
those of the Sicilian bronzes, there can remain very
little doubt of the fact.

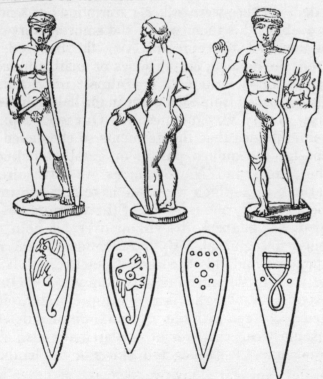

Sicilian bronzes in the Meyrick collection, and Norman shields from the
Bayeux tapestry.

These shields, besides the holders, as the straps

[15] Meyrick, Critical Inquiry, vol. i.

were called through which the arm passed, had a long strip of leather which went round the neck and formed an additional support for it, while it enabled them to use both hands with greater facility. (Vide the last in the preceding engraving, which presents the inner side, with the strap twisted.) This extra strap was called the guige, and the Norman poet remarks the advantage it gave his countrymen over the Saxons, who, he says, did not know how to joust (tilt), nor to carry arms on horseback. " When they wished to strike with their battle-axe, they were forced to hold it with both hands. To strike strong, and at the same time to cover themselves, was what they could not do :" for the Anglo-Saxon shield was, as we have before mentioned, held at arm's length by the clenched hand (a distinction particularly attended to in the tapestry). The wielders, therefore, of double-handed weapons either could not carry such a protection or must drop it for the blow.

Some of the Norman shields bear the rude effigies of a dragon, griffin, serpent, or lion ; others, crosses, rings, and various fantastic devices, but no regular heraldic bearings. A griffin is observable on one of the Sicilian shields, but, as might be expected, in better drawing.

In the Bayeux tapestry, William and his principal knights are seen with lances, ornamented with small flags or streamers, which were termed in the language of that day Gonfanons or Gonfalons. Upwards of seven hundred years have elapsed since the Conquest; the lance has again become an English military weapon, and the streamer is still attached to it.

In the Norman army we perceive archers, both mounted and on foot ; that nation excelling in the use of the bow, which had been much neglected, if not totally discontinued, in England during the Saxon era. Henry of Huntingdon makes William speak of the Saxons as a nation not even having arrows. A random shaft, it is well known, struck Harold in the eye at the battle of Hastings; and to the arrows of the Normans, generally, the issue of the contest is attributed by our early historians.

Clubs are seen in the hands of William and his half-brother Odo, Bishop of Bayeux.

The ' Roman de Rou' says of the latter,—

> " Sur un cheval tout blanc seoit
> Toute la gent le congnoissoit;
> Un baston tenoit en son poing[16]."

The which "baston," we learn from the Bayeux tapestry, was not the leading-staff afterwards introduced, but a good stout cudgel, with which he " encouraged the youths[17]."

Balistarii, or slingers, were in both armies, and slightly accoutred. The battle-axes and bills of the Saxon infantry are recorded as making terrible havoc amongst the Normans[18]. The Norman spur is the same as that of the Saxons.

THE ANGLO-NORMAN LADIES

were attired similarly to the Anglo-Saxon. They wore the long tunic, and over it a garment answering to the Saxon *gunna* or gown, but which of course the Normans called " robe [19];" and the veil or head-cloth, which in like manner they rendered *couvre-chef,* from whence our word kerchief. The principal novelty is in the gown or *robe,* which was laced close to fit the figure, as we shall shortly discover,

[16] Mémoires de L'Acadamie des Inscriptions, tom. xii. p. 466.
[17] " Hic Odo Eps. baculum tenens confortat."
[18] Wace speaks of gisarmes, but he evidently uses a Norman name for the Saxon weapon. For a description of the gisarme see page 88.
[19] It was sometimes short like the Saxon *gunna;* at others, equally long with the under tunic.

Anglo-Norman Ladies, from Illum. MS. Cotton, Nero, C. 4.

and has sleeves tight to the wrist, and then suddenly widening and falling to some depth. The borders of the dresses are of gold and very broad. The hair, when seen, is long, and sometimes platted in two or more divisions, after the Gothic fashion.

The two figures engraved above, are copied from some illuminations illustrative of scripture history, which we consider to have been executed in France about this period, as they exhibit all those peculiarities of costume which distinguished the commencement of the Norman era, and provoked the wrath and satire of the cotemporary chroniclers. The female to the right is from a miniature representing the presentation of the infant Jesus in the temple, and bears the sacrifice of "a pair of turtle doves, or two young pigeons[20]."

[20] St. Luke, chap. ii. ver. 24.

Her hands are covered with the curious mufflers,
alluded to in page 36; they are in form exactly like
the single one on the left hand of the Anglo-Saxon
females, but have long streamers attached to them,
and over the right-hand one is a thin gauze or fine
linen cloth, in which the doves are carried, the end
appearing to pass under the sleeve of the left arm.
The painter's skill has perhaps not seconded his
intention in this respect, but, as it has nothing to do
with the costume, we will not waste our time in speculations upon it.   The mufflers themselves are very
singular, and too distinctly drawn to admit of a doubt
respecting their form or object.

A Bishop of the close of the 11th century, Cotton MS. Nero, C. 4.

ECCLESIASTICAL COSTUME.

The figure of a bishop of this period, represents him in a bonnet, slightly sinking in the centre, with the pendent ornaments of the mitre (vittæ or infulæ) attached to the side of it. The chasuble retains its original shape; the dalmatica appears to be arched at the sides ; the pastoral staff is exceedingly plain, and reminds us strongly of the Roman *lituus*, which is said by some writers to have been its prototype.

CHAPTER VI.

REIGNS OF WILLIAM II., HENRY I., AND STEPHEN,
A.D. 1087—1154.

Royal habits of the commencement of the 12th century, from Cotton MS.
Nero, C. 4.

THE Normans and the Flemings who accompanied
the Conqueror into England, and those who followed
him in great numbers after his establishment upon
the throne, are said by our early historians to have
been remarkable for their ostentation and love of
finery. Personal decoration was their chief study,

and new fashions were continually introduced by them [1].

Habits of the commencement of the 12th century, from Cotton MS. Nero, C. 34; and a psalter in the collection of the late Mr. Douce.

THE DRESS OF THE COMMON PEOPLE

continued to be a short tunic with sleeves. The better sort wore chaussés and shoes, or short boots, and in bad weather, or when travelling, covered the head and shoulders with a cloak or mantle, having a cowl attached to it, and called by the Normans the *capa.* The Phrygian-shaped cap is still worn, and a hat appears in one illumination of this date resembling the Roman *petasus,* or a modern English carter's.

THE HABITS OF THE NOBILITY

were of course more influenced by fashion, and the reign of Rufus is stigmatized by the writers of the period for many shameful abuses and innovations. The

[1] Strutt's Dress and Habits.

king himself set the example, and clergy and laity became alike infected with the love of extravagant and costly clothing. The short tunic was lengthened and worn fuller, and the sleeves particularly so. The long tunic, worn on state occasions, and the *interula,* or linen vestment worn beneath it, positively trailed upon the ground. The sleeves were also of length and breadth sufficient to cover the whole hand[2]. But that gloves were now worn, at least by the higher classes, we find from the account of the Bishop of Durham's escape from the Tower during the reign of Henry I., as, having " forgotten his gloves," he rubbed the skin off his hands to the bone in sliding down the rope from his window[3]. The mantles were made of the finest cloth, and lined with rich furs[4]; one presented to Henry I. by Robert Bloet, Bishop of Lincoln, was lined with black sables. with white spots, and cost £100[5]. With the shorter tunic a shorter cloak was worn, lined with the most precious furs, and called the *rheno*[6]. Peaked-toed boots and shoes, of an absurd shape, excited the wrath and contempt of the monkish historians. Ordericus Vitalis says they were invented by some one deformed in the foot. The peaked-toed boots, called *ocreæ rostratæ,* were strictly forbidden to the clergy. The shoes called *pigaciæ* had their points made like a scorpion's tail, and a courtier named Robert stuffed his out with tow, and caused them to curl round in form of a ram's horn, a fashion which took mightily amongst the nobles, and obtained for its originator the cognomen of Cornadu[7].

[2] Ordericus Vitalis. Vide also engraving at head of chapter.
[3] Ordericus Vitalis, p. 780, 787. [4] Ordericus Vitalis.
[5] Malmsbury, lib. v. p. 98; Henry Huntingdon, p. 222.
[6] Ordericus Vitalis.
[7] These peaked toes are alluded to by Anna Comnena, who mentions them as encumbering the dismounted cavalry of the Franks. Alexias, lib. v. p. 140. The Greek term has been ignorantly trans-

We have noticed the extraordinary custom of shaving the back of the head as well as the face, in use amongst the Norman-French. On their establishment in England this unbecoming custom appears soon to have been abandoned, and with the usual caprice of fashion the Anglo-Normans seem to have run into the opposite extreme ; for William of Malmsbury, the same writer whose lamentations over the cropping system we lately quoted, is compelled, during the reign of Rufus, to reprobate the long hair, the loose flowing garments, the extravagant pointed shoes, and the unweaponed effeminate appearance of the youths of that day[8].

In 1104, when Henry I. was in Normandy, a prelate named Serlo, preached so eloquently against the fashion of wearing long hair, that the monarch and his courtiers were moved to tears; and, taking advantage of the impression he had produced, the enthusiastic prelate whipped a pair of scissors out of his sleeves, and cropped the whole congregation !

This was followed up by a royal edict prohibiting the wearing of long hair, but in the next reign, that of Stephen, the old fashion was revived, when in 1139 it received a sudden check from an exceedingly trifling circumstance. A young soldier, whose chief pride lay in the beauty of his locks, which hung down almost to his knees, dreamed one night that a person came to him and strangled him with his own luxuriant ringlets. This dream had such an effect upon him that he forthwith trimmed them to a rational length. His companions followed his example, and superstition spreading the alarm, cropping became again the order of the day. But this reformation,

lated " spurs." Gibbon's Decline and Fall of the Roman Empire, c. 56, note.
   [8] A decree was passed against long hair by the Council of Rouen in 1095, but without effect.

adds the historian, was of very short duration; scarcely had a year elapsed before the people returned to their former follies, and such especially as would be thought courtiers permitted their hair to grow to such a shameful length, that they resembled women rather than men; those whom nature had denied abundance of hair supplying the deficiency by artificial means. Wigs therefore may date in England from the time of Stephen; and should signs to shops become again the fashion, our perruquiers are bound in gratitude to distinguish theirs by three Sagittarii, the device assumed by that monarch, according to tradition, in consequence of his having ascended the throne while the sun was in Sagittarius.

The fashion of wearing long beards re-appeared during the reign of Henry I. and was equally reprobated by the clergy. Both Serlo in his sermon, and Ordericus Vitalis in his Ecclesiastical History, compare the men of their day to "filthy goats."

THE ARMOUR AND WEAPONS

of the time of the Conquest continued with little variation to the close of the twelfth century.

William Rufus (1087—1100) is represented on his great seal in a scaly suit of steel or leather armour, with, in lieu of the nasal helmet, a new head-piece, called by the Normans a *chapelle-de-fer*, an iron cap of a very Tartar-like shape, which will be better understood by referring to the engraving. He carries a gonfanon and a kite-shaped shield.

Henry I. (1100—1135) on his great seal wears a hauberk of flat rings; and the seal of Milo Fitzwalter, Constable of England and Governor of Gloucester, during his reign exhibits the baron in a suit of mascled or quilted armour of the same shape as those in the Bayeux tapestry, with a gonfanon, a kite-shaped shield, and a chapelle-de-fer. (Vide engraving.)

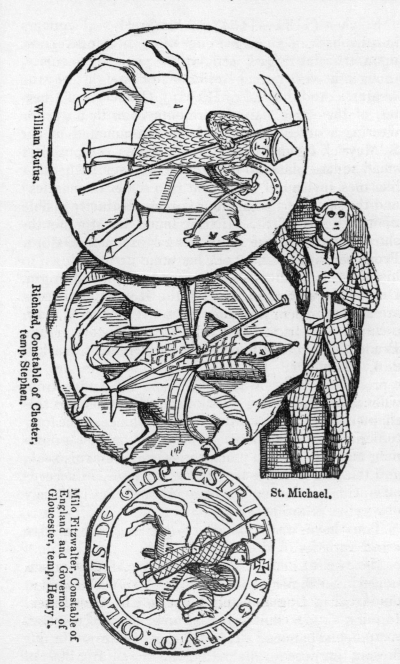

William Rufus.

Richard, Constable of Chester, temp. Stephen.

St. Michael.

Milo Fitzwalter, Constable of England and Governor of Gloucester, temp. Henry I.

Stephen (1135—1154) on his great seal appears
in a hauberk of rings set edgewise, an improvement
upon the flat-ringed armour in point of security,
though a very great addition of weight to the
wearer. And the seal of Richard, Constable of Chester, of the same period, presents us with a warrior
wearing a suit of what has been denominated by Sir
S. Meyrick *tegulated* armour, it being composed of
small square plates of steel, lapping over each other
like tiles, instead of being cut into scales or mascles ;
and the same sort of armour is more distinctly visible
upon a figure of St. Michael, found in Monmouth-
shire, and now in the Ashmolean Museum at Oxford.
From beneath the hauberk his tunic streams down to
his heels, a Frankish fashion, and of oriental origin.
On the Trajan column some of the Roman auxiliaries
are seen attired in flowing tunics, over which is worn
a cuirass or lorica ; and in a MS. copy of Aurelius
Prudentius in the Bibliotheque du Roi, Paris, marked
283, illuminated by the Franks, warriors are so
represented. The MS. of the time of Rufus, from
whence our engravings at the commencement of this
chapter are copied, affords another instance of the long
tunic under the hauberk. The nasal helmet, gonfanon, and kite-shaped shield appear also on this seal ;
and the long-pointed toes to the chaussés, in accordance with the fashion above mentioned, are curiously
illustrative of the period.

Thus have we evidence of the existence of five
or six varieties of body armour during the first half
of the twelfth century, independently of those mentioned in Sir S. Meyrick's letter, to which we alluded in
our last chapter, and also in the same writer's ' Critical
Inquiry,' under the terms of trelliced or broigned,
rustred, and banded. It is sufficient, however, for our
present purpose to state that the ingenuity, both of
armourers and warriors, was naturally in continual ex-

ertion, to invent such defences for the body as would
be proof against all the various weapons, invented
with equal rapidity, for the purposes of destruction; and that consequently alterations and improvements were taking place every day of great
importance to the actual wearer, but too minute for
delineation then, or for distinction now, when time
has half obliterated the details of objects at first but
imperfectly represented by the rude artists of this
dark but interesting period.

Referring then the more curious inquirer to the
elaborate treatise above mentioned, we will confine
ourselves to observing that the hauberk, covered with
flat rings, or with rings set upon their edges, and closely
stitched together, which is denominated single mail, is
the most obvious armour discernible from the close of
the tenth century to the reign of Edward I., and that
scales and mascles are the principal varieties[9]. The
collar of the hauberk was about this period (i. e. the
reigns of Rufus and Henry I.) drawn up over the
chin and mouth, and fastened to the nasal, so that the
eyes were alone visible. We have noticed this in the
Bayeux tapestry, and it occurs in the illuminations
prefixed to Canute's copy of the Gospels, which, from
the long toes to the shoes of the monarchs, are certainly as late as the reign of Rufus. When Magnus
Barefoot, King of Norway (1093—1103), led his
forces to Britain, he was opposed near the Isle of
Anglesea by two earls, Hugh the Proud and Hugh
the Fat. The king shot an arrow against the former,
and at the same moment another arrow was launched
in the same direction by one of his followers. The
earl was so enveloped in mail (*allbrynjathur*) that
no part was exposed but his eyes, and both the arrows

---

[9] Anna Comnena mentions the French knights, at the close
of the eleventh century, wearing both ringed and scaled armour,
p. 397.

striking at once on the earl's face, one of them broke
his nasal (*nef-biorg hialmsins*), whilst the other perforated the eye and brain, so that he dropped down
dead[10].

This custom of hooking up the collar to the nasal,
was followed by the introduction of steel cheek-pieces,
either pendent to the sides of the helmet, in addition
to the neck-piece behind, like the Persian and Indian
helmets both ancient and modern, or worn beneath
like a half mask, with apertures for the eyes. Of
this latter description are the cheek-pieces of William,
Count of Flanders, the grandson of the Conqueror,
who died in 1128, and who wears over them a round-
topped helmet without a nasal (the *stàl hufu*, or
steel cap of the Danes and Norwegians, who called
the helmet with pendent flaps *hangandi stàl hufur*,
and the cheek-pieces themselves *kind-skiæzm*, or
kinn-biorg). The Normans called all these defences
for the face by the simple but natural term *ventaille*,
or *aventaille* (i. e. *avant-taille*); and the word being
afterwards applied to the visor, has occasioned many
writers to confound things of which the use was the
same, but the shape and material totally different.

The second seal of Henry I. represents him without
a helmet, the cowl of mail being drawn over a steel
cap called a *coif-de-fer* in contradistinction to the
chapelle-de-fer worn over the mail.

The spur remains a single goad, and the shield of
the kite-form; but from being slightly curved it has
become, in Stephen's time, almost semi-cylindrical.
It is still undistinguished by heraldic bearings.
Stephen is said to have adopted the sign Sagittarius
for his device, as we have already stated, but his
shield is perfectly plain, and his gonfanon bears a
simple cross; on his seal is a star or sun, and on
that of Henry I. a flower.

[10] Saga, Mag. Burf. c. 11.

Female costume of the reigns of Rufus and Henry I.

Fig. *a*, from Cotton MS. Nero, C. iv.; *b*, from a psalter of the 12th century, in the collection of the late Mr. Douce; *c*, a sleeve; *d*, the border of a tunic, from the same psalter.

THE FEMALE COSTUME,

from 1087 to 1154, presents us with but one striking novelty, and that by no means an improvement. The rage for lengthening every portion of the dress was not confined to the male sex. The sleeves of the tunics, and the veils or kerchiefs of the ladies, appear to have been so long in the reigns of Rufus and Henry I. as to be tied up in knots to avoid treading on them, and the trains or skirts of the garments lie in immense rolls at the feet. In a MS. of the close of the eleventh century, the satirical illuminator has intro-

duced the father of all evil in female apparel, with the
skirts, as well as the sleeves of the tunic, so knotted.
The garment is also laced up the front, a fashion
which we hear much of in the twelfth and thirteenth
centuries. In other illuminations of nearly the same
date, the cuffs of the sleeves hang from the wrist like
pendent canoes (vide figs. *b* and *c*), and are doubly
curious from having furnished the shape of the old
heraldic maunch, or sleeve, first borne by the family
of De Hastings. William de Hastings, the founder of
the family, was steward of the household to Henry I.,
in whose reign the illuminations in which we discover this singularly-shaped sleeve, were, it is most
probable, executed.

Arms of the family of De Hastings, from the tomb of William de Valence,
Earl of Pembroke, Westminster Abbey.

Over the long robe or tunic is occasionally seen a
shorter garment of the same fashion, which answers
to the description of the *super-tunica*, or *sur-cote*, first
mentioned by the Norman writers. In the illuminations we have last mentioned it is chequered and
spotted, most likely to represent embroidery, and
terminates a little below the knee with an indented
border, the commencement of a fashion against
which the first statute was promulgated by Henry II.
at the close of this century, but which defied and sur-
vived that and all similar enactments. We mentioned, in the last chapter, the plaited hair of the
Norman ladies; in some instances the plaits appear

to have been encased in silk, or bound round with riband (vide fig. *a*) : indeed the dress of both sexes is now distinguished by oriental character. The costume of England, to the close of the tenth century, had "more of the antique Roman than the Dane" in it. But the Normans had adopted the Saracenic and Byzantine fashions they found diffused through the south of Europe; and an English female of the twelfth century could scarcely have been distinguished, by her attire, from a lady of the Lower Empire, or indeed from a modern "maid of Athens."

Chapter VII.

REIGNS OF HENRY II., RICHARD I., AND JOHN,
A. D. 1154—1216.

WE have now arrived at a period when a new and
most valuable source of information is opened for
our assistance. The monumental effigies of the illustrious dead, sculptured in their habits as they
lived, and in a style of art remarkable for so dark
an age, many elaborately coloured and gilt, and all
of the full size of the figure, take precedence of every
other authority, until the paintings of Holbein and
Vandyke appear to place the breathing originals before us.

The earliest monumental effigy of an English
sovereign is that of Henry II. in the Abbey of
Fontevraud, Normandy. A modern French writer,
who states as his authorities MSS. preserved in the
ecclesiastical archives, says, " the body of the unfortunate monarch vested in his royal habits, the
crown of gold on his head and the sceptre in his
hand, was placed on a bier richly ornamented, and
borne in great state to the celebrated Abbey of Fontevraud, which he had chosen as the place of his
interment, and there set in the nave of the great
church, where he was buried." This account tallies
with that of Matthew Paris, who says, " he was arrayed in the royal investments, having a golden
crown on the head and gloves on the hands, boots
wrought with gold on the feet, and spurs, a great
ring on the finger and a sceptre in the hand, and
girt with a sword ; he lay with his face uncovered."

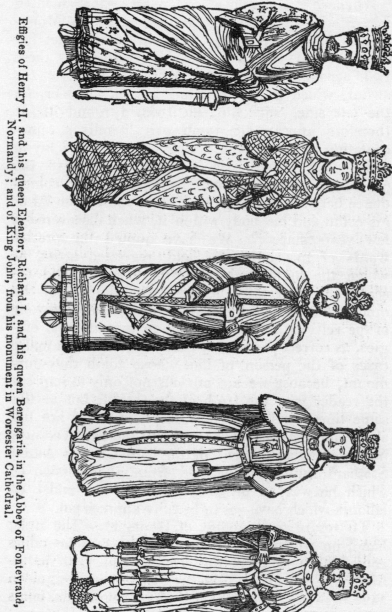

Effigies of Henry II. and his queen Eleanor, Richard I. and his queen Berengaria, in the Abbey of Fontevraud, Normandy; and of King John, from his monument in Worcester Cathedral.

" When we examine the effigy," observes the lamented
Mr. Stothard, in his admirable work, ' the Monumental Effigies of Great Britain,' "we cannot fail
of remarking, that it is already described by these
two accounts; the only variation being in the
sword, which is not girt, but lies on the bier, on
the left side, with the belt twisted round it. It
therefore appears the tomb was literally a representation of the deceased king, as if he still lay in
state. Nor can we, without supposing such was the
custom, otherwise account for the singular coinci-
dence between the effigy of King John on the lid of
his coffin and his body within it, when discovered a
few years since [1]." We have quoted the precise
words of this admirable and regretted artist, to
whom the highest character for accuracy and research is universally accorded, in support of the
opinion entertained by our best antiquaries in favour
of the reliance to be placed upon monumental effigies, as correct portraits of the costume, and in many
cases of the person of him whose tomb they sur-
mount, because we are anxious not only to impress
the reader with the truth of this belief, but at the
same time to point out how deeply indebted are the
artists and antiquaries of Europe to the perseverance,
intelligence, and talent of the late Charles Alfred
Stothard, untimely snatched from a profession of
which he was an ornament, and in the midst of
labours which have yet to be fully appreciated.

To return to the effigy of Henry II. The right
hand, on which was the great ring, is broken, but
contains a portion of the sceptre, which, to judge
from certain marks on the breast of the figure, must
have been remarkably short. The beard is painted
and pencilled like a miniature, to represent its being
closely shaven (the old Norman custom at this time

[1] Monumental Effigies.

returned to). The mantle is fastened by a fibula on
the right shoulder; its colour was originally (for it
has been painted several times, as Mr. Stothard discovered by scraping it) of a deep reddish chocolate.
The dalmatica or long tunic is crimson, starred or
flowered with gold. The boots are green, with gold
spurs fastened by red leathers. The gloves have
jewels on the centre of the back of the hand, a mark
of royalty or high ecclesiastical rank. The crown
has been many years broken, and an injudicious attempt has been made to restore it with plaster of
Paris. It is represented in our engraving without
these modern additions, and above it is placed the
crown as given by Montfaucon in his copy of the
same effigy, which, though very inaccurately drawn
and carelessly engraved, shows that it was surrounded with leaves, like that of Richard I. on his
effigy in the same abbey. This latter effigy and that
of King John at Worcester present the same general
features, with very slight variation. Richard and
John are both attired, like their father, in the dalmatica and mantle, with boots, spurs, and jewelled
gloves. The dalmatica of John is shorter than those
of Henry or Richard, and discovers more of the
under tunic; it also appears to have been made
fuller. Richard's mantle is fastened on the breast;
John's depends from the shoulders, without any
visible fastening, and discloses the jewelled collar of
the dalmatica. Both are represented with beards
and moustaches, which came again into fashion towards the close of Richard's reign. In the early
part of it a seditious Londoner was called William
with the Beard, from his obstinately wearing it in
defiance of the old Norman custom, revived, as we
have already stated, by Henry II.

From these effigies, and from the illuminated MSS.
of the period, we learn, therefore, that

THE CORONATION ROBES

of Henry II., Richard I., and John were composed
of two tunics (the upper, with loose sleeves, called a
dalmatica), of nearly equal lengths, and girded round
the waist by a rich belt, over which was worn the
mantle, splendidly embroidered ; the crown, the
sword, the jewelled gloves, boots, and spurs without
rowels. The same dress was worn also on state
occasions; and the

COSTUME OF THE NOBLES,

during the latter half of the twelfth century, approached
as nearly as possible, in form and magnificence, the
habit of their kings. Henry II. is said to have introduced a mantle, called the cloak of Anjou, which,
being shorter than those worn in the previous reigns,
obtained for him the cognomen of *Court Manteau.*
Of the splendour and character of the decorations of
the mantles of this period we may judge from the
description of one belonging to Richard I., which is
said to have been nearly covered with half moons and
shining orbs of solid silver, in imitation of the system
of the heavenly bodies. During the reign of Henry II.
the fashion of indenting the borders of the tunics
and mantles seems to have been introduced, as in the
last year but one of that monarch's reign a statute
was passed prohibiting certain classes the wearing of
cut or jagged garments [2]. Stockings and chaussés
were worn as usual, and the Saxon word *hose*
occurs in a wardrobe roll of King John's time,
as well as the Latin *caligæ.* Sandals of purple
cloth and *sotulares* or *subtalares* (the shoes or soles
worn with them), fretted with gold, are enumerated as parts of the dress belonging to the same
monarch. By sandals are certainly meant the leg-

[2] Gervase of Dover and John of Brompton, sub anno 1188.

bandages, no longer worn in rolls, but regularly
crossing each other the whole way up the leg from
the very point of the toes, and frequently all of gold
stuff or gilt leather.   Gloves, some short, some reaching nearly to the elbows, embroidered at the tops, and
jewelled on the backs, if appertaining to princes or
prelates, become frequent.   The covering for the
head was still the Phrygian-shaped cap, or the capuchon of the cloak ; but the hair, in the reign of
John, was curled with crisping irons, and bound with
fillets or ribands ; and the beaux of the period continually went abroad without caps, that its beauty
might be seen and admired.   Beards and moustaches were worn or not, as the fancy directed, all
legislation concerning them being disregarded or
abandoned.

Seal of Henry II.

THE MILITARY HABITS

during the reign of Henry II. underwent no distinguishable change ; but those of the reign of
Richard I. and John present us with some striking
novelties.   The shield emblazoned with heraldic

bearings, the long tunic worn under and the sur
cote or surcoat worn over the coat of mail, usually
made of silk of one uniform colour, but sometimes
variegated, sometimes richly embroidered, and sometimes altogether of cloth of gold or silver.   Both the
seals of Richard I. represent him with the long tunic
under the hauberk, and his brother John is represented in a surcoat.   It has been conjectured that
the custom originated with the crusaders, both for the
purpose of distinguishing the many different leaders
serving under the cross, and to veil the iron armour
so apt to heat excessively when exposed to the direct
rays of the sun.   The date of its first appearance in

Seals of Richard I.

Fig. *a*, his first seal; *b*, his second seal; *c*, part of the same, imperfect.
See note 3.

Europe, and the circumstance of the knights of St.
John and of the Temple being so attired in their monumental effigies, are certainly arguments in favour of
the supposition.   The helmet, towards the close of
the twelfth century, had assumed almost the shape
of a sugar-loaf, but suddenly, during the reign of

Richard I., it lost its lofty cone, and subsided into a
flat-topped steel cap, with a hoop of iron passing
under the chin, the face being protected by a moveable grating affixed to a hinge on one side, and fastened by a pin on the other, so that it opened like a
wicket, and might be taken off or put on 'as occasion
required. This was called the *ventail* or *aventaille*,
as the earlier defences for the face had been before it.
Richard wears a most complete one on his second 'seal,
and his helmet is surmounted by a very curious fan-
like crest, on which appears the figure of a lion. The
imitations of the impressions preserved in England
have occasioned strange speculations upon this ornament ; but the copy of a perfect one, lately discovered
in France, is herewith presented to our readers[3].
Besides the surcoat, two other military garments are
common to this period : the *wambeys* or *gambeson*,
and the *haqueton* or *acketon*. They were wadded
and quilted tunics, the first, according to Sir S. Meyrick, of leather stuffed with wool, and the second of
buckskin filled with cotton. Both these were worn
as defences by those who could not afford hauberks,
but they were also worn under the hauberk by persons of distinction, and sometimes by them in lieu
of it, as fancy or convenience might dictate. In the
latter case these garments were stitched with silk or

[3] Monsieur Achille Deville, who discovered this impression attached to a charter dated 18th May, 1198, in the archives of the
department of the Seine Inférieure, amongst other records of the
Abbey of St. George de Bocherville, observes :—" Ce casque est
couronné par un large cimier, sur lequel on remarque la figure du
lion. Sandford veut voir des brins de genet dans la crete du
cimier, qui serait placé là sans doute, selon lui, comme un souvenir
de famille. Quant à moi, j'y verrais tout au plus des brins de
baleine, si ce n'est même des piquants de fer attendu le roideur
et l'arrangement symetrique de ce singulier ornement." Vide his
Account published at Caen, 1830. The upper part of the imperfect seal, so often copied in England, is given in our engraving
behind the perfect one.

Effigies of Geoffrey de Magnaville, Earl of Essex, in the Temple Church, London; and of William Longespee, Earl of Salisbury, in Salisbury Cathedral.

gold thread, and rendered extremely ornamental. The word *gamboisé* or *gamboised*, from this circumstance, was afterwards applied to saddles and other padded, stitched, or quilted articles. We have alluded to the gambeson before, in our description of the Norman Knights, represented in the Bayeux tapestry. The northmen, both Danes and Norwegians, called it the panzar or panzara, improperly translated coat of mail. According to their sagas and poems, it was sometimes worn over the hauberk like the surcoat: in that case it was without sleeves.

The *plastron-de-fer*, or steel plate, introduced

during this century to prevent the pressure of the hauberk upon the chest, was sometimes worn under the gambeson, sometimes between it and the hauberk. In a combat between Richard Cœur de Lion, then Earl of Poitou, and a knight named William de Barris, they charged each other so furiously that their lances pierced through their shields, hauberks, and gambesons, and were only prevented by their plas-trons from transfixing their bodies. In later times we shall find the plastron called the *gorget*, and some-times the *harbergeon* or *haubergeon*, a word frequently confounded with " hauberk," of which it is evidently the diminutive, and meaning literally the " little throat-guard" when of plate, or the little coat or jacket of mail when composed of chain ; a specimen of the latter is to be found in the effigy of Helie, Comte de Maine, engraved in Montfaucon's ' Mo-narchie Française.'

The shields of the reign of Richard and John have gradually decreased in length, and becoming less arched at the top approach the triangular form, which was afterwards denominated heater-shaped. Instead of being flat, however, they are semi-cylindrical, and are decorated, for the first time, with the regular heraldic bearings ; John's early seal (before his accession) exhibiting two lions passant regardant, and Richard's first seal a lion rampant, presumed, as only half the shield is visible on account of the curve, to be one of two lions combatant. On the second seals of both monarchs their shields are bla-zoned with three lions, as quartered ever since in the English arms.

To the spear, sword, battle-axe, and bow, we have now to add the arbaleste or cross-bow, introduced during the reign of Richard I., who was killed by a shaft from that formidable weapon. It continued in use till the final triumph of musketry.

The gisarme is mentioned by Wace, who wrote in the reign of Henry II. This very ancient weapon, written by various authorities *gisarme, guisarme, guissarme, guysarme, gysarme, juisarme, jusarme, quisarme*, has had as many derivations and descriptions allotted to it as modes of spelling. By some it has been called a *partizan*, by others a *bipennis* or double axe, a cutting weapon used in lieu of a sword, a sharp weapon (*arma acuta*, or *arme aiguisée*). Skinner derives the name from *bisarma*, and Barbazan from *acuere*. In the old Provençal language it is also spelt *ghizarma*. (Vide ' Glossaire de la Langue Romain, par J. B. Roquefort,' tom. i.) Now, the lance or javelin of the Gauls and Franks was called the *gæsum*, and is thus described by the scholiast Agathias, a lawyer and native of Myrina, who wrote in the sixth century : "It is of moderate length, and covered with iron, bent on each side in the form of hooks, which they make use of to wound the enemy, or entangle his buckler in such a manner that, his body being exposed, they may run him through with their swords." This description tallies better than any other with the weapon in later times called the *guisarme*, which was a lance with a hook at the side; and the corruption of *gæsum* into *gisarme* is easy and probable.

The spur remains spear-shaped.

THE FEMALE COSTUME

of this half century presents the same general appearance as that of its predecessor. The robe has, however, lost its extravagant cuffs, and the sleeves are made tight and terminate at the wrist. A rich girdle loosely encircles the waist, and Berengaria, queen of Richard I., is represented with a small pouch called an *aulmonière*, and in form like a modern reticule, depending from it on the left side.

Green appears to have been the prevailing colour of this garment in the reign of John. We have the king's warrant for making two robes for the queen, each of them to consist of five ells of cloth, and one of them to be of green and the other of brunet. Du Cange cites a cotemporary register to prove that a green robe, lined with cendal, was estimated at sixty shillings; and Matthew Paris, and other ancient historians, speaking of the flight of Longchamp, Bishop of Ely, state that he disguised himself in a woman's tunic of green, with a capa (the Norman mantle with a capuchon) of the same colour.

State robes and mantles appear to have been splendidly embroidered. The effigy of Eleanor, queen of Henry II., exhibits a robe and mantle covered with golden crescents. We have just spoken of a similar one in the possession of her son, Richard I. Her crown, like that of her royal husband, has been broken. Montfaucon's representation of it is therefore placed above the figure, but that of Queen Berengaria, which has escaped with less damage, would be perhaps the better guide for its restoration. Montfaucon's copies are lamentably incorrect.

Pelisses (*pelices, pelissons*), richly furred (whence their name), were worn in winter under the mantle or capa. King John orders a grey pelisson, with nine bars of fur, to be made for the queen. It appears to have been a dress fitting close to the body. A garment called *bliaut* or *bliaus*, which appears to have been only another name for the surcoat or supertunic, as we find it worn also by knights over their armour, is also frequently mentioned as lined with fur for the winter [4]. The wimple is first mentioned

---

[4] In this *bliaus* we may discover the modern French *blouse*, a tunic or smock-frock.

in the reign of John. It appears to have been sometimes but another name for the veil or kerchief, at
others a separate article of attire worn under the veil,
as in the conventual costume to this day, which is in
all but colour the usual dress of the thirteenth century.
The wimple, properly so called, wrapped round the
head and the chin, and was bound on the forehead
by a golden or jewelled fillet amongst the wealthy,
by a plain silken one amongst the humbler classes.
Wimples and fillets of silk were forbidden to the nuns,
who wore them then, as now, of white linen.

Short boots were worn, as well as shoes, by the
ladies. King John orders four pair of women's boots,
one of them to be *fretatus de giris*, embroidered
with circles, and several instances occur of similarly
embroidered boots at this period, but the robe was
worn so long that little but the tips of the toes are
to be seen in the effigies or illuminations, and the
colour of as much as is visible in the latter is generally black.

Gloves seem not to have been generally worn by
ladies of the twelfth century.

THE HABITS OF THE CLERGY

continued exceedingly sumptuous. The princely
splendour of Becket occasioned the French rustics to
exclaim, during his progress to Paris, " What a won-
derful personage the King of England must be, if his
Chancellor can travel in such state !" and the accounts of his magnificence in that city are so extraordinary, that Lord Lyttleton, in his History of Henry
II., declares them to be incredible. The story of
Henry's struggle with Becket in the open street, when
the monarch pulled the new scarlet capa, lined with
rich furs, from the back of the priest, to give to the
shivering beggar beside him, is told by every his-

torian ; but these are only notices of his secular garments.   In the sacred vestments of the clergy of this
period, the principal novelty is the approach of the
mitre to the form with which we are familiar.

Mitres from the tomb of King John in Worcester Cathedral.

CHAPTER VIII.

REIGN OF HENRY III., A. D. 1216—1272.

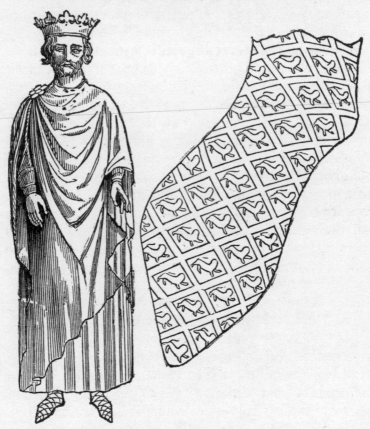

Effigy of Henry III. in Westminster Abbey.

THE long reign of Henry III. embraces the greater portion of the thirteenth century, but its costume is more remarkable for increase of splendour than for alteration of form. Matthew Paris, the monk of St. Alban's, a faithful and cotemporary historian, and an eye-witness of much of the pageantry he describes, repre-

sents himself disgusted rather than pleased by the
excessive foppery of the times. The effigy of

THE KING,

in his monument in the chapel of Edward the Confessor, at Westminster, represents him, as usual, in
the royal robes ; but they are of the simplest description,—a long and very full tunic and a mantle
fastened by a fibula on the right shoulder, both devoid
of ornament or border. The boots are, however, exceedingly splendid, illustrating the expression *fretatus de auro*, and each square of the fret containing a
lion or leopard. When Henry conferred the honour
of knighthood on William de Valence, A.D. 1247, he
was arrayed in vestments of a newly-introduced and
most magnificent material called cloth of Baldekins [1],
from its being manufactured at Baldeck, as Babylon
was then called. According to Du Cange, it was
a very rich silk woven with gold [2] : on his head he
wore a coronet or small circle of gold called in the
language of that day a chaplet or garland. In an inventory of the jewels belonging to Henry, made in the
last year of his reign, mention is made of five garlands
of gold of Paris work, a large and precious crown,
three other crowns enriched with gems, and an imperial cap splendidly jewelled, and valued at five hundred marks. An order is extant for the making of
robes of various colours fringed with gold, and one
is especially commanded to be made of the best pur-
ple-coloured samite (a rich silk), embroidered with
three little leopards in front and three behind. This
latter is called a *quintis* or *cointise*, a name given to
a peculiarly-fashioned gown or tunic of that day, but
of which we have no satisfactory description. That

[1] Matthew Paris, Hist. Ang. sub anno 1247.
[2] Du Cange, in voce " Baldekins."

it was the cut of the garment that distinguished it we
have proof, however, in the lines of William de
Lorris, who, in his ' Roman de la Rose,' written at
the close of this century, describing the dress of Mirth,
says he was vested

> " D'une robe moult deguisée
> Qui fut en maint lieu incissée,
> Et decoppée par *cointise*."
>
> *Rom. de la Rose*, l. 839.

which is thus translated by Chaucer :—

> " Wrought was his robe in straunge gise,
> And all to slyttered for *queintise*,
> In many a place lowe and hie."

i. e. slyttered or slit all to pieces in a quaint or fanciful
manner or for whim's sake ; *quinte* in French sig-
nifying fancy, whim, caprice ; and *quinteux*, *quin-
teuse*, fanciful, whimish, freakish. The scarf afterwards worn round the crest of the helmet was called a
cointise, and as its edges were frequently jagged, it is
not improbable that the robes or tunics with jagged
borders and sleeves, expressly forbidden to certain
classes as early as 1188, and frequently met with
hereafter, may have obtained, on their first appearance, the appellation of cointises.

THE NOBILITY

who attended at the marriage of the daughter of
Henry III. to Alexander, King of Scotland, A. D. 1251,
are also stated by Matthew Paris to have been attired
" in vestments of silk, commonly called çointises," on
the day the ceremony was performed, but on the following day they were laid aside, and new robes
assumed. The materials for dress became more
numerous and costly during this century. Velvet is
mentioned under the Latin name of *villosa*, and the

French *villuse* or velours[3], and a rich stuff manufactured in the Cyclades, and therefore called *cyclas*
or *ciclaton*[4], gave its name to a garment like a
dalmatica or super-tunic worn by both sexes. It was
known in Germany as early as the year 1096, when
Judith, daughter of the King of Bohemia, wore a
cyclas embroidered or interwoven with gold; but
we first hear of it in England at the coronation of
Henry III. and his queen, when the citizens who
attended the ceremony wore cyclades worked with
gold over vestments of silk. To the furs of sables,
foxes, &c. we now find added those of ermines, martens, and squirrels, the vair and the minevair or
miniver. Two mantles lined with ermine are ordered
by Henry for his queen and himself, and Matthew
Paris speaks of the doubled or lined garments for
the winter belonging to the king and his courtiers.

THE GENERAL MALE COSTUME, 1216—1272,

consists of the tunic, the cyclas or cointise, girded or
not, according to the fancy, chaussés or stockings, and
drawers; the latter are distinctly visible in this reign
in consequence of the tunic being open in front,
sometimes as high as the waist, for greater freedom
in action. Mantles and cloaks are only seen in state or
travelling dresses, and for the latter purpose we read
of a garment called the *super-totus* or over-all, an
improvement on the capa, being more ample, and
having large sleeves as well as a capuchon. It is
sometimes called *balandrana*, being latinized from the
French *balandran*, a cloak for foul weather, and
under that name was forbidden to the monks of the
order of St. Benedict, in common with other garments
appertaining to the laity. The shoes and boots have

---

[3] Mat. Paris in Vita Abbatum, et Du Cange in voce.
[4] Monach. Pegaviensis, sub anno 1096.

again become long-toed. They are either embroidered in chequers or frets, or painted black, according to the rank or situation of the wearer. The shoes of Mirth, in the ' Roman de la Rose,' are described as " decouppés a làs," rendered by Chaucer, "decoped and with lace," whereby we may either understand them cut or divided by lace into the frets aforesaid, or that they were open and laced up the side as we find them in the next century. Capuchons or cowls are worn with indented edges, round caps or bonnets and hats, not unlike the modern beaver ; but a white coif tied under the chin is most frequently seen upon the heads of persons hunting or on horseback, heralds, messengers, &c., who may have adopted it as more secure in hard riding.

When mentioning the herald, it may be as well to remark, that he is as yet undistinguished by a tabard, wearing only a small shield of arms at the girdle of his tunic.

The hair is worn in flowing curls, but the face is in general closely shaved.

THE MILITARY HABIT

underwent several changes during this reign. Quilted and padded armour of silk, cloth, buckram, or leather, came still more into use, and from the peculiar work with which it was now ornamented obtained the name of *pourpoint* and *counterpoint*. A complete suit, consisting of a sleeved tunic and chaussés, was frequently worn by the knights of this period beneath the surcoat, which was considerably lengthened, and during this reign first emblazoned with the arms of the wearer. The flat-ringed armour has nearly disappeared, and that composed of rings set up edgeways seems to have been the most generally worn mail of the thirteenth century. But during Henry's

Effigy in Malvern Church, Gloucestershire, surrounded by helmets, &c. of
the reign of Henry III., from Matthew Paris's Lives of the two Offas.

reign a new species was introduced from Asia, where
it is still worn. This was the chain mail, and consisted of four rings connected by a fifth, all of which
were so fastened with rivets that they formed a complete garment of themselves without the leathern
foundation; and this shirt of chain was worn loose
over the gambeson or aketon, being itself covered
by the surcoat. The capuchon and chaussés were
also made of interlaced rings, but the former is frequently separate from the tunic, and hangs over the
surcoat; and instances occur of an additional cap or
coif of mail worn over the capuchon. Small plates
of iron or steel were worn upon the shoulders, elbows,

and knees, called, according to their position, *epau-lières* or *poleyns, coutes* or *coudes*, and *genouillères*, and with these additional defences commenced the last grand change that " cased in complete steel" the chivalry of Europe.

The flat-topped cylindrical helmet of the reigns of Richard and John descended no lower than the ears, the face being covered by the aventaille ; but in this reign it covered the whole head and rested on the shoulders, and by degrees assumed a barrel form, bulging at the sides. These great helmets were only worn when in positive action, being too heavy and cumbrous for general use, and when forcibly turned round upon the shoulders by a vigorous stroke of a lance severely hurt the wearer.   In the romance of ' Lancelot du Lac,' the helmet of a knight is said to have been so turned that the edges grazed his shoulders, and " ses armes estoient toutes ensang-lentées."   Apertures for sight and breathing were cut in them in the shape of a cross, to which was added sometimes a cluster of simple perforations.

A convex plate of steel, so perforated, is seen worn as a simple mask by some warriors, being tied round the head over the capuchon of mail, with or without a helmet, and skull-caps or chapelles-de-fer, with or without nasals, are common amongst esquires, archers, and men-at-arms.

The archers in Matthew Paris's lives of the two Offas are represented in ringed hauberks, with sleeves to the elbow, over which are seen vests of leather, defended by four circular iron plates.

The knight's shield is flatter and straight at top, and generally emblazoned. Round targets, fancifully ornamented, occur, and the martel-de-fer (a pointed hammer or small pick-axe) was added to the offensive weapons, making sad havoc with the various species of mail, breaking the links of chain and picking off the scales and plates, leaving fatal openings for the passage of the sword and the lance.

The rowelled spur is first seen on the great seal of Henry III., but it is not common before the reign of Edward I.

Effigy of Aveline, Countess of Lancaster, in Westminster Abbey; and two female heads, from a MS. of the 13th century.

THE FEMALE COSTUME

still consisted of the robe or gown with long light sleeves, over which was sometimes worn a super-tunic, surcoat, or *cyclas*, and for state occasions a mantle, all composed of the most magnificent materials. The *peplum* or veil, and the wimple, was frequently of gold tissue or richly embroidered silk, and over the

veil was occasionally placed a diadem, circlet, or garland, and sometimes a round hat or cap.   Isabel, the
sister of Henry III., is described by Matthew Paris
as taking off her hat and her veil, in order that the
people might see her face ; or it might be her garland or chaplet, as the golden circlet was called ; for
the word he uses is *capellum*, and the chaplet is
continually called *chapeau* and *chappel* by the French
writers.

> " Et s'amie lui fit *chappeau*
> De roses gracieux et beaux."
>
> *Roman de la Rose.*

In another part of the same poem we find a chaplet
of roses worn over the garland of gold.

> " Ung *chappel* de roses tout frais
> Eut dessus le *chappel* d'Orfrays."

Cloth stockings embroidered with gold are amongst
the articles of dress ordered by Henry III. for his
sister Isabel.

In the 'Squier of Low Degree,' a romance written
towards the end of the thirteenth century, the King of
Hungary is made thus to address his daughter :—

> " To-morrow ye shall yn hunting fare,
> And yede my daughter in a chare ;
> Yt shall be covered with velvet red,
> And clothes of fine gold all about your head;
> With damask white and azure blewe
> Well *diappered* with lillies new ;
> Your mantle of ryche degree,
> Purple pall and ermyne free."

The word *diaper* is derived by some writers from
" D'Ipres," i. e. " of Ypres," a town in Flanders,
famous for its manufactory of rich stuffs and fine
linen before the year 1200. Du Cange derives it
from the Italian *diaspro*, the jasper, which it resem-

bles in its shifting lights; but the first is by far the most plausible conjecture; and though we read of diapers of Antioch, it is only because Ypres having given its name to its peculiar manufacture, any similar cloth received the same appellation. Thus we see in the lines above quoted, that the "*damask* white and azure blewe" is to be well "*diappered* with lilies," that is to say, covered all over with a pattern of lilies, in the style of the cloth made at Ypres. In the same manner, Damascus itself having obtained a reputation for its manufactures of ornamental stuffs and steel, to *damask* a sword blade, became a familiar phrase, and damasks of Ypres might have been spoken of with as much propriety as diapers of Damascus or of Antioch.

The fashion of wearing the hair was completely altered during this reign. The plaited tails were unbound, and the hair turned up behind, and confined in a net or caul of gold thread; but the veil and wimple frequently prevent its being seen on the monumental effigies of this period.

The richly embroidered

GARMENTS OF THE CLERGY

at this period occasioned Innocent IV. to exclaim, "O England, thou garden of delights, thou art truly an inexhaustible fountain of riches! From thy abundance much may be exacted!" and he forthwith proceeded to exact as much as he could, by forwarding bulls to several English prelates, enjoining them to send a certain quantity of such embroidered vestments to Rome for the use of the clergy there. Some of these sacerdotal habits were nearly covered with gold and precious stones, and others were exquisitely embroidered with figures of animals and flowers. The red hat is said to have been first given

to the cardinals by Pope Innocent at the Council of
Lyons in 1245; and, according to De Curbio, they
wore it for the first time in 1246, on occasion of an
interview between the Pope and Louis IX. of France.
It was not flat, as at present, but of the shape here
represented from a MS. of the commencement of the
fourteenth century, marked, Royal MS. 16, G. 6.

During this reign the two orders of friars [5], the
Dominicans, or preaching friars, and the Franciscans,
or friars minors, were established in this country.   St.
Dominic founded his order in the year 1215, and
the first Englishman that is recorded to have become
a Dominican was the ecclesiastical physician, Johannes Ægidius.   Forty-three houses of this order
were in time raised in England, where from their
black cloak and capuchon they were popularly termed
Black Friars.   The Franciscans planted themselves
at Canterbury in 1220, and at Northampton soon
after.   Their grey vestments obtained for them the
additional name of Grey Friars.

[5] From frères (brothers).   "A frère there was, a wanton and a
merry."   Chaucer's Canterbury Tales.

CHAPTER IX.

REIGNS OF EDWARD I. AND II., 1272—1327.

Regal costume.

Fig. *a*, Edward I., from a seal attached to a charter of the city of Hereford ; *b*, regal personage, from a MS. of this reign, in the library of H. R. H. the Duke of Sussex.

EDWARD I., 1272—1307.

EDWARD I., that chivalric and temperate prince, who, despite a ferocity which was perhaps the vice of his age more than the bent of his natural disposition, must be ranked as one of the greatest monarchs that ever swayed the English sceptre, was as simple in his dress as he was magnificent in his liberalities. He never wore his crown after the day of his coronation, and preferred to the royal garments of purple the dress of a common citizen. Being asked one day why he did not wear richer apparel, he answered, with the consciousness of real worth, that it was absurd to suppose he could be more estimable in fine than in simple clothing. Under such a king it is natural to suppose that foppery could not flourish, and we therefore hear of no preposterous fashions amongst the knights and nobles of his court. The shafts of satire are directed in this reign against the ladies only.

There is no monumental effigy of Edward; but on opening his tomb in Westminster Abbey, A.D. 1774, his corpse was discovered arrayed in a dalmatica or tunic of red silk damask, and a mantle of crimson satin fastened on the shoulder with a gilt buckle or clasp four inches in length, and decorated with imitative gems and pearls. The sceptre was in his hand, and a stole was crossed over his breast of rich white tissue, studded with gilt quatrefoils in philagree-work, and embroidered with pearls in the shape of what are called true-lovers' knots. The gloves, it is presumed, had perished, for the ornaments belonging to the backs of them were found lying on the hands. The body from the knees downwards was wrapped in a piece of cloth of gold, which was not removed. The regal ornaments were all of metal gilt, and the stones and pearls false; a piece of economy unusual at this period. In a fine MS. of this time, in the library of his Royal Highness the Duke of Sussex, several figures in regal costume have a stole crossed on their breasts splendidly embroidered, and one of these we have selected for the engraving at

the commencement of this chapter. The crowned
head beside it is that of Edward I. from a seal.

Costume of the close of the 13th century, from the Painted Chamber at
Westminster.—Vide p. 106-7.

THE HABITS OF THE NOBLES

were becomingly magnificent. The long tunic and
mantle, varied sometimes by the cyclas, and the
bliaus composed of rich stuffs [1] and lined with ermine
and other costly furs, was the general costume of the

---

[1] The rich stuff called "cloth of tars" is mentioned in this reign.
It was latinized *tarsicus* and *tartarinus,* and we read of dalma-
ticas and tunics of slate-colour, and light blue cloth of tars embroidered with branches and bezants of gold. Visitat. Thesau.
St. Paul, Lond. sub anno 1195.

Civil costume of the reign of Edward I., from a MS. Royal, 16, G. 6.

court.   Caps of various shapes, and a hat like the
classical petasus slung behind to be assumed at pleasure, become frequent.   (Vide fig. *a*, *b*, *c*, in the engraving from the Painted Chamber.)   Buttons closely
set from the wrist to the elbow appear about this
time (vide figure on horseback), and in a MS. poem,
certainly not later than the year 1300, particular
mention is made of this fashion:—

> " His robe was all of gold beganne,
>   Well chrislike maked I understande;
>   *Botones* azurd (azure) everilke ane
>   *From his elboth to his hande.*"

MS. *Cotton, Julius V.*

Gloves are more generally worn by noblemen and
officers of state.   Some are splendidly embroidered

up the sides (vide fig. *d*, from the Painted Chamber)
or round the tops.   The hose are richly fretted with
gold and various coloured silks (fig. *e*, Ibid.).

The hair and beard are crisped and curled with
great precision.

On the investment of the young Prince of Wales,
afterwards Edward II., with the military belt of
knighthood, purple robes, fine linen garments, and
mantles woven with gold were liberally distributed
to his young knight companions, who crowded in
their glittering dresses the gardens of the Temple,
which were set apart for their reception, and received
much injury in this novel service.

Edward Crouchback, Earl of
Lancaster, Westminster Abbey.

Brass, in Gorleston Church, Suffolk.

In the

MILITARY HABITS

we have first to notice the more general usage of the emblazoned surcoat. The cyclas, the bliaus, and the cointise, all worn over the shirt of mail as well as over the more peaceful tunic, were richly embroidered either with fanciful devices or the armorial bearings of the owner[2]. Towards the close of this reign those curious ornaments called *ailettes*, or little wings, from their situation and appearance, are seen on the shoulders of knights either in battle or in the lists, but they did not become general till the next reign. They were of various shapes; sometimes emblazoned like the surcoat, shield, and banner, with the arms of the knight; sometimes plain or charged with a simple St. George's cross[3]. The barrel-shaped helmet is frequently surmounted by the heraldic crest, and this picturesque decoration becomes henceforward a principal feature of the chivalric equipment[4].

[2] Roman de Garin and of Percival de Galois; and Giuart, Hist. Franc. sub anno 1304.

[3] Vide figure at the head of this section, from a brass formerly in Gorleston Church, Suffolk, engraved in Stothard's Monumental Effigies. It is quite of the close of the reign of Edward I.

[4] In a MS. of this period (L'Histoire de l'Ancien Monde), preserved in the library of his Royal Highness the Duke of Sussex, and before quoted, some of these helmets appear to be decorated with a feather instead of a crest (vide engraving from it, p. 109): as it is worn by more than one knight in the same illumination, it can scarcely be itself a crest, and is therefore remarkable as an instance of the feather being worn as a simple decoration in the helmet earlier than the fifteenth century. It certainly was not a custom or fashion in England previous to the reign of Henry V., or in the innumerable illuminations of the thirteenth and fourteenth centuries frequent instances must have occurred. In the present case, as the history terminates with the reign of Mithridates, and its embellishments represent

Military costume, temp. Edward I., from a MS. in the library of H. R. H. the Duke of Sussex.

The top of the helmet inclines to a cone in some

the deeds of Polynices, Theseus, the Amazons, &c. &c., the introduction of the feather might have been an unusual stretch of fancy in the illuminator, suggested by the mention of the plumed helmets of the heroic ages.

instances; and the front, seen in profile, presents almost an angular appearance. Skull-caps, or chapels-de-fer, both spherical and conical, the latter the prototype of the *bascinet*, and indeed already so called, are worn over the mail-coif, and commonly with the nasal, which disappears after this reign.

From the Painted Chamber at Westminster.

The mail gloves of the hauberk are now divided into separate fingers, and leathern gauntlets appear reaching higher than the wrist, but not yet plated.

The shield is now sometimes flat and nearly triangular or heater-shaped; sometimes pear-shaped and semi-cylindrical.

From the Painted Chamber at Westminster.

The lance has lost its gonfanon; and the *pennon*, which resembles it in its swallow-tailed form, but longer and broader, becomes a military ensign, and is generally charged with the crest, badge, or war-cry of the knight; his arms being emblazoned on the banner, which is in shape a parallelogram. Vide engravings, pages 109, 110.

Edward I. had banners emblazoned with the arms of England, gules, three lions passant regardant; of St George, argent, a cross gules; of St. Edmund, azure, three crowns Or; and of St. Edward the Confessor, azure, a cross fleury between six martlets Or.

In the old French poem on the siege of Karlaveroc, by Edward I., A. D. 1300, the author, speaking of the array of English knights, says,

' La ont meinte riche garnement
Borde sur cendeaus et samis,
Meint beau penon en lance mis,
Meint baniere deploye."

Cotton MS. Caligula, A. 18.

There have they many rich ornaments
Broidered on cendals and samites (silks and satins),
Many a fair penon fixed on a lance,
Many a banner displayed.

And he forthwith enumerates the knights and their
separate *cote armures* with laudable minuteness.

From the Painted Chamber at Westminster.

The *falchion*, a peculiarly shaped broad-bladed
sword; the *estoc*, a small stabbing sword; the *anelace* or *anelas*, a broad dagger tapering to a very fine
point; and the *coutel* or *cultelas* (whence *cutlass*),
a military knife, are added to the offensive weapons.
The mace also first appears in illuminations, though
it may have been introduced during the earlier crusades, as it is evidently of oriental origin.

THE FEMALE COSTUME

of this period has been severely satirized by cotemporary writers, as we have already remarked, and we
are inclined to think unjustly so; for, in nearly all
the illuminations of this reign it appears elegantly
simple, particularly when compared with that of
the reign of Rufus, the tasteless and extravagant

fashions of which certainly provoked and deserved
both ridicule and reprobation.

The authors of the famous ' Roman de la Rose,
William de Lorris, who died in 1260, and John de
Meun, his continuator, who finished the poem about
the year 1304, are amongst the most bitter of these
satirists, particularly the latter, who, it has been
acknowledged, extended his sarcasms beyond the
bounds of truth and decency. It is true that they were
both Frenchmen, and that their philippic is directed
against their own countrywomen; but the same style
of costume was generally prevalent at the same
period throughout Europe, and England then, as
now, adopted the most whimsical fashions of her
continental neighbours. A double marriage in the
year 1298 contributed also, not a little, to the introduction of French fashions; Edward I. marrying the
sister, and his son, the Prince of Wales, the daughter
of Philip IV. of France, surnamed Le Bel. The
ladies of the reign of Edward I. appear in the robe
or kirtle [5], made high in the neck, with long tight
sleeves, and a train, over which is generally seen
another vestment, the surcoat, super-tunic, or cyclas [6],
without sleeves, but as long in the skirt as the gown
itself, and sometimes held up by one hand to keep it
out of the way of the feet. To these two garments
are added, as occasion may require, the mantle, fast-

[5] Vide p. 117, where the kirtle and mantle are alone mentioned.

[6] The sosquenie, surquayne, or suckeney was an exterior garment at this period. William de Lorris says it is the handsomest
dress a woman can wear:—

> " Nulle robe n'est si belle,
> A dame ne à damoiselle;
> Femme est plus cointe et plus mignotte,
> En *surquayne* que en cotte."

Chaucer translates "surquayne," "*rockette*;" but no dress like a
rochet is seen upon female figures of this reign. *Sousquenille* is
still French for a coachman or groom's frock.

ened on the shoulders by cords and tassels. Indeed
the effigy of Aveline, Countess of Lancaster, given
in the last chapter, presents very nearly the costume
of this reign ; it being quite of the close of that of
Henry III. A. D. 1269. The effigy of Eleanor,
queen of Edward I., is remarkable for its simplicity, and the absence of any kind of head-tire ;
her hair streaming naturally upon her shoulders
from under the regal diadem. But in illuminations of this period, the hair of married ladies and
noble dames is generally gathered up behind into
a caul of golden network, over which is worn the
peplus or veil, and sometimes upon that a round
low-crowned cap ; while the younger females are
depicted with flowing ringlets, bound by a simple
garland, or fillets of gold or silk, or by the still more
becoming chaplet of real flowers. The authors of
the ' Roman de la Rose' mention all these articles of
apparel, and thereby confirm the authenticity of the
illuminations, while they fail in proving their charges
of folly and extravagance, except perhaps in two
points ; the first being the unnecessary length of
the trains, in allusion to which the satirist advises
the ladies, if their legs be not handsome, nor their
feet small and delicate, to wear long robes trailing
on the pavement to hide them ; those, on the contrary, who have pretty feet are counselled to elevate
their robes, as if for air and convenience, that all who
are passing by may see and admire them. And another poet of the thirteenth century compares the ladies
of his day to peacocks and magpies ; " for the pies,"
says he, " naturally bear feathers of various colours ;
so the ladies delight in strange habits and diversity
of ornaments. The pies have long tails that trail in
the dirt ; so that the ladies make their tails a thousand times longer than those of peacocks and pies.'
The second rational complaint is against a very ugly

species of wimple called a gorget, which appears about this time. John de Meun describes it as

Female of the reign of Edward I. with the gorget and long trailing robe, from Sloane MS. 3983.

wrapped two or three times round the neck, and then being fastened with a great quantity of pins, it was raised on either side the face as high as the ears. " *Par Dieu!*" exclaims the poet ; " I have often thought in my heart when I have seen a lady so closely tied up, that her neckcloth was nailed to her chin, or that she had the pins hooked into her flesh ;" and certainly he is so far correct, as the reader will acknowledge, on referring to the annexed figure from an illumination of this date. But, unless it be to the projections of the gorget on each side that he alludes, we are at a loss to discover what he means by their hoods being thrown back, and their horns advanced as if to wound the men, and propped up by gibbets or brackets. Strutt applies these observations to the horned head-dress, so frequently met with in later

illuminations, but there is not the slightest indication
of such a fashion prevailing at this time in any MS.
we have inspected; and though many of the head-
dresses are far from becoming, they do not, in our
eyes, at all bear out the remarks of the satirist. Some
evanescent caprice may, however, have provoked the
simile, but it has not been handed down to us by the
pencil.

Female head-dresses, temp. Edward I. Royal MS. 15, D. 2.

Of ornaments, we have a long list furnished us by
the same authors; but unless they were worn by
persons who could not afford such splendour, we
perceive nothing in the articles themselves to carp at.
Jewels, buckles of gold, rings, earrings, and chaplets
of fresh flowers, or goldsmith's work in imitation of

them, are very natural and elegant ornaments for a
female, and to carry the worth of one hundred pounds
in gold and silver upon the head is only a reproach
where it is incompatible with the circumstances of
the wearer. The golden net-caul, termed *crestine*,
creton, *crespine*, *crespinette*, was an elegant addition
to the female costume of this period, and formed for
the two next centuries an important article of a lady's
wardrobe.

The injurious practice of tight lacing we have
already discovered in existence during the reign of
Rufus or Henry I.; and, in a MS. copy of the ' Lay
of Syr Launfal,' written about the year 1300, we
have the following description of two damsels, whom
the knight unexpectedly meets in a forest :—

> " Their kirtles were of Inde sendel,
> *Y-laced small, jolyf, and well,*
> There might none gayer go ;
> Their mantels were of green velvet,
> Y-bordered with gold right well y-sette,
> Y-pellured with gris and gros ;
> Their heads were dight well withal,
> Everich had on a jolyf coronal,
> With sixty gems and mo.
>
>   *   *   *   *
>
> Their kerchiefs were well schyre,
> Arrayed with rich gold wyre."

The second line in the French original is still stronger ;
they are said to have been *Lacies moult estreitement*,
" very straitly or tightly laced." The Lady Triamore,
in the same romance, is also described as

> " Clad in purple pall,
> With gentyll body and middle small."

And, in another poem, we read of a lady with a
splendid girdle of beaten gold, embellished with
emeralds and rubies, " about her middle small."

By the first quotation we perceive also that the
kirtle was at this time an exterior garment, like the
robe or gown, if not, indeed, another term for the
same thing. " Inde sendel" may mean either *Indian*
silk or *light blue* silk ; the words *Inde* and *Pers* being
frequently used to express that colour. *Sarcenet* or
saracennet, from its Saracenic or oriental origin, was
known about this period. The robe of Largesse or
Liberality, in ' the Roman de la Rose,' is said to
have been

> "———bonne et belle,
> D'une coute toute nouvelle,
> D'un pourpre *Sarraxinesche*."—Line 1172.

Gauze, latinized *gazzatum*, and thought to have
derived its name from being manufactured at Gaza,
in Palestine, *Brunetta* or *burnetta*, and several other
fine and delicate stuffs, are mentioned by writers of
this reign [7]. Tartan, in French *tyretaine*, in Latin
tiretanus, was a fine woollen cloth, much used for
ladies' robes, and generally of a scarlet colour [8].
John de Meun speaks of

> " Robbes faites par grand devises,
> De beaux draps de soies et de laine,
> De scarlate de *tiretaine*."
>
> *Roman de la Rose.*

There is no visible alteration in the

ECCLESIASTICAL COSTUME.

The initial letter of Edward's name in a MS. of his
reign furnishes us with the appearance of an arch-

[7] Brunettam nigram, gazzatum, et alium quemcumque pannum
notabiliter delicatum interdicimus universi. Concil. Budense, anno
1279, cap. 61.

[8] From whence, probably, its name, the *tient* or colour of *Tyre ;*
scarlet being indifferently used for purple by the early writers,
and including " all the gradations of colours formed by a mixture
of blue and red, from indigo to crimson." Vide Illustrations of
Northern Antiquities, 4to. Edinb. 1814, p. 36.

bishop in his official vestments.   The mitre has very
nearly its modern form[9].

Coronation of Edward I. from an initial letter, MS. Harleian, 926.

THE DRESS OF THE COMMONALTY

also remains as in the last century, or indeed as from
the time of the Conquest, with the addition of the

[9] A rich and curiously wrought stuff, called *checkeratus*, was
worn at this period by the superior clergy (capa cum nodolis checkeratus subtilis operis facta de casula episcopi Fulconis.   Visit.
Thesauri, S. Pauli, Lond. A. D. 1295); and *marble cloth*, a thick
stuff manufactured of party-coloured worsted, and sometimes
adorned with figures of animals and other devices, besides the
veined pattern from which it derived its name, is also mentioned
in the same account, "Tunica de quodam panno marmoreo spisso,
cum notis et grifonibus."

bliaus or blouse (the smock-frock of the present day),
made generally of canvas or fustian, and worn by
both sexes. *Russet*, *birrus* or *burreau*, *cordetum*,
and *sarcilis*, are also quoted by the indefatigable
Strutt, as coarse woollen cloths used for the garments
of the lower orders during the thirteenth century.
Cowls, with points or tails to them, are worn more
than caps, and the blacksmith has already his brown
leathern apron, with the square bib to it, as worn
by his brother craftsmen to this hour.

EDWARD II., 1307—1327.

The twenty troublesome years of the reign of Edward II. were remarkable for the increase of luxury
in proportion to the decline of honour and virtue.
Excited by the example of the profligate and presump-
tuous Gaveston, "the esquire endeavoured to outshine the knight, the knight the baron, the baron the
earl, and the earl the king himself, in the richness of
his apparel;" and towards the latter end of this reign
we begin to discover the party-coloured, strait, and
shortened habits worn in the reign of Edward III.,
and the long tippets or streamers at the elbows of
them. The sleeves of the dalmatica, on the effigy in
p. 121, are so terminated. The capuchon, instead of
being worn as a cowl, was sometimes twisted into a
fanciful form and placed upon the top of the head
like a modern toque, or simply folded and balanced
upon it, as the women of the Pays de Basque wear
it in summer to this day; the former fashion being
an approach to the chaperon of the following reigns.
The beard of the king is carefully curled, and his
hair, cut square on the forehead, hangs in wavy
ringlets below his ears. Amongst other indignities

Effigy of Edward II., Gloucester Cathedral.

said to have been heaped upon this miserable monarch, our readers will remember the traditionary story of the shaving of his cherished beard with cold and dirty water by the road-side on his way to Carnarvon Castle.

Beards were worn apparently by persons in years, great officers of state, and knights templars, but not generally; for Peter Anger, valet to Edward II., when setting out on a pilgrimage to the Holy Land, obtained letters of safe conduct from the king, because, having vowed not to shave his beard, he was afraid he should be taken for a knight templar, and consequently insulted; the persecution and suppression of that renowned order having commenced at this period.

Military costume.

Fig. *a*, from a brass in Minster Church, Isle of Sheppey ; *b* and *c*, Illum.
MS. Sloane collection, 346; *d* and *e*, from MS. Royal, 20, D. 4.

THE MILITARY HABIT

of this period is generally recognized by a greater
admixture of plate with the chain. The hauberk
and chaussés are now nearly covered with wrought
iron. Brassarts connect the shoulder with the elbow-
pieces, and avant-bras or vant-braces defend the arm
from the latter to the wrist. Greaves of one plate
protect the fore-part of the leg, and on the breast are
fastened sometimes one, sometimes two round plates,
called *mamelières* from their position, to which are
appended chains, attached at the other end, one to
the sword-hilt and the other to the helmet, which at
the moment of action was placed over the *coif de*

mailles or the *bascinet,* which latter appears in this reign in a more important shape, without the nasal, and occasionally with a moveable visor, which renders the helmet unnecessary. The flat-topped, barrel-shaped helmet seems to have been abandoned about this period ; and that important piece of armour, which at the close of Edward's reign had been tending towards the conical, now assumed the sugar-loaf or egg-like form. The conical-topped helmet, with the angular projection in front, outlived the new fashion, however, as we shall find in the next reign. It was still surmounted with the heraldic crest or the fan-shaped ornament of the reign of Henry III., or a scarf called the cointise was tied to a ring at the top of it, and sometimes the cointise was attached to the crest itself. The ailettes were more generally worn, and a neck-guard of chain was added to the bascinet and called the *camail,* either corrupted from *cap-mail,* or from its resembling the lower part of the capuchon, commonly worn by all classes, but which among the higher ranks was made of camel's-hair, and therefore termed *camelin* by the French, and *camelotum* by the Latin writers, from whence our word *camlet,* afterwards applied to an inferior stuff made in imitation of it[10]. At this period camlet is always ranked with silk, satin, velvet, and the richest materials.

The cyclas or surcoat is sometimes considerably shorter in front than behind. Vide fig. *a* in the engraving, p. 122.

The shield is triangular or pear-shaped, sometimes flat, sometimes semi-cylindrical. To the offensive weapons were added about this time the *scimitar,*

---

[10] The latter derivation is given according to Sir Samuel Meyrick. Mr. Kempe, in his introduction to Stothard's Monumental Effigies, deduces the term camail from cap-mail. We know of no cotemporary authority for either derivation.

borrowed from the Turks, and a sort of pole-axe, called the *godenda* or *godendac.*

The *falcastrum*, a sort of bill or gisarme, is recommended for sea-fights, and described as a scythe firmly fixed to a very long spear. This shape was afterwards preserved, in the double-bladed weapon formed of one piece of iron and called the guisarme, down to the close of the fifteenth century, after the ancient weapon of that name mentioned by Robert Wace as early as the time of Henry II.

THE FEMALE COSTUME

appears to have undergone no particular alteration; the ugly gorget is still occasionally worn, vide p. 125; but the head is perhaps more generally uncovered in

Female costume, temp. Edward II.
Figs, *a* and *b*, from a MS. Sloane collection, 346; *c*, from Royal MS. marked 14, E. 3.

this reign than in the last; and in one manuscript of this date (Sloane Collect. 346), we perceive the hair ornamented with fret-work in a very peculiar style. Vide fig. *a*. The coverchief, or a capuchon like that of the men, is twisted fantastically and placed on the top of the head (fig. *c*). The *apron* is seen upon a female figure of this date (fig. *b*). It is afterwards mentioned by Chaucer as the *barme*, or *lap-cloth.*

Female costume, temp. Edward II., from a brass in Minster Church, Isle of Sheppey.

THE ECCLESIASTICAL COSTUME

presents no variation, but

LEGAL PERSONAGES

begin now to be distinguished by their habits.

Lawyers were originally priests, and of course wore the tonsure ; but when the clergy were forbidden to intermeddle with secular affairs, the lay lawyers continued the practice of shaving the head, and wore the coif for distinction-sake. It was at first made of linen, and afterwards of white silk. The serjeant-at-law's habit anciently was a long priest-like robe, lined with fur, and a white linen coif. Judges wear caps and capes of fur. Vide plates 80 and 81, in 2d vol. of Strutt's ' Dress and Habits.'

CHAPTER X.

REIGN OF EDWARD III., A.D. 1327—1377.

Effigy of Edward III. in Westminster Abbey, and of his second son William of Hatfield in York Cathedral.

Fig. *a*, termination of the sleeve of Edward, buttoned up the side; *b*, pattern on the shoes; *c*, pattern of border of the robe; *d*, coronet of William; *e*, pattern on the jupon or cote-hardie; *f*, pattern on military belt; *g*, embroidery on the shoes.

THE reign of Edward III. is one of the most important eras in the History of Costume. The complete changes that take place in every habit, civil or

military, render its effigies and illuminations more
distinctly conspicuous than those perhaps of any other
period, from the Conquest to the days of Elizabeth.
The effigy of this great monarch is remarkable for its
noble simplicity. The number of the royal vestments
does not exceed that of his predecessors, but their
form is rather different. The dalmatica is lower in
the neck and shorter in the sleeves than the under
tunic, and the sleeves of the latter come lower than
the wrist, and are decorated by a closely-set row of
very small buttons, the continuation of a fashion of
the reign of Edward I. His shoes or buskins are
richly embroidered, and his hair and beard are
patriarchal. He bears the remains of a sceptre in
each hand; the crown has been removed or lost
from the effigy.

The habits of

THE NOBILITY

in general were by no means so simple. The long
robes and tunics of the preceding reigns vanished
altogether, and a close-fitting body garment, called
a *cote-hardie*, buttoned all the way down the front,
and reaching to the middle of the thigh, became
the prevailing dress of the higher classes. It
was sometimes magnificently embroidered, and the
splendid military belt was worn by every knight,
buckled across the hips over this new and peculiar
garment. From the sleeves of this *cote*, which sometimes only descended to the elbow (discovering the
sleeves of an under vest or doublet, buttoned from
thence to the wrist), depended long slips of cloth,
generally painted white in the illuminations, which
were called *tippets*, and over this dress was worn
occasionally a mantle, exceedingly long, and fastened
by four or five large buttons upon the right shoulder,

so that when suffered to hang loose it covered the wearer entirely to the feet; but the front part being thrown back over the left shoulder, it hung in folds behind, and formed a sort of *cope* upon the breast, as may be seen in the effigy of William of Hatfield, son of Edward III., at the head of this chapter. His mantle, it will be perceived, is cut at the edges into the form of leaves, a fashion very prevalent at this period, and which we first noticed as early as the reign of Henry II.

The frequent tournaments and pageants of this period, as Mr. Strutt observes, contributed not a little to promote the succession of new fashions. The knights, who attended them from all parts of Europe, were usually decorated with some quaint device suggested by gallantry, and endeavoured to outstrip each other in brilliancy of appearance [1]. In a wardrobe roll of this reign, orders are given for a jupon of blue tartan, powdered with blue garters decorated with buckles and pendents of silver-gilt; also for a doublet of linen, having round the skirts and sleeves a border of long green cloth embroidered with clouds and vine branches of gold, and this motto dictated by the king, " It is as it is." Upon

---

[1] Many foreign fashions were introduced by the foreign knights assembled at the round table at Windsor, in the nineteenth year of Edward's reign. "The Englishmen haunted so much unto the foly of strangers," says Dowglas, the monk of Glastonbury, "that every year they changed them in diverse shapes and disguisings of clothing, now long, now large, now wide, now strait, and every day clothingges new and destitute and devest from all honesty of old arraye or good usage; and another time to short clothes, and so strait waisted, with full sleeves and tapetes (tippets) of surcoats, and hodes, over long and large, all so nagged (jagged) and knib on every side, and all so shattered, and also buttoned, that I with truth shall say, they seem more like to tormentors or devils in their clothing, and also in their shoying (shoeing) and other array, than they seemed to be like men." MS. Harleian Collect.

another garment made for the king's own use, this distich is commanded to be wrought :—

> " Hay! Hay! the whythe swan,
> By Gode's soul I am the man."

In the thirty-seventh year of this reign, A.D. 1363, the Commons exhibited a complaint in Parliament against the general usage of expensive apparel not suited either to the degree or income of the people; and an act was passed by which the following regulations were insisted upon :—

Furs of ermine and lettice, and embellishments of pearls, excepting for a head-dress, were strictly forbidden to any but the royal family, and nobles possessing upwards of one thousand pounds per annum.

Cloths of gold and silver, and habits embroidered with jewellery, lined with pure miniver and other expensive furs, were permitted only to knights and ladies whose incomes exceeded four hundred marks yearly.

Knights whose income exceeded two hundred marks, or squires possessing two hundred pounds in lands or tenements, were permitted to wear cloth of silver, with ribands, girdles, &c. reasonably embellished with silver, and woollen cloth, of the value of six marks the whole piece; but all persons under the rank of knighthood, or of less property than the last mentioned, were confined to the use of cloth not exceeding four marks the whole piece, and were prohibited wearing silks and embroidered garments of any sort, or embellishing their apparel with any kind of ornaments of gold, silver, or jewellery. Rings, buckles, ouches, girdles, and ribands, were all forbidden decorations to them, and the penalty annexed to the infringement of this statute was the forfeiture of the dress or ornament so made or worn.

The Scots had a rhyme about this period which ran thus :—

"Long beirds hertiless,
Peynted hoods witless,
Gay cotes graceless,
Maketh Englonde thriftless[2]."

And we accordingly find the beard worn long and pointed ; and capuchons, with long peaks, tails, or tippets, as they were called, hanging behind, and closely buttoned up to the chin in front. The " gay cotes graceless" are the splendidly embroidered *cote-hardies* already described, and which it was considered by the graver and older nobility as foppish and degrading to wear.

Caps of several shapes continue to be worn, and the knight's *chapeau* is frequently met with in nearly its present heraldic form ; but one of the most important novelties in civil costume is the occasional appearance of feathers—or rather a feather—for it is always single, and generally worn upright in front of the bonnet or cap. Beaver hats are spoken of about this time. They were probably manufactured in Flanders, and these caps and hats were frequently worn over the capuchon.

The golden chaplets or fillets round the heads of princes or princesses of the blood royal begin to be surmounted with pearls or leaves about this period, and assume the form of coronets, but without uniformity of pattern to distinguish the particular rank. Vide effigies of John of Eltham, Earl of Cornwall, son of Edward II. ; Edward the Black Prince ; William of Hatfield ; Blanch de la Tour, &c.

[2] These stanzas were fastened on the door of St. Peter's Church at Stangate, and a writer in a MS. chronicle adds, "for all that tyme the Englishemen were clothed all in cootes and hoodes peynted (painted) with letters and flowers, and semely with long beardes ;" but " peynted" may also mean pointed or peaked, a peculiar feature of the capuchon at this period.

Female Costume, temp. Edward III.

Fig. *a*, from MS. Royal, 19, D. 2; *b*, effigy of Blanch de la Tour, daughter of Edward III., Westminster Abbey; *c*, head-dress of the latter, side view.

THE HABITS OF THE LADIES

of this reign were exceedingly sumptuous and extravagant, "passing the men in all manner of arraies and curious clothing;" and several distinct fashions appear to have existed at the same period. One consisted of the gown or kirtle, with tight sleeves, sometimes reaching to the wrist, sometimes only to the elbow, and, in the latter case, with the same pendent streamers or tippets attached to them, that we have noticed in the dress of the other sex. The gown was cut rather lower in the neck, fitted remarkably close to the waist[3], and was occasionally worn so long, not only

[3] "They wered such strait clothes," says the Monk of Glastonbury, "that they had long fox-tails sewed within their garments to

in the train but in front, as to be necessarily held up when walking.

Another, and newer fashion, was the wearing of a sort of spencer, jacket, or waistcoat, for it resembles either, or rather all three, faced and bordered with furs, according to the rank of the wearer. It has sometimes sleeves reaching to the wrist, at others it seems to be little more than the skeleton, if we may so speak, of a garment, with long and full skirts, wanting sides as well as sleeves, or at least the armholes cut so large that the girdle of the kirtle worn under it is visible at the hips [4].

The cote-hardie was also worn by the ladies in this reign, buttoned down the front like that of the men, sometimes with tippets at the elbows, and there is an appearance of pockets in some of the illuminations of this period. Vide fig. *a*, at the head of this section.

In the vision of Pierce Ploughman, written, it is supposed, about 1350, the poet speaks of a woman richly clothed, her garments purpled, faced, or trimmed with fine furs, her robe of a scarlet colour in grain, and splendidly adorned with ribands of red gold, interspersed with precious stones of great value. Her head-tire, he says, he has not time to describe, but she wore a crown that even the king had no better. Her fingers were all embellished with rings of gold, set with diamonds, rubies, and sapphires, and also with oriental stones or amulets to prevent any venomous infection. At the tournaments and public shows the ladies rode in party-coloured tunics, one

holde them forth;" upon the principle, indeed, of a much satirized modern accessory, as the holy father tells us in no very equivocal language.

[4] The effigy of Blanch de la Tour, daughter of Edward III., deceased 1340, affords us a good specimen of this sideless garment. Vide fig. *b*, at the head of this section.

half being of one colour and the other half of another, with short hoods and *liripipes* (the long tails or tippets of the hoods) wrapped about their heads like chords.

Their girdles were handsomely ornamented with gold and silver, and they wore small swords, "commonly called daggers," before them in pouches, and thus habited they were mounted on the finest horses that could be procured, and ornamented with the richest furniture.

By "short hoods" we should have presumed those were meant of which we have given a representation and description in the last reign—that is to say, the capuchon twisted up in a fantastic form, and placed lightly upon the top of the head; but the *liripipe* or tippet, being bound about the head like a chord, brings to our recollection the figure of Charles le Bon, Count of Flanders, engraved in Montfaucon's Monarchie Française, who wears the capuchon of this period without the cape on the shoulders, and the tippet tied about his head precisely as described above.

Charles le Bon, Count of Flanders.

The fashion of wearing daggers stuck through pouches became very general amongst knights and gentlemen about this period; and we may therefore fairly presume, that the ladies then, as now, affected male attire in their riding habits, with peculiar alterations, caprices of their own, which were in turn eagerly caught at and imitated by the fops and gallants of the day[5].

The splendid embroidery of this period is well represented on the brasses at Lynn in Norfolk, dated 1343, 1364, engraved in Mr. Cotman's fine collection of monumental brasses.

Fig. *a*, effigy of Sir Oliver Ingham, Ingham Church, Norfolk; *b*, visored bascinet, from the brass of Sir Hugh Hastings, A.D. 1347, in Cotman's monumental brasses.

[5] The author of the Eulogium, cited by Camden, supports us in this opinion, for, speaking of the dress of the men in Richard II.'s time, he says, "their hoods are little, tied under the chin, and buttoned *like the women's*." Vide page 153 of this work.

THE MILITARY HABITS

of this reign present several striking novelties. The improved visored bascinet and camail, worn always for war (vide fig. *b*), the crested helmet being reserved for the lists. The magnificent jupon, emblazoned with the wearer's arms, or richly and fancifully embroidered—its constant and sumptuous companion the military belt—the casing of the body so nearly in complete steel, that plate armour may be said to commence from this period—are all unequivocal testimonies of the chivalric spirit of the age, and the splendour with which it was considered incumbent and politic to invest the honourable profession of arms. The earliest military effigies of this reign still exhibit the cyclas shorter in front than behind, or the surcoat with indented borders. The effigy of Sir Oliver Ingham affords us a good specimen of the mixed armour at the commencement of this reign, and that of the Black Prince a splendid one of the plate armour at its close. To the latter effigy, however, we have preferred for illustration the initial letter of the grant of the Duchy of Aquitaine, by Edward III. to the Black Prince, as the costume is the same, with the addition of pourpoint over the cuisses or thigh pieces, a very prevalent fashion during this and the following reign.

The principal causes of the adoption of plate armour were, according to Sir S. Meyrick, the excessive weight of the chain mail, with its accompanying garments. Indeed it was so great that the knights sometimes sank under it, suffocated with the heat, as well as the burden. The new steel-back and breastplate enabled the wearer to dispense with the hauberk and the plastron, and the jupon was a much lighter and less cumbrous garment than either the surcoat or cyclas. Besides, if of well tempered metal the

plate could not be pierced or pushed into the body
of the knight, as the hauberk was apt to be if the
gambeson or hacketon was imperfect underneath, the
breast only having at that time the additional protection of a steel plate.

Edward III. and the Black Prince, from the initial letter to the grant of
the Duchy of Aquitaine.

This great improvement was of Italian origin. The
Florentine annals give the year 1315 as the date of a

new regulation in armour, by which every horseman
who went to battle was to have his helmet, breast-
plate, gauntlets, cuisses and jambes, all of iron, a pre-
caution taken on account of the disadvantage which
their cavalry had suffered from their *light* armour at
the battle of Catina, so that what was adopted by them
to supply a deficiency was assumed by the soldiers of
Northern Europe as a relief from their superabun-
dance of defensive armour.

The various pieces for the limbs, worn during this
reign, were the *brassarts*, *demi-brassarts*, and *vant* or
vambraces for the arms ; the *cuissarts* or *cuisses* for
the thighs, and the *greaves* or *jambs* (steel boots) for
the legs, with *sollerets* of over-lapping plates for the
feet. The backs of the leathern gauntlets were also
furnished with overlapping plates, and the knuckles
armed with knobs or spikes of iron, called *gads* or
gadlings, the tops from the wrist being of steel and
lined with velvet. In a trial by combat adjudged
between John de Visconti and Sir Thomas de la
Marche, fought before Edward III. in close lists, at
Westminster, Sir Thomas de la Marche gained the
advantage by striking the gadlings of his gauntlets
into the face of his adversay. The gauntlets of Edward the Black Prince are of brass or laton, and the
gadlings instead of being spikes are made in the
shape of lions or leopards. They hang above his
tomb in Canterbury Cathedral, with his velvet surcoat, which is gamboised (that is, stuffed with wool
and stitched in perpendicular lines), and emblazoned
with the arms of France and England, quarterly ;
his tilting helmet, his shield made of the famous
cuir-bouilli (vide page 163), and the scabbard of
his estoc or small stabbing-sword ; the sword itself
having been taken away, as is reported by Oliver
Cromwell. The helmet and gauntlets are engraved
on p. 139. The shape of the former is scarcely

changed from that of the helmet of the preceding
reign.   It is conical to fit the bascinet, which has
assumed the same form, and over it was worn the
knight's cap and crest, the former being an addition
to the military costume of this period.

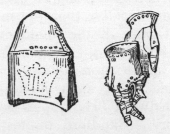

Tilting helmet and gauntlets of Edward the Black Prince, in Canterbury
Cathedral.

It is impossible for us to pass from this subject
without a few words upon the long-disputed origin
of the famous " Prince of Wales' feathers," and the no
less famous epithet of " the Black Prince," by which
the hero of Cressy and Poitiers was distinguished.
First, then, of the feathers.

On a seal appended to a grant of Prince Edward
to his brother, John of Gaunt, dated 1370, *twenty-
five years after the battle of Cressy*, Edward is seen
seated on a throne, as sovereign prince of Aquitaine,
with a *single* feather and a *blank* scroll on each side
of him, and the same badge occurs again upon the
seal to another grant in 1374.   This is, we believe,
their *earliest known appearance*.   The popular tradition of three feathers having been the *crest, arms,*
or *badge* of John, King of Bohemia, slain at the
battle of Cressy, *is not traceable to any credible
authority*.   It is first mentioned by Camden, in his
' Remains,' who says, " the victorious Black Prince,
his (Edward III.'s) sonne, used sometimes one
feather, sometimes three, in token, as some say, of his
speedy execution in all his services, as the posts in

the Roman times were called *pterophori*, and wore
feathers to signifie their flying post haste ; *but the
truth is* that he wonne them at the battle of Cressy
from John, King of Bohemia, whome he there slew."
The learned writer, however, neglects to state upon
what authority he asserts this to be "the truth [6];"
and it is rather singular that the minute and pictorial Froissart, and all the cotemporary historians,
Walsingham, Knighton, Giovanni Villani, &c. &c.
should make *no allusion whatever* to so interesting an incident. Yet such is the case. Barnes,
in his Life of Edward III., quotes Sandford's Genealogical History. Sandford quotes Camden, and
Camden quotes *nobody ;* but admits that, even in
his time, it was a disputed point, by giving another
and not very improbable derivation circulated at that
period.

The German motto "Ich Diene [7]," generally rendered "I serve," first seen upon the tomb of Prince
Edward, at Canterbury, has perhaps helped to give
currency, if it did not give birth, to the belief of the
Bohemian origin of the feathers ; but Camden himself did not credit this part of the story, for he goes
on to state, though still without quoting his authority,
that to the feathers, the prince himself "adjoined
the old English word 'ic dien' (thegn), that is, 'I
serve;' according to that of the apostle, 'the heir,
while he is a childe, differeth nothing from a servant.'"

[6] We are therefore also inclined to doubt the story of Edward
slaying the King of Bohemia, if bv the words "whom he there
slew," Camden would imply his having done so in personal combat. It is very improbable that the generous and chivalrous
Edward would have ruthlessly cut down a brave *blind* old man ;
and the cotemporary historians content themselves with the mere
statement of the fact of his being *found slain,* after the battle, beside the two knights who had guided him into the melée. Walsingham, p. 157 ; Froissart, c. 130.

[7] "Dien" is spelt on the tomb with a final *e.*

Now it certainly may be argued, on the other hand, that the King of Bohemia did feudal service to the King of France, as Count of Luxembourg, at the battle of Cressy; and there appears no reason for Edward's selecting a German motto (for it is absurd to call it old English) to express his own service to his father, supposing it, as Camden has done, to have been assumed with that modesty and filial affection for which the prince was as much renowned as for his valour: but the crest of John of Bohemia was the entire wing or pinion of an eagle, apparently from its shape, as may be seen on his seal engraved in Olivarius Vredius (vide fig. *a* in annexed engraving), and not one or three distinct ostrich feathers. In the same work, it is true, however, that we do meet with crests of wings or pinions surmounted by

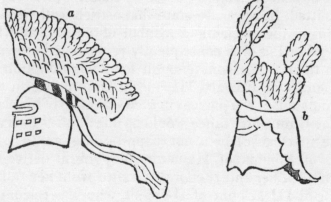

Helmet of John, King of Bohemia, and another from seals in Olivarius Vredius.

distinct feathers (vide fig. *b*), and one or three such might have been plucked from the crest of the King of Bohemia as a symbol of triumph; and granted as a memorial of victory and heraldic distinction by Edward III. to his gallant son. Yet " to vouch this is no proof ;" and again we ask, is it likely so interesting a fact could have passed unnoticed by all the cotemporary historians ? Again, the feathers are borne *singly* by not only all the brothers and descendants of Edward, but by Thomas de Mowbray, Duke of Norfolk, who must either have borne them by grant from Richard II., or, in consequence of his descent by the female side, from Thomas de Brotherton, fifth son of Edward I.; and how is this to be reconciled with the tradition of Cressy? John of Gaunt bore them ermine for difference [8].

It may, after all, have been but a fanciful badge adopted by the prince from caprice, or suggested by some very trivial circumstance or quaint conceit, no longer recollected, as were hundreds of devices of that period, to account for which stories have been ingeniously invented in after ages, and implicitly believed from the mere force of repetition. In such a case discovery is almost hopeless. Having already mentioned one classical derivation quoted by Camden, we may be permitted, however, to state that ostrich feathers were amongst the ancients a symbol of equity, and the Egyptian Isis was consequently represented crowned with them. Reasons enough for their adoption by the family of Edward III. might be founded on this circumstance: the justice (in their opinion) of his claim to the throne of France would be one; and " I serve " (in a just cause) be a not inappropriate motto [9]; as sons of Phillipa of Hainault, they might derive the ostrich feather and the foreign motto from her father, William III., Count of Hainault, who was celebrated for his justice. Again, the vulgar belief of the extraordinary digestive powers of the ostrich has afforded a remarkable simile to a foreign writer of Prince Ed-

[8] They were so blazoned in the window facing his tomb in old St. Paul's Cathedral. The difference afterwards is said to have been made in the quill of the feather; the king's being gold, the prince's argent, the Duke of Lancaster's ermine, and the Duke of Somerset's, compony, argent and azure. Ashmole's Hist. of the Order of the Garter.

[9] The motto of the garter is supposed by Sir E. Ashmole to allude to the same claim.

ward's own time, one who claims indeed to have been
his companion in arms at the battle of Poictiers,
where he says, " many a hero, *like the ostrich*, was
obliged to digest both iron and steel, or to overcome
in death the sensations inflicted by the spear and the
javelin." Amongst the far-fetched conceits of the
middle ages of knighthood, may be found more
obscure and fantastical devices than an ostrich feather
assumed, in allusion to the bearer's appetite for, or
mastery over, iron and steel. The German for an
ostrich, also, is *strauss*—(*der strauss vogel*), which,
curiously enough, signified anciently " a fight, combat, or scuffle," though it is now obsolete in that
sense. Here is another sufficient reason for the
adoption of an ostrich feather by the prince as a
general allusion to his warlike propensities, or by the
whole family of Edward III. as a type of their determination to fight in support of his French claim;
and as to the motto, suppose, as Camden asserts,
that it had no connexion originally with the badge,
but was merely associated with it accidentally. It
certainly appears on the tomb at Canterbury upon
the small scrolls attached to the three feathers, and
upon the large one over each shield that contains
them. But what says the prince in his will? "We
will that round the said tomb shall be twelve esco-
cheons of laton, each of the breadth of a foot, six of
which shall be of our arms entire, and the other six
of ostrich feathers : and that upon each escocheon
shall be written ; that is to say, upon those of our
arms, and *upon the others of ostrich feathers*,
' Houmout'" (high spirit). Here is another puz-
zle! The motto " Ich Dien" is not mentioned, yet
it has in every instance been placed with and over
the feathers, and the word " Houmout" only over
the shield of arms by those who minutely fulfilled
the directions of the will in every other particular !

The motto, "Ich Dien," does *not* appear on the scrolls of the feathers on the seals of the Black Prince, of Thomas Duke of Gloucester, or of Richard II., or Henry V. when Prince of Wales, or on the monumental tablet of John, Duke of Bedford, but it *does* appear on the seal of Edward Plantagenet, Duke of York, slain at Agincourt, and who was no way connected with Wales—a sufficient proof that it can have no relation to that principality. Richard II. is seen in an illumination in a Harleian MS., in a surcoat powdered with golden ostrich feathers, and the bardings of his horse and his pennon are similarly blazoned. Sir Roger de Clarendon, the natural son of Edward the Black Prince, bore for his arms Or, on a bend Sable, three ostrich feathers Argent, the quills transfixed through as many scrolls of the first. To his son Richard, the Black Prince leaves a blue vestment embroidered with gold roses and ostrich feathers, and " a hall of worsted" (that is, tapestry for a hall), embroidered with mermaids of the sea, and the border paly red and black, embroidered with swans with ladies' heads, and ostrich feathers; and he gives " a hall of ostrich feathers, of black tapestry, with a red border wrought with swans with ladies' heads," to the church of Canterbury; but in no case does he mention the motto " Ich Dien ;" and the feathers *singly*, as we have already observed, appear with *blank* scrolls upon the seals or tombs of nearly all the princes of the houses of York and Lancaster, down to Arthur, Prince of Wales, son of Henry VII., upon whose monument at Worcester they *first appear as a plume in a coronet*, as well as singly; plumes having come into fashion towards the close of the fifteenth century.

The story of Edward being called the Black Prince from the colour of his armour has already been exploded by Sir Samuel Meyrick, and rested on no better foundation than did the tradition of the feathers. Barnes, in his Life of Edward III., merely says, " Edward, the young Prince of Wales, whom, from this time, the French began to call *Le Neoir*, or the Black Prince," and quotes apparently a certain chapter of Froissart, in which decidedly there is no mention of any such title. At tournaments he might have worn a sable surcoat, with ostrich feathers upon it, in accordance with his shield of peace, and the caparisons of his horse being of the same funereal hue might have suggested the appellation ; but it is equally probable that he was called " the black" from the terrors his deeds inspired in the bosoms of his enemies ; and Æneas Sylvius, the historian of Bohemia, expressly says, " on the feast of St. Ruffus the battle of Cressy was fought between the French and the English ; hence is that day still accounted *black*, dismal, and unlucky, which took away the lives of two kings by the sword of the enemy," alluding to John, King of Bohemia, and James, King of Majorca ; the fall of the latter monarch is, however, disputed. The *first* mention of Edward as the Black Prince, in England, occurs in a parliamentary paper of *the second year of the reign of Richard II.*

In the twenty-second year of Edward III.'s reign was founded the most noble Order of the Garter. The circumstance that suggested his choice of this symbol is another mystery; but all writers of any credit combine to reject the popular tradition, which assigns it to the accidental fall of a lady's garter (the Queen's or a Countess of Salisbury's) at a grand festival, and the motto, " *Honi soit qui mal y pense,*" to the gallant indignation of the monarch at the sneer of his courtiers. Sir E. Ashmole, in his History of the Order, considers the garter as a symbol of union, and in this opinion he is followed by Sir Walter Scott and Sir Samuel Meyrick. We are not aware of any evidence that would shake such high authority; but one curious question occurs to us, connected with the subject of our work—costume,—from whence did Edward derive the garter? Camden says, he gave forth his *own* garter as a signal for a battle that sped well, which Du Chesne takes to be that of Cressy; but we have yet to learn that garters *were worn by men in those days.* No indication of such an article occurs upon any monument or in any illumination of the time, nor would it appear there was any need of such an assistant; the chaussés or long hose being attached to the doublet, or at least ascending to the middle of the thigh, where they were met by the drawers. The leg-bandages, abandoned in the previous century, have no affinity to the short garter and buckle, which forms the badge of this celebrated order. In the absence of all proof, however, probability is in favour of such garters being worn by the ladies, whose hose were in shape precisely the stockings of the present day, as may be seen in an illumination of the time of Edward II., engraved in Strutt's Dress and Habits, from Royal MS. 2, B. 7.

But whatever may have been the origin of the garter itself, the recorded one for the foundation of the order is the uniting not only of the native knights one with another, but of foreigners with them in the bonds of unity and peace, and our principal business is with the vestments by which they were distinguished. These were originally a mantle, tunic, and capuchon, of the fashion of the time, all of blue woollen cloth; those of the knights companions differing only from the sovereign's by the tunic being lined with miniver instead of ermine. All the three garments were powdered, that is to say, thickly embroidered with garters of blue and gold, the mantle having one larger than all the rest on the left shoulder, inclosing a shield Argent, with the cross of St. George Gules. Edward III. had 168 garters embroidered on his tunic and capuchon.

In the thirty-fourth year of his reign the colour of the tunic was changed to *black*, as a sign of humiliation, in consequence, Ashmole supposes, of the pestilence then raging; and in the thirty-seventh year it was made of cloth *sanguine in grain*, by which is generally understood *purple*. The capuchon always varied with the colour of the tunic. The garter was of blue and gold, as at present, and worn round the left knee, as appears from the effigy of Sir Richard Pembridge (an original knight), in Hereford cathedral. The effigy indeed, in its present state, has a garter round both knees; and Gough, in his ' Sepulchral Monuments,' mentions this as a curious circumstance; but the story prevalent at Hereford accounts for it in a most ludicrous manner. Part of the roof of the cathedral having fallen in, and broken the right leg of the effigy, which is of alabaster, a carpenter was employed to carve a wooden substitute, and taking for a pattern the (in both senses of the word) *left* leg, he very carefully placed a garter round that of his own fabrication. It is perhaps a more curious circumstance, that the garter is not visible on the monuments of Edward the Black Prince, Sir Oliver Ingham[10], or of any other original knight of the Garter except Sir Richard Pembridge, or in any illumination of the period, and that no mention of a garter, to be worn round the knee, occurs in any wardrobe account of the time!

[10] Gough says, it does appear on the effigy of Sir Oliver; but the accurate Stothard has not represented or noticed it.

MOURNING HABITS

first appear in monuments and illuminations of this
reign; and the earliest mention of them also seems
to be by Chaucer and Froissart, both writers of this
period.   Chaucer, in his 'Knight's Tale,' speaks of
Palamon's appearing at Arcite's funeral

> " In clothes *black* dropped all with tears ;"

and in his 'Troylus and Creseyde' he describes his
heroine

> " In widdowe's habit large of samite *brown ;*"

and in another place says,

> " Creyseyde was in widowe's habite *blacke ;*"

and in another, when separating from Troylus, he
makes her say,

> " ———my clothes evereh one
> Shall *blacke* ben in tolequyn (token), herte swete,
> That I am as oute of this worlde agone."

Froissart tells us, that the Earl of Foix, on hearing
of the death of his son Gaston, sent for his barber,
and was close shaved, and clothed himself and all
his household in black.   At the funeral of the Earl
of Flanders, he says, all the nobles and attendants
wore black gowns; and on the death of John, King
of France, the King of Cyprus clothed himself in
black mourning, by which distinction it would seem
that some other colours were occasionally worn,
such as the " samite brown" of Chaucer's Creseyde.
The figures on the tomb of Sir Roger de Kerdeston,
who died A.D. 1337, represent the relations of the
deceased knight, and wear their own coloured clothes
under the mourning cloak.

Chapter XI.

REIGN OF RICHARD II., 1377—1399.

THE march of foppery was accelerated under the reign of the weak and luxurious Richard of Bordeaux. "Fashions from proud Italy," and many imported by Queen Anne from Bohemia, infected even the menial servants. The vanity of the common people in their dress was so great, says Knighton, that it was impossible to distinguish the rich from the poor, the high from the low, the clergy from the laity, by their appearance. What it was impossible to do then we may be surely excused attempting now, and therefore we shall confine ourselves to dividing the male from the female dress, the civil from the military [1].

CIVIL COSTUME.

To begin with the king himself. He was perhaps the greatest fop of the day. He had a coat estimated at thirty thousand marks, the value of which must have arisen chiefly from the quantity of precious stones with which it was embroidered—this fashion obtaining greatly during the fourteenth century, as did that also of working letters and mottoes on the dress, and cutting the edges of the mantles, &c. into the shape of leaves and other devices. The curious and authentic portrait of Richard, preserved in the Jerusalem Chamber at Westminster Abbey, represents

[1] Chaucer's Canterbury Tales, however, furnishes us with some characteristic dresses, which we shall notice in regular rotation.

Civil costume of the reign of Richard II., from illuminations in a MS.
metrical history of his deposition, marked Harleian, 1319.

him in a robe embroidered all over with roses and
the initial letter of his name. A few sumptuary laws
were enacted by Richard, but they were little attended
to, and extravagance of every description seemed the
object of the entire population. Harding, speaking
of the king's train and servants, says—

"There was great pride among the officers
And of all men surpassing their compeers
Of rich array and more costious
Than was before or sith and more precious.
     *   *   *   *   *   *   *
Yemen and gromes in cloth of silk arrayed,
Sattin and damask in doublettes and in gownes.
In cloth of greene and scarlet, for unpayed (unpaid for)."

Cut worke was great both in court and townes,
Bothe in men's hoodes and also in their gownes,
Broudur (embroidery) and furre and goldsmith's worke all newe
In many a wyse each day they did renewe."

Chronicle, chap. 193.

And the poet declares that all this he heard Robert
Ireleffe say, who was clerk of the green cloth to
Richard II.

Chaucer, who wrote his 'Canterbury Tales' towards
the close of this reign, puts a two-fold lamentation
into the mouth of the parson concerning the " sinful
costly array of clothing." First as to " the sin in
superfluity of clothing, which maketh it so dear, to
the harm of the people, not only to the cost of the
embrouding, the disguising, indenting or barring,
ounding, paling, winding or bending[2], and semblable
waste of cloth in vanity ; but there is also the costly
furring in their gowns, so much pounsoning (pouncing)
of chisel to make holes, so much dagging of shears,
with the superfluity in length of the aforesaid gowns,
trailing in the dung and in the mire on horseback
and eke on foot, as well of man as of woman." * * *
And secondly, " upon that other side, to speak of the
horrible disordinate scantiness of clothing as be these
cut *slops* or *hanselines*[3]," that through their short-

[2] Most of these are heraldic terms. " Barring" signifies striping
horizontally ; " paling," longitudinal divisions ; " bending," diagonal
stripes ; and " ounding" or " undeing," a waved pattern or edge.
" Indenting" and " winding" need no explanation.

[3] Strutt has not attempted a derivation for this word. " Hanse-
lein" is the German diminutive of the familiar name " Hans"
(Jack), and has, we imagine, been applied in a punning sense
to the short or little jack which Froissart mentions at this
time as a garment of German origin ; for he tells us that
Henry, Duke of Lancaster, on his return to England, entered
London in a courte jacques of cloth of gold, " à la fachon
D'Almayne." The little jack or jaques was afterwards called
jaquette by the French, and jacket by the English, as the shortened
roc or tunic had been called roquette and rocket previously. The

ness, he says, and the wrapping of their hose, which
are departed of two colours, white and red[4], white and
blue, white and black, or black and red, make the
wearer seem as though " the fire of St. Anthony, or
other such mischance," had cankered and consumed
one-half of their bodies. These party-coloured dresses,
which commenced about the reign of Edward II., are
certainly more singular than elegant, and have a particularly grotesque appearance, when, as in an illumination representing John of Gaunt sitting to decide
the claims on the coronation of his nephew Richard
II. (Cotton MS., marked D. 6), the long robe is
divided exactly in half, one side being blue and the
other white, the colours of the house of Lancaster.
The party-coloured hose, too, renders uncertain the
fellowship of the legs, and the common term of
a pair perfectly inadmissible. Knighton says the
fashions were continually changing, every one endea-
vouring to outshine his neighbour in the richness
of his habit and the novelty of its form. The author of an anonymous work called the ' Eulogium,'
cited by Camden, and apparently of this date, says,
the commons were besotted in excess of apparel,
" some in wide surcoats reaching to their loins, some

epithet "cut slop," also applied to it, shows that it was a shortened
garment. Slops, we are told in the next century, are mourning
coats or cassocks. The word here occurs for the first time that
we are aware of, and seems to be derived from the German
schleppe, which signifies " anything trailing." (*Schleppe kleid* is
" a gown with a train.") " These cut slops or hanseleins," therefore, evidently means these shortened gowns or coats, or little jacks.

[4] White and red were the colours assumed by Richard II. as
his livery, and were consequently much worn by the courtiers of
his reign. The mayor, accompanied by the citizens of London
in a very large company on horseback, met Richard II. and his
queen on Blackheath, all of them being clothed in the king's
colours—that is to say, in party-coloured gowns of white and red,
and conducted them first to St. Paul's Church and then to the
Royal Palace at Westminster. (Knighton.)

in a garment reaching to their heels, close before, and strutting out on the sides, so that at the back they make men seem like women, and this they call by a ridiculous name, *gowne.* Their hoods are little, tied under the chin, and buttoned like the women's, but set with gold, silver, and precious stones. Their lirripipes or tippets pass round the neck, and, hanging down before, reach to the heels, all jagged. They have another weed of silk which they call a *paltock*[5]. Their hose are of two colours, or pied with more, which they tie to their paltocks, with white lachets called *herlots*, without any breeches. Their girdles are of gold and silver, and some of them worth twenty marks. Their shoes and *pattens* are snouted and picked (piked), more than a finger long, crooking upwards, which they call *crackowes*, resembling devil's claws, and fastened to the knees with chains of gold and silver." These crackowes were evidently named after the city of Cracow, and were no doubt amongst the fashions imported from Poland, which had been incorporated with the kingdom of Bohemia by John, the grandfather of Richard's queen Anne. Not that the long-toed shoe was a novelty, as we have already noticed them as early as the reign of Rufus ; but the fastening of them to the knee might have been the

[5] This "weed" is mentioned by Pierce Ploughman, and was therefore introduced during the reign of Edward III. It appears to have been of Spanish origin, and was most probably brought into fashion by the knights in the service of John of Gaunt or Edward the Black Prince, whose connection and communication with Spain was so near and so frequent. *Paletoque* still exists in the Spanish dictionary, and is rendered a kind of dress like a scapulary, which was a monk's frock, generally without sleeves (according to Du Chesne). The word *paletoque* seems compounded of *palla*, a cloak, and *toque*, a head-dress, which would induce a belief that the paltock had a hood or cowl attached to it. It had either been originally, or it afterwards became the dress of the common people, as *paleto* signifies, in Spanish, a clown, and the word *paltoquet*, in French, means clownish.

peculiar fashion of Cracow. We have no illumination exhibiting them so fastened, although the points are represented of a preposterous length ; but there is the appearance of a chain at the knee of one figure, in a miniature of this date (Royal MS. 20, B. 6) ; and Major Hamilton Smith, in his ' Ancient Costume of England,' mentions a portrait of James I. of Scotland, existing at Kielberg, near Tubigen in Swabia, a seat of the family of Von Lystrums, wherein the peaks of the monarch's shoes are fastened by chains of gold to his girdle.

The tight sleeves of the preceding reigns were now out of fashion, and the Monk of Evesham speaks of the deep wide sleeves, commonly called *pokys*, shaped like a bagpipe, and worn indifferently by servants as well as masters. They were denominated, he says, the devil's receptacles, for whatever could be stolen was popped into them. Some were so long and so wide that they reached to the feet, others to the knees, and were full of slits. As the servants were bringing up pottage, sauces, &c., their sleeves " would go into them, and have the first taste ;" and all that they could procure was meant to clothe their uncurable carcasses with those pokys or sleeves, while the rest of their habit was short.

Chaucer's squire, in the ' Canterbury Tales,' is described as wearing a short gown, with " sleeves long and wide." His dress was also embroidered,

> " As it were a mede
> Alle full of fresshe flowres white a rede."

His locks

> " were crull as they were laide in presse."

His yeoman was clad in "a cote and hoode of grene," his horn slung in a green baldrick, a silver figure of St. Christopher was on his breast, and a gay or handsome bracer on his arm. A sword and buckler hung on one side of him, and a dagger on the other ; a sheaf of arrows, with peacocks' feathers, was tucked beneath his girdle, and he bore "a mighty bow" in his hand. In the 'Friar's Tale' another yeoman is described wearing a *courtepy* of green, and a hat with black fringes.

The franklin, or country gentleman, is merely stated to have worn an anelace or knife, and a gipciere or purse of silk hanging at his girdle, white as milk.

The merchant is represented in "motley" (i. e. party-colours), with a forked beard and a "Flaundrish beaver hat," his boots clasped "fayre and fetously."

The doctor of physic was clothed "in sanguin and in perse" (i. e. purple and light blue), lined with taffata, and sendal or cendal. In the 'Testament of Cresseyde,' Chaucer speaks of a physician in a scarlet gown, and "furred well, as such a one ought to be;" and he may mean scarlet by "sanguin," as scarlet and purple were terms used indifferently one for the other.

The sergeant-at-law's dress was a medley coat, with a girdle of silk, ornamented with small bars or stripes of different colours [6].

The reeve or steward wore a long surcoat; he had a rusty sword by his side, his beard was closely shaven, and his hair rounded at the ears and docked on the top of the crown like a priest's.

The miller was clothed in a white coat and a blue hood, and was armed with a sword and buckler. His hose on holydays were of red cloth, when he also twisted the tippet of his hood about his head,

---

[6] A Harleian MS., marked 980, informs us that the sergeant-at-law's robe was formerly party-coloured, in order to command respect, as well to his person as to his profession. He wore a cape about his shoulders, furred with lamb's skin, a hood with two labels upon it, and a coif of white silk, when in the exercise of his profession.

a fashion amongst the gallants, as we have remarked in page 134.

The poor ploughman wore a tabard, with his hat, scrip, and staff.

The shipman was dressed in a gown of *falding* to the knee, with a dagger slung under one arm by a lace round his neck.

The haberdasher, carpenter, weaver, dyer, and tapestry-worker, all wealthy burghers of London,

> " were yclothed in a livery
> Of a solempne and grete fraternite."

Their clothes were new, and the chapes of their knives and their pouches and girdles ornamented with silver.

The clergy, as Knighton has already told us, were not to be known from the laity ; and the ploughman in the 'Canterbury Tales' rails at them for riding glittering with gold upon high horses, gayer than any common knight might go, wearing golden girdles and gowns of scarlet and green, ornamented with cut-work, and the long piked shoes, nay, being armed even like men of war, with broad bucklers and long swords and baldricks, with keen basilards or daggers. Many priests, he says, have mitres embellished with pearls, like the head of a queen, and a staff of gold set with jewels. In addition to this, Chaucer has introduced a monk amongst his pilgrims dressed in open defiance of the regulations of the church. The sleeves of his tunic are edged with the *fur de gris*, " the finest in the land." His hood is fastened beneath his chin with a golden pin, curiously wrought, the great end being fashioned like a true-lover's knot, or having one engraved on it. His supple boots and the bells upon his horse's bridle are mentioned as instances of his foppery and love of display. Even the parish-clerk, described by the miller, is said to be spruce and foppish in his dress. His hose were red, his kirtle sky-blue, set about with many points, and over it a surplice white as a blossom. His shoes had "Paules windows carven" on them—that is to say, they were cut or embroidered lattice-wise, a fashion more or less prevalent during the thirteenth and fourteenth centuries. Hats, caps, and high bonnets are worn as well as chaperons. The latter have sometimes a single feather in front. Vide engraving at page 150.

The hair was worn long, and curled with great care, as we have already found that of the squire described. The beard was forked, and the moustache in all knightly effigies is long, and drooping on each side of the mouth over the camail.

To the decoration of the garter we have, in this reign, to add the badge of the white hart, assumed by Richard II., and worn by all his courtiers and adherents both male and female, either embroidered on their dresses, or suspended by chains or collars round their necks. This device seems to have been derived from his mother, whose cognizance was a white hind. Rymer mentions that in the ninth year of his reign Richard pawned certain jewels, "à la guyse de cerfs blancs;" and in the wardrobe accounts of his twenty-second year is an entry of a belt and sheath of a sword of red velvet, embroidered with white harts, crowned, and with rosemary branches. An ancient author, quoted by Holingshed (sub anno 1399), says, " that amongst the few friends that attended this unfortunate prince after his capture by the Earl of Northumberland was Jenico D'Artois, a Gascoine, that still wore the cognizance or device of his master, King Richard, that is to saye, a white hart, and would not put it from him neither for persuasion nor threats ; by reason whereof, when the Duke of Hereford understood it, he caused him to be committed to prison within the castle of Chester.

This man was the last (as saith mine author) which bare that device, and showed well thereby his constant heart towards his master." The white hart still remains, painted of a colossal size, on the wall over the door leading to the east cloister from the south aisle of Westminster Abbey. It is generally represented crowned, collared, and chained, and couchant under a tree. Other badges of this monarch were the sun in splendour [7], and the pod of the Planta Genista, or broom, with which the robe of his monumental effigy is covered.

The surcoat of the knights of the garter was, in the seventh year of Richard II., made of "violet in grain;" in the eleventh year it was white, and in the twelfth and nineteenth of " long blue cloth." Vide Ashmole's History of the Order.

Military costume, temp. Richard II., from Harleian MS. 1319.

[7] Gower, Bib. Cotton, Tiberius, A. 4, fol. 153.

THE MILITARY COSTUME

partook of the sumptuous extravagance of the age.
The alterations made in the armour during the reign
of Edward III. were perfected in that of his grandson, and the era of plate may be said to commence
from the accession of Richard II. The camail, the
gussets of chain at the joints, and the indented edge
of the chain apron, are all that remain to be seen of
the complete suit of double-ringed mail worn at the
commencement of this century. Milan was the grand
emporium from whence the most splendid suits were
forwarded to the chivalry of Europe. The armour
made expressly for Henry, Duke of Hereford, to wear
in the famous duel at Coventry, was manufactured at
Milan by order of Galeazzo Visconti, to whom the
duke had written on the subject. The jupon and
military girdle introduced in the last reign were still
worn ; but the loose surcoat or blouse seems to have
come again into fashion at the close of this century.
It is generally, however, represented as fancifully
embroidered, instead of being emblazoned like the
jupon. The most characteristic novelty is the visor,
ventàille or *bavière* (as it was indifferently called), of
the bascinet, which, from having been simply convex,
has now assumed a shape that will be best understood from the engraving of a specimen in the collection at Goodrich Court, one of the only two
visored bascinets of this period known to exist. The
other is now in the Tower, having been bought for
the national collection at the sale of Mr. Brocas's
armour, March 22, 1834.

Visored bascinet of the time of Richard II.

As a most interesting and curious authority, we subjoin the following engraving from an illuminated MS. copy of the 'Roman de la Rose' of this date, in the collection of the late Francis Douce, Esq., F.S.A., in which are several figures of females armed with sword, spear, and shield, and wearing the visored bascinet and camail, most faithfully delineated.

Helmets of the time of Richard II. on two female figures in an illuminated copy of the Roman de la Rose, in the collection of the late F. Douce, Esq.

Some of these extraordinary visors were hooked like the beak of a bird: the bascinet itself was richly ornamented round the edges, and a band or fillet of the most splendid workmanship sometimes encircles it like a diadem. The "bacinet a visiere" was worn only for war. In tournaments the visor was removed, and the helmet, surmounted by its mantling wreath and crest, placed over the bascinet. Chaucer has the following stirring picture of the preparation for a joust in the Knight's Tale :—

> " There mayst thou see devising of harneis
> So uncouth and so riche and wrought so wele
> Of goldsmithry, of 'broudry, and of stele,
> The sheldes bright, testeres [8], and trappures,
> Gold hewin helmes, hawberks, and coat armures,
> Lordis in paramentes [9] on their coursers,
> Knightis of retinue and eke esquires
> Nailing of speres and helmes buckling,
> Gigging [10] of shields, with laniers lacing
> As there need is, they were nothing idyl.
> The foming stedis on the goldin bridyl
> Gnawing, and fast the armourers also
> With fyle and hammer, riding to and fro ;
> Yeomen on foot, and commons many a one,
> With shorte staves thick as they may gone,
> Pipes, trompes, nakoners, and clariouns,
> Meet in the battaile blowen bloody sounds."

The terms hauberk and haubergeon, in this reign, occasioned a good deal of confusion, from the circumstance of both the military garments originally so called being superseded by defences of plate, to which the old names are applied. The knight, in the prologue to the 'Canterbury Tales,' is said to have worn a gipon (jupon) of fustian, " alle besmotred with his habergeon." Now this appears to mean that the habergeon was worn over the jupon, and therefore by gipon we are not to understand the splendidly emblazoned garment generally at this period covering

[8] " Testieres," horse armour for the head.

[9] " Paramentes," robes of state.

[10] " Gigging," " guiging," that is, arranging the guige or strap of the shield which went round the neck.

the breast-plate or plastron, but a plain fustian just-au-corps, and by habergeon, the plastron or breast-plate itself.   In the French metrical history of the deposition of Richard II. (Harleian MS. 1319) Bolingbroke is seen with a breast-plate, worn over a black jupon or just-au-corps.   In the rhyme of Sir Topas, Chaucer gives a fuller description of the dress and arms of a knight.   He first put on

> " Of cloth of lake fin and clere
> A breche and eke a sherte,
> And next his sherte an haketon,
> And *over that* an habergeon
> For piercing of his herte."

Here again the habergeon is apparently the plastron; but he continues,

> " And *over that* a fin hauberk
> Was all ywrought of Jewes work,
> Ful strong it was of *plate*,
> And *over that* his cote-armure
> As white as is the lily floure
> In which he wold debate."

Here the hauberk is distinctly said to be also of plate, and worn over the habergeon, being itself covered by the jupon or surcoat, emblazoned with his armorial bearings. We have quoted this passage merely to show that the terms hauberk and haber-geon no longer designate chain or ringed armour only, and thereby prevent our readers being puzzled, like poor Mr. Mills, who argued himself into a fever upon the subject for want of that very simple key to the riddle[11].

The jambeaux or jambs (leg-pieces) of Chaucer's Sir Topas were of cuir-bouly (cuir-bouilli), a pre-paration of leather much used at this period, not only for armour, but for effigies and various works of art.

[11] History of Chivalry, 2 vols, 8vo.   London, 1825.

" His swerde's sheth of ivory,
His helme of latoun bright,
His sadel was of rewel bone,
His bridel as the sonne shone,
Or as the mone light,
His spere was of fin cypres,
* * * * *
The hed ful sharpe y-ground."

His shield was gilt, and emblazoned with a boar's head and a " charboncle," and his crest was a tower, out of which sprung a lily.

THE FEMALE COSTUME

of this reign was as splendid and fantastic as the male. The party-coloured dresses of the previous reigns were still in vogue, with numerous varieties of the cote-hardie, the waistcoat or spencer-like vest, described in the last chapter, some of them probably Bohemian fashions introduced by Queen Anne. Gower, in his ' Confessio Amantis,' particularly alludes to " the new guise of Beme," and describes, in the same poem, a route of ladies mounted on fair white ambling horses, with splendid saddles, " evrich one ride on side" (i. e. sideways), another fashion said to have been introduced by Anne of Bohemia, and at this time a mark of high rank. They were clothed all alike in rich copes and kirtles, " departed white and blue," and embroidered all over with the most fanciful devices ; their bodies were long and small, and they had crowns on their heads, the least costly of which could not be purchased " for all the gold of Crœsus' hall."

The following engravings represent five female figures, taken from various illuminations of this period. Figures *a* and *b* exhibit very clearly the sideless garment faced with fur, and terminating in long full skirts, described in the last chapter, and worn over

the kirtle.   Figure c shows a lady " in kirtle alone," as
the ancient romances tell us they sometimes " served
in hall," with the " gentil body and middle small,"
much spoken of in this and the previous century, and
the girdle over the hips with the gysire attached to
it, part of which only is seen in figure b.   In figure
d the exterior garment is so long as to be gathered
up and carried over the arm ; and figure e presents
us with a shorter but more splendid variety of it, with
an opening up the side bordered with ermine.

The long white tippets or streamers from the elbow
are still worn, but towards the close of the reign they
are less frequent, and when they do occur, are wider,
and of the same stuff as the dress.   The gowns, kirtles, and mantles were frequently emblazoned with

Female costume, close of the 14th century.

Fig. *a*, from Royal MS. 16, G. 5; *b*, Royal MS. 20, C. 1; *c* and *d*, Harleian, 4379; *e*, from the Liber Regalis, Westminster Abbey.

armorial bearings (like the jupons or surcoats of the knights, or the tabard of the herald, which first appears about this time[12]), or covered with devices (as

[12] Previous to the fifteenth century heralds are represented with merely an escutcheon or badge at their girdles; and Chaucer, in 'the Flower and the Leaf,' alludes expressly to this fashion:—

> " And after them came a great company
>   Of heraudis and pursevaunts eke
>   Arrayed in clothes of white velvet,
>   And every man had on a chapelet
>   *Scotchonis* and eke horse harneis indede
>   They had in *sute* of them who fore them yede."

we have just learned from Gower) and mottoes, like the garments of the other sex. "Bien et loyaulment" is a motto mentioned by Chaucer as worked on the facings and borders of a lady's dress, and the trains of the gowns were so enormously long that a tract was written by some divine in this reign, entitled ' Contra Caudas Dominarum' (Against the tails of the ladies).

The parson, in the ' Canterbury Tales,' speaks in general terms of the outrageous array of the women.

We have read in the last chapter of the quaint attire of ladies attending tournaments and public shows, and in this reign we hear of four and twenty ladies[13] riding from the tower to the jousts in Smithfield, leading four and twenty knights in chains of gold and silver. The knights, ladies, and all other attendants at the tournaments, having their dresses, shields, and trappings decorated with Richard's livery of the white hart, with a crown of gold round its neck, and a chain hanging thereto[14].

The hair was still worn in a gold fret or caul of network, surmounted frequently by a chaplet of goldsmith's work, a coronet, or a veil, according to the wearer's rank or fancy.

> " A fret of golde she had next her here."
>
> CHAUCER, ' Legend of Good Women.'
>
> " And everich on her head
> A rich fret of golde, which withouten drede
> Was full of stately net stones set,
> And every lady had a chapelet
> On her head of branches fair and green," &c.
>
> IBID. ' The Flowre and the Leaf.'

In this latter instance the chaplet is allegorical, but it

[13] Froissart says "sixty."
[14] Caxton, Addition to Polychronicon, c. 6, fol. 397. We should not quote Caxton for the reign of Richard II. were he not supported by Froissart.

is continually seen in illuminations of this period, composed of jewels disposed like natural flowers. Of less exalted dames we have a portrait or two in the 'Canterbury Tales.' The Wanton Wife of Bath wore coverchiefs

> " full fine of ground,
> I durste swere that they weiged a pound,
>   the Sonday were upon her hedde,
> Hire hosen weren of fine scarlet redde,
> Ful streite yteyed and shoon full moist and newe,
> *   *   *   *   *   *   *
> Upon an ambler easily she sat,
> Ywimpled well and on hire hede an hat
> As brode as is a bokeler or a targe.
> A fote mantel about hire hippes large,
> And on hire feet a paire of sporres sharpe."

The carpenter's wife's outer garment is not described, but her girdle was barred with silk; the collar of her shift and the tapes of her white *volupere* (we are not certain of the article of dress thereby alluded to) were embroidered with black silk; her apron or barm-cloth was as white as morning milk. She had a broad silken fillet round her head, a leather purse attached to her girdle " tasselled with silk and pearled with latoun," (that is, studded or impearled with little metal buttons, vide that worn by fig. c, in p. 165); on her low collar she wore a brooch as big as the boss of a buckler, and her shoes were laced high upon her legs.

THE MOURNING HABITS

of this reign are represented in the ' Liber Regalis' (a splendid MS. so entitled, preserved in Westminster Abbey), by which we perceive that the usual garments were now made of black as well as the cloak worn during the ceremony. They are of the fashion of the time, and furred with ermine.

Parliament assembled for the deposition of Richard II, from an illumination in the Harleian MS. No. 1319.

The preceding representation of the Parliament that deposed Richard II., taken from the French metrical history before mentioned, shows the lay, spiritual, and legal peers in their usual costumes. The bishops are in cowls near the throne; the judges in coifs and furred robes; the Earls of Westmoreland and Northumberland are standing in front; the Duke of Hereford in the high cap on the left of the throne; and Exeter, Salisbury, and the other peers are seated opposite the judges.

CHAPTER XII.

REIGNS OF HENRY IV. AND V., 1399—1422.

Effigy of Henry IV., and of his queen, Joan of Navarre.

REIGN OF HENRY IV., 1399—1411.

THE effigy of Henry IV. is the most splendid of our regal series. The crown is remarkable for its magnificence. It is probably an imitation of the splendid " Harry Crown," broken and distributed by

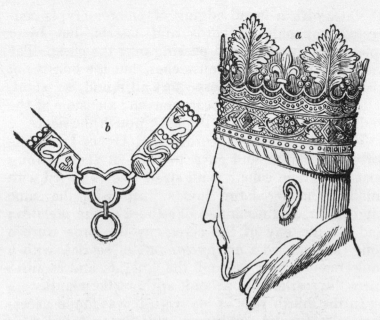

Fig. *a*, the crown of Henry IV., from his effigy; *b*, the collar of Esses, round the neck of the Queen.

Henry V., and its pieces pawned in 1415, for wages to the knights serving in the expedition to France. " A great fleur-de-lys, part of the said crown, garnished with one great balays, and one other balays, one ruby, three great sapphires, and ten great pearls, was pledged to Sir John Colvyl, and to John Pudsey, Esq., to Maurice Brunne, and to John Saundish, each a pinnacle of the aforesaid crown, garnished with two sapphires, one square balays, and six pearls." These costly fragments were redeemed in the eighth and ninth years of King Henry VI.[1]

The long tunic with pocket-holes in front is richly embroidered at the openings and the borders of the sleeves. A cope covers the shoulders and descends in front to the girdle. The inner tunic has a roll collar sitting close up the neck, and the mantle

---

[1] Rymer's Fœdera, vol. ix.

of state, with a broad edging of embroidery, is connected not only by cords and tassels, but by a splendidly-jewelled band passing over the chest. The face has beard and moustaches, but the hair is not visible, being cropped very short all round, so short, indeed, that the poll appears shaven; a custom at the end of this reign and continued through the next.

The day before his coronation, Henry IV. made forty-six knights, and gave to each of them a long coat of a green colour, with strait sleeves furred with miniver, having large hoods lined with the same kind of fur, and fashioned like those of the prelates; and on the day of the ceremony the lords wore a long tunic, called a *houppelande*[2], of scarlet, with a long mantle over it, and the knights and esquires wore the scarlet houppelande without the mantle.

In the fourth year of his reign it was found necessary to revive the sumptuary laws enacted, but to so little purpose, by his predecessors. They were revived, and with considerable additions, but seemingly with as little effect. " No man not being a banneret, or person of high estate," was permitted to wear cloth of gold, of crimson, or cloth of velvet, or motley velvet, or large hanging sleeves open or closed, or gowns so long as to touch the ground, or to use the furs of ermine, lettice, or marten, excepting only " gens d'armes quant ils sont armez ;" an odd exception at first sight, but it alludes to the loose surcoat over the armour, and the caps and hoods that were worn till the trumpet sounded, and the bascinet was hastily assumed for action.

Decorations of gold and silver were forbidden to all who possessed less than two hundred pounds in

---

[2] The Spanish word *hopa* is rendered " a long cassock with sleeves ;" and *hopalanda*, " the train of a gown worn by students." The houppelande was most probably therefore derived from Spain.

goods and chattels, or twenty pounds per annum, unless they were heirs to estates of fifty marks per annum, or to five hundred pounds' worth of goods and chattels.

Four years afterwards it was ordained that no man, let his condition be what it might, should be permitted to wear a gown or garment cut or slashed into pieces in the form of letters, rose leaves, and posies of various kinds, or any such-like devices, under the penalty of forfeiting the same, and the offending tailor was to be imprisoned during the king's pleasure.

Sergeants belonging to the court (it is left uncertain whether sergeants-at-law or sergeants-at-arms are alluded to) were by this additional statute privileged to wear such hoods as they pleased for the honour of the king and the dignity of their station. The mayors, for the time being, of London, Warwick, and other free towns, are also exempted from any prohibition.

That these statutes were as little regarded as ever, we have sufficient proof in the complaints of Occleve the poet, from whose poem of ' Pride and waste-clothing of Lorde's Men, which is azens (against) their Estate,' we shall quote a few stanzas, modernizing in some degree the spelling for the benefit of the general reader.

After a few introductory lines, he says,—

" But this methinketh an abusion,
To see one walk in a robe of scarlet,
Twelve yards wide, with pendant sleeves down
On the ground, and the furrur thereon set,
Amounting unto twenty pounds or bett (better);
And if he for it paid, hath he no good
Left him wherewith to buy himself a hood.
     *   *   *   *   *   *

Some afar men might loras know,
By their array, from other folk ; or now (but now)
A man shall study or muse a long throw
Which is which : O lords, it fits you,
Amend this, for it is in your prow (power).
If in you and your men no difference
Be in array, less is your reverence.

Also there is another new jett,
A foul waste of cloth, and excessive.
There goeth no less in a man's tippet
Than a yard of broad cloth by my life.

    *   *   *   *   *   *

What is a lord without his men ?
I put case, that his foes him assail
Suddenly in the street, what help shall he
Whose sleeves encumbrous so side trail
Do to his lord,—he may not him avail ;
In such a case he is but a woman ;
He may not stand him in stead of a man ;
His arms two have right enough to do,
And somewhat more, his sleeves up to hold.

    *   *   *   *   *   *

Who now most may bear on his back at once,
Of cloth and furrour (furs) hath a fresh renown,
He is a lusty man clepyd for the nones :
Now have these lords little need of brooms
To sweep away the filth out of the street,
Since side sleeves of pennyless grodms
Will it up lick, be it dry or wet.

    *   *   *   *   *   *

If a wight virtuous, but narrow-clothed,
To lords' courts now-a-days go,
His company is to myk (many) folk lothed.
Men pass by him both to and fro,
And scorn him for he is arrayed so.
To their conceit there is no wight virtuous
But he whose array is outrageous."

Were it not for the style, would not any one suppose the latter lines had been written yesterday ?

A decoration makes its appearance in this reign, and is worn by the distinguished of both sexes, the origin of which is differently accounted for. We allude to the collar of SS or Esses[3]. Camden says it was composed of a repetition of that letter, which was the initial of Sanctus Simo Simplicius, an eminent Roman lawyer, and that it was particularly worn by persons of that profession. Other writers contend that it was an additional compliment of Edward III. to the Countess of Salisbury. But its non-appearance till the reign of Henry IV. is a sufficient answer to that supposition. Sir Samuel Meyrick, with much greater probability, suggests, that we should consider it the initial letter of Henry's motto, " Souveraine," which he had borne while Earl of Derby, and which, as he afterwards became sovereign, appeared auspicious. The initial of a common motto of the middle ages, " Souveniez vous de moy" (Souvenez vous de moi), has also been mentioned as a derivation, and supported by the remark, that a " fleur-de-souvenance," the " forget-me-not," occasionally linked the double SS together ; but we incline to the opinion of Sir Samuel Meyrick, and at the same time we must remark the singularity of the circumstance, that the origin of such popular and celebrated decorations and badges as the feather of the Prince of Wales, the Order of the Garter, and the collar of SS, should be to this day a mystery to the most learned and indefatigable antiquaries.

A great gold collar called of Ilkington, lavishly garnished with rubies, sapphires, and pearls, is spoken of as the jewel of the Prince of Wales, afterwards Henry V., and was pawned by him for five hun-

[3] See it engraved, page 171 of this work, as it appears round the neck of Joan of Navarre, queen of Henry IV.

dred pounds to the Bishop of Worcester, when
raising funds for the French expedition in 1415 [4].

Another collar called Pusan or Pysane d'Or,
from its being manufactured at Pisa, worked with
antelopes, and set with precious stones, was pawned
at the same time to the mayor and city of London [5],
and most probably had belonged to Henry IV., whose
supporter and badge was an antelope. A gold chain
wrought with letters and crowns, a sword garnished
with ostrich feathers (the prince's), a gypsire of
purple velvet garnished with gold, and numberless
other jewels, &c., were pledged at the same time to
various persons, and had formed part of the royal
paraphernalia during this reign.

No alteration is noticed in the robes of the Order
of the Garter during this reign.   In the

ARMS AND ARMOUR

of the knights of the reign of Henry IV. we have no
novelty to remark, except that the soleret or steel
shoe was sometimes supplied by footed stirrups, and
the jambs or leg-pieces in such cases terminated at
the instep.   Increase of splendour is however visible
in the military equipment.   A rich wreath or band
surrounds the bascinet of the knight, and the border of
the jupon is still cut into elegant foliage, notwithstanding the strict prohibition of the statute.   Hall, the
chronicler, gives an elaborate account of the armour
worn at the grand tournament at Windsor by the
knights who conspired against Henry; and this
description Mr. Gough has unsuspiciously copied
into the preface to his ' Sepulchral Monuments,' and
Mr. Sharon Turner, more recently, into his ' History
of England.'   The mention however of lamboys,
pass-guards, and other pieces of armour not known

[4] Rymer's Fœdera, vol. ix.   [5] Ibid. page 299.

before the time of Henry VII., shows the whole
account to be a fabrication of the ingenious chronicler, who (like others of his craft and period) is only
an authority for his own time, when, if he chooses to
embellish a pageant or a banquet, he describes at
least fashions that are known to him, and gives the
various articles of apparel the names by which they
were then distinguished.

With regard to

Female head-dress of the reign of Henry IV., from the effigy of Lady De
Thorpe, Ashwelthorpe Church, Norfolk.

THE FEMALE COSTUME,

the fashions of the reign of Richard II. appear to
have been continued with little variation (vide
effigy of Joan of Navarre at the head of this chapter) ; the long-trained gowns, with the *sur-cols* or
ventes (stomachers) trimmed with fur, have entirely
displaced the super-tunic, and the reticulated head-
dress (as the hair gathered into a gold caul at the
sides has been denominated), sometimes covered
with a kerchief or veil, assumes in this reign a
square, and in the two following a heart-shaped
appearance, which seems to have awakened the
wrath and satire of the moralists and poets of
the time. Great confusion exists respecting the
horned head-dress in the works of Strutt, who, as
we have before mentioned, applies some obscure

lines of Jean de Meun to this fashion, and mixes
them up with the observations of a writer nearly a
hundred years later. This writer is a Norman knight,
who compiled a work for the use of his three young
daughters about the close of the fourteenth century
or beginning of the fifteenth century, and therein we
have the horned head-dress more clearly described.
The writer introduces a holy bishop declaiming from
the pulpit against the fashionable follies of the fair
sex, whom he accuses of being marvellously arrayed
in diverse and quaint manners, and particularly with
high horns. He compares them to horned snails,
to harts, and to unicorns, and proceeds to relate a
story of a gentlewoman who came to a feast having
the head so strangely attired with long pins, that her
head-dress resembled a gibbet, and she was consequently scorned by the whole company, who said she
carried a gallows on her head. This description
tallies well enough with the fashion observable in
this reign. The reticulated head-dress, spreading
out on each side, might, when covered with a veil,
be fairly enough assimilated to the cross-tree or
square gibbet of those times, and when the veil is
thrown over one of the heart-shaped head-dresses,
and suffered to sink in the centre, it may also be
called horned ; but there is another and more complete horned head-dress that became fashionable in
England during the reign of Henry V., and had
probably been so for some time previously in France,
from whence it travelled, we may presume, in the
suite of Queen Katherine. Of that, however, anon.
The square head-dress is the most remarkable during
this reign. A fine specimen is engraved in preceding
page, from the effigy of Lady De Thorpe.
    The French MS. before quoted contains many
strictures upon the female costume of this period.
The writer inveighs against the superfluous quanti-

ties of fur on the tails of the gowns, on the sleeves,
and the hoods; and adds, the use of great purfles
and slit coats was introduced by wanton women,
and afterwards adopted by the princesses and ladies
of England, and with them he wishes it may continue. He laments that the love of useless fashions
was so prevalent amongst the lower classes of people,
saying, "there is a custom now amongst serving-
women of low estate which is very common, namely,
to put fur on the collars of their garments, which
hang down to the middle of their backs. They put
fur also upon the bottom, which falls about their heels
and is daubed with the mire, &c." And, to deter his
daughters from extravagance and superfluity in dress,
he recounts a legend of a knight, who, having lost
his wife, applied to a hermit to ascertain if her soul
had taken an upward or a downward direction. The
good man, after long praying, fell asleep in his
chapel, and dreamed that he saw the soul of the
fair lady weighed in a balance, with St. Michael on
one side and the devil on the other. In the scale
which contained the soul were placed the good deeds
of her life, and in the opposite one her evil actions,
and beside the scale lay her fine costly clothing in
the care of a fiend. The devil then said to St.
Michael: this woman had ten diverse gowns and as
many coats, and you well know that a smaller number would have been sufficient for every thing necessary, according to the law of God, and that with the
value of one of these gowns or coats no less than
forty poor men might have been clothed and kept
from the cold, and that the mere waste cloth in
them would have saved two or three from perishing;
so saying, the foul fiend gathered up all her gay
garments, rings, and jewels, and flung them into the
scale with her evil actions, which instantly prepon-

derated, and St. Michael immediately left the lady and her wardrobe at the devil's disposal.

Strutt has quoted another short story from the same work, which we will add here as throwing a little more light upon the cote-hardie.

The eldest of two sisters was promised by her father to a young knight, possessed of a large estate. The day was appointed for the gentleman to make his visit, he not having as yet seen either of them, and the ladies were informed of his coming, that they might be prepared to receive him. The affianced bride, who was the handsomest of the two, being desirous to show her elegant shape and slender waist to the best advantage, clothed herself in a cote-hardie, which sat very strait and close upon her, without any lining or facing of fur, though it was in winter, and exceedingly cold. The consequence was, that she appeared pale and miserable, like one perishing with the severity of the weather; while her sister, who, regardless of her shape, had attired herself rationally with thick garments lined with fur, looked warm and healthy, and ruddy as a rose. The young knight was fascinated by her who had the least beauty and the most prudence, and having obtained the father's consent to the change, left the mortified sister to shiver in single blessedness.

The sumptuary laws passed in this reign prohibit the wearing of furs of ermine, lettice, pure minivers or grey, by the wives of esquires, unless they are noble themselves, or their husbands mayors of London, Warwick, or other free towns. The queen's gentlewomen and the chief maiden attendant upon a princess, a duchess, or a countess, are likewise permitted to wear the richer furs.

REIGN OF HENRY V., 1411—1422.

THE CIVIL COSTUME

of this short but busy reign differs in no visible degree from its immediate precursors. The long and short gowns, with sweeping sleeves, fancifully indented at the edges, or the pokys or bagpipe sleeves, mentioned by the monk of Evesham, formed the general upper garments of high and low, according to their own goodwill and pleasure, and in contempt of all parliamentary enactments.

A *peti* or *pettite coat* of red damask is mentioned as remaining amongst the apparel of Henry V., and as it is described to have had open sleeves, there can be no doubt it was but a *little coat*, and that the garment had no affinity to its highly-honoured namesake. The mention of gowns, houppelands, chaperons, &c. in the same inventory, proves the duration of the fashions of the last reign. *Heukes* of scarlet cloth and camlet, and *pilches* of grey fur, are novel articles. The first was no doubt a cloak similar to that still called a heuke by the Moors of Barbary and Morocco. The latter word is a corruption of the Latin *pelliceus*, or the Saxon *pylce*, and was an outer garment of fur used in cold or bad weather. Chaucer says,

"After grete hete comith colde,
No man cast his pilche away."

Gallages or *galloches* occur in the same inventory; and Henry V.'s partiality to short boots or buskins, called by the French *housseaulx* and *bottines*, is proved by an anecdote in Monstrelet's Chronicles.

"When the rumour of Henry's death had reached the French court, Messire Sarazin D'Arly inquired of a relation, who had just returned from Picardy, if he knew any thing relative to the decease of the King of England; to which he replied in the affirmative,

and said that he had seen the body of that monarch
lying in state in the church of St. Offram at Abbe-
ville. 'But are you sure,' said Sarazin, 'that you
have not been deceived?' 'Perfectly sure,' replied
the other. 'But will you swear that he had not his
buskins on his legs?' 'Truly, he had not,' said his
relation. 'Then, by my faith!' exclaimed Sarazin,
'I will not believe he is dead if he have not left them
behind him in France [6];'" that is, in the provinces
belonging to the French crown, the greater part of
Picardy being at this time an English province.

In an old English poem on the siege of Rouen,
A. D. 1418, Henry is described as riding

> " On a broune stede,
> Of blak damaske was his wede,
> A peytrelle of golde full brygt
> Aboute his necke hynge down rigt,
> And a pendaunte behind him did honge
> Unto the erthe, it was so longe [7]."

The *peytrelle* or *poitral* was a piece of horse-
furniture of this period; but if by "*his* necke" is
meant the king's, and not his "broune stede's," we
must presume it to have been some golden collar
thus called, as "hanging down from about his neck"
could hardly be the description of a breast-plate:
besides which, he is not supposed to be armed, but
entering in his garments of peace—a weed of black
damask. The long "pendaunte" was most probably
a pennon carried behind him and no part of his attire.

Beards were not much worn in this reign, and the
hair was cut close round above the ears in a very
unbecoming fashion. Whiskers are not seen, and
moustaches are only partially worn. The general
character indeed of the whole of the fifteenth century
is a closely shorn chin.

[6] Chroniques, tom. i. sub anno 1422.
[7] Vide Archæologia, vol. xxii.

In the first year of Henry V.'s reign the colour of the surcoat and chaperon of the knights of the Garter was changed again to white. The whole of the dress was still of cloth [8].

Military costume of the reign of Henry V.

Figs. *a* and *b*, from illum. MS. Royal, 15, D. 3; *c*, from effigy of Michael de la Pole, Earl of Suffolk, in Wingfield Church, Suffolk; *d*, from the effigy of Sir Robert Grushill, Hoveringham Church, Notts.

THE MILITARY EQUIPMENT

of this period is remarkable for the introduction of the panache [9]; the graceful decoration of feathers

[8] Ashmole's Hist. of the Order.

[9] The word "panache" is generally used instead of "plume" for the feathers placed upright on the apex of the helmet or bascinet, the latter term being applied when worn on the side or behind, as in later specimens. It is remarked by Mr. Fosbrooke in his Encyclopædia of Antiquities, that the knight wore three feathers,

having been hitherto confined to heraldic crests upon helmets, and never appearing as a mere ornament in

Tilting helmet of the commencement of the 15th century with heraldic crest, from the tomb of Sir Edward de Thorpe, Ashwelthorpe Church, Norfolk.

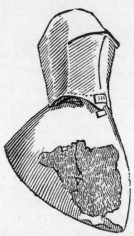

Tilting helmet and shield, from the tomb of Henry V., Westminster Abbey.

and the esquire one; but there appears no rule for this. Persons of the highest rank are as often seen with one feather on their helmet as with three.

England till the reign of Henry V.[10] Its effect in
the civil bonnet or hood, where we have seen it, from
the time of Edward III., induced some leader of
consequence, we presume, to transfer it to the bascinet, upon the apex of which it now appears falling
gracefully backward, a tube or hollow knob being

Helmet of Louis, Duc de Bourbon, engraved in Montfaucon.

placed there to contain it. The bascinet itself under-
goes a change about this time, taking the shape of
the head behind, and approaching the form of the
salade or sallet, a German head-piece, introduced in

[10] We have mentioned the apparent solitary exception in page
108 of this work, temp. Edw. I. Sir Samuel (then Doctor)
Meyrick first called attention to the curious circumstance of
feathers being first worn as ornaments in the reign of Henry V.
Mr. Mills, in his History of Chivalry, remarks that that gentleman's
"not being able to find any instance of their being thus worn,
goes but very little way to prove the negative." This is un-
courteous enough; but it is equally unjust: for their non-appearance in the thousands of earlier illuminations the learned Doctor
had examined, coupled with their simultaneous appearance in all
of that period, and continual occurrence afterwards, *does* go a
very long way to prove it. Besides, Mr. Mills prefaces this observation by stating that Dr. Meyrick had contended that "feathers
were not used as *crests* till the fifteenth century;" which he
never did do, but on the contrary, contends that they *were* used as
crests (that is to say *heraldic crests*) *only*, and not as a mere
plume or ornament, which an antiquary would not call a crest in
speaking of English armour of the middle ages. Vide Meyrick's
Critical Enquiry into Ancient Arms and Armour, 3 vols. 4to.

Bascinet, of the reign of Henry V., in the Meyrick collection.

the next reign. The great crested helmet or heaume was now only worn for the tournament. A bascinet of this time is here engraved from one at Goodrich Court, having a tube for the panache, and holes for fixing the camail round the edge, the lining or cap within, and the orle or chaplet without.

The jupon and military belt are still worn, but not so frequently; but the distinguishing character of the military effigies and illuminations of this reign is, the absence of both jupon and surcoat, and the appendage of a skirt composed of horizontal steel bands, called taces, to the globular breast-plate (vide fig. *d*, page 183) ; so that when the hause-col or steel gorget is worn instead of or over the camail, as in figs. *c* and *d*, the whole suit of armour is of plate.

Another peculiarity of the period is, the anomalous fashion of wearing large hanging sleeves of cloth, silk, or richer materials, with the armour (vide fig. *a*). Sometimes they are part of a surcoat or a cloak thrown over the whole suit, and sometimes the sleeves only are seen covering the arm to the wrist; and it is not quite evident from the illuminations whether in that case the body-armour conceals the rest of the garment, or whether they are detached articles fastened to the shoulder. When the sleeves are not worn, the shoulders appear covered with overlapping plates called *pauldrons*, and two circular plates called *pallettes*, are sometimes fastened to them in front so as to protect the armpit. Lance-rests in the form of hooks, placed just below the right breast, and breast-plates of two pieces, the lower one rising to a point in the centre and fastened upon the upper by an ornamented buckle, are also characteristic of this reign. The lower plate was called the placard. St. Remy, a writer who was present at the battle of Agincourt, describes Henry himself, at break of day, hearing three masses, one after the other, armed in all his armour excepting that for his head and his *cote d'armes* (i. e. emblazoned surcoat or jupon). After masses had been said they brought him the armour for his head, which was a very handsome bascinet, a barierre (query baviere), upon which he had a very rich crown of gold circled like an imperial crown, that is, arched over—the earliest instance of an arched crown worn by an English monarch[11].

Monstrelet tells us the archers were, for the most, without armour and in jackets, with their hose loose, and hatchets or swords hanging to their girdles; some, indeed, were bare-footed, and without hats or caps. St. Remy confirms this account, using the word " pourpoints" for jackets; but adds, that some wore caps of boiled leather (the cuir-bouilli), or wicker-work crossed over with iron.

Two-handed swords, with flaming or waved blades, first appear in this reign; but they were used more for state than for war: a pole-axe was generally carried by commanders from the present period to the reign of Edward IV.

THE FEMALE COSTUME

of this reign is distinguished by a head-dress which

[11] Elmham gives a similar but a more vague and fanciful account. Henry's crown was twice struck and injured by the blows of his enemies. The Duke D'Alençon struck off part of it with his battle-axe, and one of the points or flowers was cut off by a French esquire, who, with seventeen others, swore to perform some such feat or perish. Monstrelet, St. Remy.

Female costume of the reign of Henry V., from MS. Royal, 15, D. 3.

may indeed be called horned.   The satirical effusions
of such writers as John de Meun, and the Knight of
Normandy, appear to have had no other effect upon
the ladies than to induce them, in the true spirit of
contradiction, to justify to the fullest extent the odious
comparisons of their censors.   There is no longer
any thing extravagant in the charge of wearing a
gibbet on the head, or rivalling the crested honours
of the brute creation.   The head-dress exhibited in
the illuminations and on the effigies of this period
is certainly as ugly and unbecoming as can well be
imagined : fortunately, however, for the painter or the
actress, the fashion does not appear to have been so
general as to render its introduction on the canvas or
the stage indispensable.   The simple golden network

Horned-head-dress of the 15th century, from the effigy of Beatrice, Countess
of Arundel, in the Church at Arundel.

confining the hair, and a quaint but elegant head-tire
consisting of a roll of rich stuff, sometimes descending
in a peak on the forehead, or circling the brow like
a turban, exist to extricate the lovers of the picturesque
from so disagreeable a dilemma. Taste is ever the
true friend of fashion, and can see and amend her
follies while most admiring her inventions.

The robe or gown with a long train and hanging
or tabard sleeves, and the cote-hardie with its spencer-
like variety, are seen as in the last reign ; but where
girdles are worn, the waist is considerably shorter.
An inner tunic is sometimes discernible by its sleeves,
which descend beyond those of the robe and cover
the hand, as in the time of Henry I. ; gloves not
yet forming a usual portion of the female attire.

The effigy of William of Colchester, Abbot of
Westminster from 1386 to 1420, engraved in Stothard's work from the monument in Westminster
Abbey, may be referred to as a fine specimen of the
ecclesiastical costume of this period.

Chapter XIII.

REIGNS OF HENRY VI. AND EDWARD IV., 1420—1483.

John Talbot, Earl of Shrewsbury, in the habit of the Order of the Garter, presenting a book to King Henry VI., and his Queen, Margaret, from an illumination in the volume so presented, marked Royal, 15, E. 6.

REIGN OF HENRY VI., 1420—1461.

IF any proof were wanting of the confusion and disorder of this unfortunate monarch's reign it might be drawn from the apparel of his people, which appears to have been a jumble of all the fashions of past ages with every thing most ridiculous and extravagant that could be invented or discovered at the moment. It were a vain task to attempt a minute description or classification of the dresses of this period. The most remarkable feature of the

CIVIL COSTUME

of the middle of the fifteenth century, was the more frequent appearance of caps and hats of fantastic

Civil costume of the reign of Henry VI.

The centre figure, from a copy of Froissart, in the Harleian collection, marked 4880; the rest from a copy of Lydgate's Life of St. Ed. Harl. 2278.

shapes, and the alteration of the chaperon from an almost indescribable bundle into a regularly-formed crown within a thick roll called the roundlet, and having a long tippet attached to it which trailed on the ground, (vide fourth figure in the above engraving,) was tucked into the girdle, or wrapped

round the neck, or suspended the chaperon itself
over the shoulder when removed from the head, according to the fancy or situation of the wearer. A
single feather is sometimes worn in front of the cap
or bonnet, as in the time of Richard II. Long tight
hose with feet to them, boots or galoches coming up
to the middle of the thigh, short boots or buskins,
and shoes with high fronts and backs that turn over
each way, all of them long-toed, and some extra-
vagantly so. The gown, doublet, or jacket, instead
of being made close and high up in the neck as in
the last century, is now cut round even with the
shoulders, frequently showing the small stand-up
collar, hollowed out in front, of some under vestment, with tight sleeves that protrude through openings made in the loose ones of the gown or jacket,
which latter hang down, richly trimmed with fur, and
seemingly more for ornament than service.

The hair is worn as before, the face closely shaven.

THE STATE DRESSES

consist of long robes with or without sleeves, lined
and trimmed with furs, or having only capes or
collars of ermine descending half way to the elbow,
with bars of ermine beneath, according to the rank
of the wearer.

Garlands or coronets, and chains or collars of
gold and jewels, are worn as before.

The robes of the knights of the Garter underwent
some alteration in this reign. The colour of the surcoat and chaperon was changed to scarlet [1] in the
thirteenth year of Henry VI., and afterwards back
again to white. The number of garters to be embroidered on them was limited in this reign to one
hundred and twenty for a duke, and less by ten for

[1] And, in confirmation of this, we perceive that the surcoat of
the Earl of Shrewsbury, in the illumination engraved at the head
of this chapter, is so painted; the hood is also red but lighter.

a marquis, by twenty for an earl, and so on, down to a knight bachelor, who wore sixty. The king was unlimited, and on Henry's surcoat and hood there were one hundred and seventy-three. The mantle about this period was first made of velvet, and lined with white damask or satin[2].

Legal and other official habits are composed invariably of long and full gowns, sometimes of two colours[3], girdled round the waist, and hoods with long tippets by which they are occasionally slung over the shoulder. The gowns are trimmed and lined with furs according to the rank of the wearer.

When Henry VI. returned to England after being crowned in France, A.D. 1432, the lord-mayor of London rode to meet him at Eltham, being arrayed in crimson velvet, a great velvet hat furred, a girdle of gold about his middle, and a baldrick of gold about his neck trailing down behind him. His three henchmen[4] in one suit of red spangled with silver.

[2] Ashmole's Hist. of the Order.

[3] " Of older times," says Stow, " I read that the officers of this city wore gowns of party-colours, as the right side of one colour and the left side of another. As for example, I read in books of accounts in Guildhall, that in the nineteenth year of King Henry VI. there was bought for an officer's gown two yards of cloth coloured *mustard villars,* a colour now out of use, and two yards of cloth coloured blew, price two shillings the yard, in all eight shillings more, paid to John Pope, draper, for two gown-cloths, eight yards, of two colours, *eux ombo deux de rouge* or red medley, brune and porre (or purple) colour. Price the yard two shillings. These gowns were for Piers, Rider, and John Buckle, clerks of the chamber." *Mustard villars* has been said to be a corruption of *moitier velours,* and consequently to signify the species of stuff, and not the colour; but Stow speaks of it here as a colour distinctly. A town called *Muster de Villiers,* near Harfleur, is mentioned by the historians of the preceding reign in their accounts of Henry's expedition, and most probably gave its name to the dye or the stuff there manufactured.

[4] Pages so called. The royal henchmen were abolished by Q. Elizabeth.

The aldermen in gowns of scarlet with purple hoods, and all the commonalty of the city in white gowns and scarlet hoods, with divers cognizances embroidered on their sleeves.[5]

Figs. *a* and *b*, two salades of the reign of Henry VI., one with a moveable visor; *c*, a figure from an ivory cross-bow of the same reign showing the salade covering the face; *d*, a bill, and *e*, a dagger called *dague à roelle* from its handle; all from the originals at Goodrich Court.

THE ARMOUR

partook of the fantastic and unbridled caprices of the day. Surcoats and jupons were less worn, but it became the fashion to cover the breast-plate with silk of one colour, and the placard with silk of another. The jazerant or jazerine jacket was frequently worn

[5] Stow,

in lieu of the breast and back plates. This defence was composed of small overlapping plates of iron covered with velvet, the gilt studs that secured them forming the exterior ornament, and over this was sometimes worn the placard of steel. *Tuiles*, plates depending from the taces or skirt of the armour in front, over an apron of chain-mail, are first visible at this period. A still lighter species of armour than the jazerant, but of the same description, is mentioned by Commines about this time. " The Dukes of Berri and Bretagne," he says, " were at their ease on their hobbies, armed only with gilt nails sewn upon satin, that they might weigh the less." This sort of habit would have all the appearance of a jazerant exter-nally, and may be easily mistaken for it in illumina-tions of the fifteenth century. To the bascinet, helmet, and chapel-de-fer, was now added a new head-piece, called a *salade* or *sallet*, from the German *schale* or *shell*. Its principal characteristic is the projection behind. It had sometimes only a horizontal slit for the sight as it descended below the eyes, but at others it came no lower than the forehead and was furnished with a moveable visor. (Vide engraving on the oppo-site page.) *Casquetels* or steel caps were also in-troduced, and are seen in the illuminations of this reign with *oreillets*, round or oval plates over the ears, and sometimes with a spike at the top called a *crenel* or *charnel*. Sometimes the oreillets themselves have spikes projecting from their centres.

The armour generally is exceedingly ornamented. Every plate of that of John, Duke of Somerset, (engraved in Sandford's Genealogical History,) who died in 1444, has an exceedingly rich border to it. He also wears the splendid military belt which is seldom seen after this reign.

The spurs were screwed on to the steel shoe about this time, instead of being fastened by leathers. They were exceedingly long in the neck, and the spikes of

the rowels of formidable dimensions. (Vide figure *c,*
p. 194.)

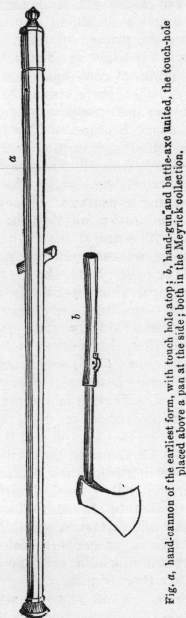

Fig. *a*, hand-cannon of the earliest form, with touch hole atop; *b*, hand-gun, and battle-axe united, the touch-hole placed above a pan at the side; both in the Meyrick collection.

The first token of a most important change in
warfare became visible during the reign of Henry VI.
The invention of cannon had suggested to the Italians
the use that might be made of a piece of ordnance
small enough to be portable, and the hand-cannon or
gonne, a simple iron tube with trunions at its sides,
and a touch-hole atop, was fixed in a stock of wood
about a cubit and a half in length, and called the
frame of the gun. It was soon however discovered
that while the touch-hole remained atop, the priming
was likely to fall off or be blown away before the
match could be applied; the perforation was consequently transferred to the side, and a small pan put
under it to hold the powder. A cover for the pan
was next invented to turn off and on by means of a
pivot, and in this stage it was used in England,
certainly as early as 1446, as appears from a roll of
purchases for the castle on Holy Island, in the
county of Durham, of that date.

A hand-cannon of the earliest sort with the touch-
hole atop, and a battle-axe with a hand-gun united
and the touch-hole placed above a pan at the side,
are engraved on the opposite page, from the originals
in the armoury at Goodrich Court.

THE FEMALE COSTUME

comprises, like that of the other sex, all the previous fashions with fantastic additions and variations
too numerous to detail in words. Gowns with enormous trains, girded tightly at the waist, and with
turn-over collars of fur or velvet coming to a point in
front, and disclosing sometimes a square-cut under
vest or stomacher of a different colour to the robe,
are of the termination of this reign. The sleeves are
of all descriptions, but the waist is exceedingly short,
as in Henry V.'s reign. The head-dresses are

Female costume, reign of Henry VI.

Figs. *a* and *b*, from Harleian MS. 2278; *c*, from the blade of a miséricorde, in the Meyrick collection; the rest from Royal MS. 15, E. 6, fol. 450.

mostly of the horned or heart shape, the latter exceedingly high, with tippets or veils sometimes attached to them. (Vide engraving above.) The Harleian MS. 2255, fol. 6, preserves "a ditty against the forked coiffures," or head-dresses which the ladies wore in the time of Henry VI., beginning

"Off God and kynde procedith al bewte."

Large turbans of the true Turkish form, made of the richest materials, are frequently seen from this period. In a poem presented by Lidgate to Henry VI. a lady is drawn sitting up in her bed with a turban on, and another with a similar head-dress attending her. (Vide figures *a* and *b*.) Isabella of Bavaria, queen

of Charles VI. of France, is seen in Montfaucon's
work with a heart-shaped head-dress of exceeding
size, and the story goes, that she carried the fashion
to such an extent, that the doors of the palace at Vin-
cennes were obliged to be altered to admit the queen
and the ladies of her suite when in full dress : but
this anecdote, if authentic, might relate to the steeple
head-dress, which succeeded the horned or hearted
shape, and was worn, as its name implies, of a portentous height [6]. Isabella is represented with one in a
another illumination copied in Johnes' edition of
Froissart, the prints to which are all engraved from
miniatures of the fifteenth instead of the fourteenth
century.

REIGN OF EDWARD IV., 1461—1483.

Lord Rivers, and Caxton, his printer, presenting a book to Edward IV. and
his family.

[6] Vide page 207.

There is no effigy of Edward IV. On his seal he
is represented in the tunic, dalmatica, and mantle with
a deep cape or cope of ermine. He is crowned with
the imperial arched diadem, its first appearance on the
seals of our English monarchs, though not in their
actual regalia. In his right hand he bears the sceptre,
and in his left the mound and cross. With a slight
variation of attitude, we perceive him similarly represented in the engraving, p. 199, copied from an illuminated MS. in the Lambeth library, wherein he is
depicted receiving a book from the hands of Lord
Rivers and Caxton the printer, and surrounded by
his queen and family. The new fashion that Edward
chose for his last state dresses was to have them
made with very full hanging sleeves, like a monk's,
lined with the most sumptuous furs, and so rolled
over his shoulders as to give his tall person an
air of peculiar grandeur[7]. He also altered the surcoat and chaperon of the Order of the Garter from
the white cloth of the last reign to purple velvet[8]. It
is probable that the velvet mantle introduced by
Henry VI. remained blue, as murrey and blue were
the colours of the house of York, and similar reasons
may have suggested the adoption of colours to the
various sovereigns; blue and white being the Lan-
castrian colours, and blue and scarlet those of the
kingdom. The lining of the surcoat was now altered from furs to white sarcenet[9].

THE GENERAL MALE COSTUME

of this period may be gathered from the following extracts from the chronicles of Monstrelet and Paradin's
Histoire de Lyons, for there was no fashion so ridiculous started in France, but then, as now, it was
immediately adopted in England. The former writer

---

[7] Monk of Croyland, 563.
[8] Ashmole, Hist, of the Order.   [9] Ibid.

Civil costume of the reign of Edward IV.
Figs. *a* and *b*, Cotton MS. Nero, D. 9; *c*, Royal, 15, E. 2, dated 1482.

tells us that the jackets, doublets, or pourpoints, were cut shorter than ever, and the sleeves of them slit, so as to show their large, loose, and white shirts; the shoulders were padded out with large waddings called *mahoitres*, and so capricious were the beaux of the period, that he who to-day was shortly clothed, was habited to-morrow down to the ground. They wore their hair so long that it came into their eyes, and they covered their heads with bonnets of cloth a quarter of an ell or more in height; all of them, as well knights as squires, wore chains of gold of the most sumptuous kind. Even boys wore doublets of silk, satin, and velvet; and almost all, especially in the courts of princes, had points at the toes of their shoes a quarter of an ell long and upwards, which they now called *poulaines*. Paradin is still more

descriptive on the subject of shoes. "The men," he
says, "wore shoes with a point before, half a foot
long; the richer and more eminent personages wore
them a foot, and princes two feet long, which was
the most ridiculous thing that ever was seen; and
when men became tired of these pointed shoes, which
were called poulaines, they adopted others in their
stead denominated duck-bills, having a bill or beak
before, of four or five fingers in length. Afterwards,
assuming a contrary fashion, they wore slippers so
very broad in front as to exceed the measure of a
good foot." p. 271.

In the third year of Edward's reign he endeavoured
to check some of these extravagances, and an act
was promulgated, by which cloth of gold, cloth of
silk of a purple colour, and fur of sables, were prohibited to all knights under the estate of lords. Bachelor knights were forbidden to wear cloth of velvet
upon velvet, unless they were knights of the Garter;
and simple esquires or gentlemen were restricted
from the use of velvet, damask, or figured satin, or
any counterfeit resembling such stuffs, except they
possessed a yearly income to the value of a hundred
pounds, or were attached to the king's court or
household.

The richer furs were also forbidden to any persons
who were not in the enjoyment of forty pounds yearly
income; and girdles of gold, silver, or silver gilt, or
any way ornamented with such materials, were also
forbidden to them.

No one under the estate of a lord was permitted to
wear the indecently-short jackets, gowns, &c. mentioned by Monstrelet, or pikes or poleines to his
shoes and boots exceeding two inches in length. No
yeoman, or person under the degree of a yeoman, was
allowed bolsters, or stuffing of wool, cotton, or *cadis*,
in his purpoint or doublet under a penalty of six

shillings and eight-pence fine and forfeiture awarded;
and to every tailor making such short or stuffed dresses,
or shoemaker or cobbler manufacturing such long-toed
shoes for unprivileged persons, Stow adds, the pain
of cursing by the clergy for the latter offence, as well
as the forfeit of twenty shillings; one noble to the
king, another to the cordwainers of London, and the
third to the chamber of London[10].

A similar statute was passed in the twenty-second
year of Edward IV., when the former statutes were
repealed, and woollen cloth manufactured out of the
king's dominions was strictly prohibited to all persons
under the rank of nobility. The lord mayor of
London ranked as a knight bachelor; and the re-
corder and aldermen of London, the mayors, bailiffs,
&c. of all cities, towns, shire towns, boroughs, cinque-
ports, and the barons of the same, were permitted
the use of apparel allotted to esquires and gentlemen
having possessions to the annual amount of forty
pounds.

The collar of suns and roses, to which was sometimes appended the white lion of the house of March,
was given by Edward IV. to his adherents, and is seen
on many of the effigies of this period. It is here engraved as seen on the effigy of the Countess of Arundel at Arundel (fig. a), and that of Sir John Crosby
in the church of Great St. Helen's, London (fig. b).
In both instances the ornament or figure appended is

[10] Chronicle, p. 419.

destroyed, but the remains of it attached to Sir J.
Crosby's collar bear evidence to its having been the
representation of some animal, if not the lion of March.
The suns and roses of the other collar are linked
by the Arundel badges of oak leaves.

Casquetel of the reign of Edward IV., in the Meyrick collection.

THE MILITARY HABIT

presents us with few striking novelties. Very globular breast-plates, immense elbow-plates, and large
tuilles (only one for each thigh) terminating in a
sharp angle, are characteristic of this reign, but they
are not universal. The sollerets were still enormously long and pointed, in accordance with the
piked shoes of the time. The steel pikes, however,
retained the old name of cracowes, while those of
the boots and shoes were new christened pouleines.
Helmets appear little worn except for tournaments,
and the visored salade is the general head-piece of
knights in battle, sometimes surmounted by a wreath
and crest. The morion first appears in this reign.
The skull-caps of steel, called *casquetels* and *capel-
lines* with the large oval ear-pieces, are frequent, and
the gorget and apron of chain-mail are indented or
escalloped at the edges. The surcoat and jupon are
seldom seen, but a tabard of arms, worn loose like
the herald's, occasionally supplies their place. The
military belt is still worn, and the jazerine jacket
and nearly all the armour of the preceding reign
may be found in illuminations of the present.

The shield is without alteration. Halberts are first mentioned about this period, though the name belonged to the earliest pole-axe, which the Germans called alle-barde or cleave-all. The *voulge*, a variety of the glaive or guisarme, and the *genetaire* or *janetaire*, a kind of Spanish lance, are added to the catalogue of offensive weapons, and the hand-gun became common. Swords and bucklers are first assigned to archers in this reign. Chanfrons, with spikes projecting from them, were adopted about 1467. Spurs as before.

Grose, on the authority of a MS. in the British Museum, says that, in the year 1471, Edward IV. landed at Ravenspur in Yorkshire, having among his troops three hundred Flemings armed with *hange-guns*, which, if not a corrupted reading for hand-guns, may have been so called from a long hasp of iron generally affixed to them, and by which they might be hung at the girdle.

THE COSTUME OF THE LADIES

of the reign of Edward IV. is no whit behind that of their lords in extravagance or splendour. Monstrelet tells us that, about the year 1467, the ladies left off the fashion of wearing tails to their gowns, and in their room substituted borders of lettice and marten skins, or of velvet and other materials, as wide and sometimes wider than a whole breadth of the stuff. They wore on their heads round caps, gradually diminishing to the height of half an ell, or three quarters, as some had them with loose kerchiefs atop, hanging down sometimes as low as the ground. They began to wear their girdles of silk much larger than they were accustomed to do, with the clasps more sumptuous, and collars or chains of gold about their necks much quainter than before (" plus cointe-

ment"), and in a greater variety. Paradin says the
ladies ornamented their heads with certain rolls of
linen[11] pointed like steeples, generally half, and sometimes three quarters of an ell in height. These were
called by some, great butterflies, from having two large
wings on each side resembling those of that insect.
The high cap was covered with a fine piece of lawn
hanging down to the ground, the greater part of which
was tucked under the arm. The ladies of a middle
rank wore caps of cloth, consisting of several breadths
or bands twisted round the head, with two wings on
the sides like ape's ears; others again, of a higher
condition, wore caps of velvet half a yard high,
which in these days would appear very strange and

[11] He calls them "fontanges."

Female costume of the reign of Edward IV.

Figs. *a* and *b*, from Royal MS. 14, E, 2 ; *c*, Ibid. 19, E. 5 , dated 1478 ; *d*, Ibid. 15, E. 4, dated 1483 ; *e*, Harleian MS. 4373 ; the others from Cotton collection, Nero, D. 9.

unseemly. It is not an easy matter, continues the author, to give a proper description in writing of the different fashions in the dresses of the ladies, and he refers the readers to the ancient tapestry and painted glass, in which they may see them more perfectly represented. "To these he might have added," says Mr. Strutt, " the illuminated MSS., wherein they are frequently enough to be met with ;" but his readers might have satisfied themselves still more completely, as indeed ours may do, by a glance at the costume of Normandy. The peasantry of Rouen, Caën,

Caux, &c., to this day wear the identical steeple caps with the butterflies' wings that, three hundred and sixty years ago, towered upon the heads of the gentle dames of Paris and London. The evanescent caprice of some high-born fair has given a national costume to the paysannes of Normandy, who have reverently copied for nearly four centuries the head-dress worn by their mothers before them.

Addison, in the Spectator, has a pleasant letter on this subject, comparing the steeple head-dress to the *commode* or *tower* of his day; and, following Paradin, he says, "The women might possibly have carried this Gothic building much higher had not a famous monk, Thomas Conecte by name, attacked it with great zeal and resolution. This holy man travelled from place to place to preach down this monstrous *commode*; and succeeded so well in it that, as the magicians sacrificed their books to the flames upon the preaching of an apostle, many of the women threw down their head-dresses in the middle of his sermon, and made a bonfire of them within sight of the pulpit. He was so renowned, as well for the sanctity of his life as his manner of preaching, that he had often a congregation of twenty thousand people, the men placing themselves on the one side of his pulpit, and the women on the other, that appeared (to use the similitude of an ingenious writer) like a forest of cedars with their heads reaching to the clouds. He so warmed and animated the people against this monstrous ornament that it lay under a kind of persecution, and, whenever it appeared in public, was pelted down by the rabble, who flung stones at the persons that wore it. But notwithstanding this prodigy vanished while the preacher was amongst them, it began to appear again some months after his departure; or, to tell it in Monsieur Paradin's own words,—the women that, like snails in a fright, had drawn in their horns, shot them out again as soon as the danger was over[12]."

In a MS. copy of Froissart, in the Harleian Library, a waggish illuminator has ridiculed the steeple cap and its appendages by drawing in the margin a swine walking upon stilts, and playing the harp ; its head being decorated after the prevailing fashion. By the sumptuary laws of this reign the wives of esquires and gentlemen, knights bachelors and knights under the rank of lord, unless they were knights of the Garter, were forbidden to wear cloth of gold, velvet upon velvet, furs of sable, or any kind of *corses* worked with gold, and to the former was forbidden the use of figured satins, and even of stuffs made in imitation of it, or of the finer cloths of velvet or gold. The wives of persons not having the yearly value of forty pounds, and widows of less possession, their daughters, &c. were forbidden to wear girdles ornamented with gold, silver, or gilt work, or any *corse of silk* made out of the realm, or any coverchief exceeding a certain price, or the furs of martens, foynes, and lettice, with a variety of minor prohibitions. The word *corse* is said by Strutt to mean here the corset or stays, it being derived from the French *corps;* and a pair of stays, consequently called at first *a pair of bodies*, from whence our word *bodice*. Something like a bodice certainly appears about this time, that is to say, the body of the dress is visibly laced in front over a sort of stomacher, as in Switzerland and many parts of the Continent to this day ; but any kind of " corses worked with gold," we take simply to mean any kind of bodies (of gowns) so embroidered, and not a corset or pair of stays, though probably their origin. The expression, " any *corse of silk* made out of the realm," has, however, certainly no reference to stays or even to the body of a gown ; for in

[12] Spectator 98. See also Argentre's Histoire de Bretagne.

Richard III.'s letter from York, quoted in page 212 of this work, there is an order for " one yard three quarters corse of silk meddled with gold," and " as much black corse of silk *for our spurs.*" So that corse here seems to signify the quality of the silk itself.

————————

Chapter XIV.

REIGNS OF EDWARD V. AND RICHARD III.,
1483—1485.

It seems absurd at first sight to separate in a work of this description two years from the three or four and twenty preceding or following them, merely because two monarchs during that short period sat upon the throne of England ; but so great a change in costume followed the accession of Henry VII. that it would be perplexing to join these reigns to his, and there are sufficient variations in the dress of Richard III.'s time from that of his brother Edward's to warrant our allotting "the crooked back tyrant," as he has been unfairly called, a chapter to himself, his unfortunate nephew being only named *pro forma.*

Of Richard III. there is no authentic representation existing. His monumental effigy, carved by order of Henry VII., was broken to pieces at the dissolution of the monasteries in the reign of Henry VIII., and the portrait on wood, in his majesty's possession, as well as those which adorn the walls of the meeting-room of the Society of Antiquaries, are supposed to have been painted during the reign of Henry VII., and whether from recollection, fancy, or from some portrait for which Richard had sat, and which is now lost or mislaid, no documents remain to satisfy us. They must therefore be considered equivocal testimony as to features, and in point of costume, being merely heads with caps on them, they are of little value to our present purpose.

Of the

CORONATION ROBES

of Richard we have a detailed account in a book, to
which is prefixed an indenture, witnessing " that Piers
Courteys, the king's wardrober, hathe taken upon
him to purvey by the 3d day Juyell next coming the
parcels ensying agaynst the coronation of our Sove-
reigne Lorde." We therein find that the day before
his coronation he was to ride from the Tower to
Westminster in a doublet and stomacher of blue cloth
of gold, " wroght with netts and pyne apples[1]," a long
gown of purple velvet furred with ermine, and a pair
of short gilt spurs. On the day of the coronation he
appears to have worn two complete sets of robes, one
of crimson velvet embroidered with gold and furred
with miniver pure, the other of purple velvet furred
with ermine; his sabatons (shoes) covered with
crimson tissue cloth of gold; his hose were of crimson satin, as were also the shirt, coat, surcoat, mantle,
and hood in which he was anointed, previously to
putting on the last symbols of royalty. During that
part of the ceremony he also wore a tabard, " like
unto a dalmatica of white sarcenet," and a coif made
of lawn, which, being put on his head after the unction,
was to be worn for the space of eight days. Two
hats of estate are also ordered with the round rolls
behind and the beeks (beaks or peaks) before.

Richard's wardrobe was at all times magnificently
furnished; he and the Duke of Buckingham being
notorious for their love of dress and finery. A man-
date still exists amongst the Harleian MSS. sent
from York by Richard to the keeper of his wardrobe
in London, August 31, 1483, wherein he specifies
the costly habits in which he was desirous of exhibit-

---

[1] This pattern is frequently seen in illuminations of the fifteenth
and sixteenth centuries.

ing himself to his northern subjects, with a descriptive detail, which, as Mr. Sharon Turner justly remarks, we should rather look for from the fop that annoyed Hotspur than from the stern and warlike Richard III.

From this and the other document before quoted we may acquire a general knowledge of the robes and habits of

THE NOBILITY.

They consisted of hose or long stockings (the Norman chaussés, in fact) tied by points, as the laces were called, to the doublet, which was sometimes open in front, about halfway down the breast, showing a placard or stomacher, over which it was laced like a peasant's bodice. This was a fashion just introduced. Over the doublet was worn either a long or a short gown, according to fancy or circumstances; the former hanging loose, the latter full of plaits before and behind, but plain at the sides, and girdled tightly about the waist. These upper vestments had sleeves of various descriptions, very full and slashed in front, so as to let the arm through, or cut open at the elbow behind, and showing the sleeve of the doublet or even of the shirt, the doublet being slashed also and laced across for ornament's sake merely.

Small caps, or " bonets" as they are called, the French word bonet (bonnet) becoming naturalized, we believe, about this period, of various shapes, but principally round and fitting the head closely, with rolls of fur round them, or the lining simply turned up, and a feather at the back or at the side, sometimes jewelled up the stem, formed the general head-dress; but the hood and tippet were also worn.

Boots reaching to the middle of the thigh and turned over with straps, like the modern top-boot, are frequently seen in illuminations of this period,

with long spurs and enormously long-pointed toes,
and a sort of clog fastened by a strap over the instep,
or merely by the pressure of two small side-pieces, is
seen vying in length with the toes of the hose or
chaussés above it.

The hair was worn extremely bushy behind and at
the sides, as in the preceding reign.

The materials of which the gowns, doublets, &c.
were made were splendid; of course, in proportion to
the fancy of the wearer. We will not say the rank
or the means, for the sumptuary laws continually
quoted have proved that, then as now, the folly of
dressing beyond both was but too common in England. Richard writes for his short gowns of crimson
cloth of gold; "that one with droppue, and that other
with nett, lined with green velvet;" gowns of green
velvet and green sattin; placards and stomachers of
purple and green sattin; doublets of purple and
tawney sattin, lined with galand cloth and outlined
with buske; "a cloke, with a cape of violet ingrained,
the both lined with black velvet;" and he had also a
long gown of purple cloth of gold, wrought with
garters and roses, and lined with white damask,
which was the gift of the queen.

The poor young prince, by right King Edward V.,
received for the ceremony of the coronation of his
usurping uncle a short gown, made of two yards and
three quarters of crimson cloth of gold, lined with
black velvet; a long gown of the same stuff, lined
with green damask; a shorter gown, made of two
yards and a quarter of purple velvet, lined with green
damask; a stomacher and doublet, made of two yards
of black satin; besides two footcloths, a *bonet* of
purple velvet, gilt spurs, and magnificent apparel for
his henchmen or pages.

To all the officers of state and to the principal
nobility cloths of gold and silver, scarlet cloth, and
silks of various colours were given as liveries and per-

quisites. To "the Duke of Bukks" (Buckingham), who stands first, eight yards of blue cloth of gold, wrought with "droops," eight yards of black velvet, and twelve yards of crimson velvet were delivered as a special gift from the king.

The henchmen or pages of the king and queen wore doublets of green satin, long gowns of crimson velvet lined with white sarcenet, and black bonnets. The kings had also provided for them long gowns of white cloth of gold and doublets of crimson satin.

We might fill pages with similar extracts from this book of the wardrober, but we have extracted as much as is necessary for our present purpose, and refer the curious reader to the document itself for the description of the horse-furniture, embroideries for banners, pennons, canopies, &c. and all the pomp and circumstance of the gorgeous ceremony amidst which Richard assumed a crown he had no right to wear, and lost, with his life, in twenty-six months from the date of his usurpation.

THE ARMOUR

of this period was most splendid. The pauldrons almost assumed the appearance of the later pass guards ; the knee and elbow pieces were much larger, generally fan-shaped, and of most elaborate workmanship. The effigy of Sir Thomas Peyton is a fine specimen of the knightly harness of Richard III.'s reign. (Vide engraving over leaf.) When covered it was by the tabard of arms, as in the reign of Edward IV. Richard, in his letter from York, expressly orders "three coats of arms, beaten with fine gold, *for our own person.*" The salade and the hausse-col, or gorget of steel, was still worn, the former surmounted by the knight's chapeau and crest, or, as in the preceding reigns, surrounded by a wreath of the wearer's colours, with a feather at

Sir Thomas Peyton, from his effigy in Isleham Church, Cambridgeshire.

the side. The salade of John, the first Howard, Duke of Norfolk, is so ornamented in a painting on glass in the possession of his Grace the present Duke, and which has been engraved by Mr. Williment, author of the ' Royal Heraldry,' &c. Richard, on his great seal, is represented with an additional cap over the chapeau, surrounded by the crown and surmounted by the lion. The crown of ornament which he wore at Bosworth was found, it will be remembered, in a bush, and brought to the victor upon the field. It had probably been struck from the chapeau in the melée.

The tilting shield is still more fantastic in shape, and the war-shield has become almost pentangular.

The sword is belted so as to hang almost in front, and the dagger is attached as usual to the right hip.

Leathern jacks, jazerine jackets, and short linen or cloth doublets, the latter generally white, with St. George's cross upon them, with long hose, are the general habits of the archers, bill-men, and guisarmiers; their head-piece also being the salade, or a round iron pot-helmet or skull-cap.

Effigy of Lady Peyton, from Isleham Church, Cambridgeshire.

THE FEMALE COSTUME

presents us with a new-fashioned head-dress. The high caps have disappeared, and the hair is entirely confined in a cap or caul of gold net or embroidered stuffs, projecting horizontally from the back of the head, and covered by a kerchief of the finest texture, stiffened out, as in the previous reign, to resemble a pair of wings. Some of these kerchiefs are extremely

large, and paved or chequered with gold; others
are simply transparent, and scarcely exceed the size
of the caul.   The gown remains as before, with turn-
over collars, and cuffs of fur or velvet.   In state
dresses the ermined jacket or waistcoat is still worn
with a kirtle and mantle, and the hair is permitted to
fall in natural ringlets down the shoulders.   Anne,
the queen of Richard III., wore, the day before her
coronation, a kirtle and mantle of white cloth of gold,
trimmed with Venice gold, and furred with ermine—
the mantle being additionally "garnished with seventy
annulets of silver gilt and gylt."   Her coronation robes,
like her husband's, were composed—the first set of
crimson velvet, furred with miniver; and the second
of purple velvet, furred with ermine; her shoes being
of crimson tissue cloth of gold.

Female costume, reign of Richard III., from an Illum, Royal MS, 16, F. 2,

CHAPTER XV.

REIGN OF HENRY VII., 1485—1509.

AT length we have emerged into the broad light of day. The pencils of Holbein, of Rubens, and Vandyke will henceforth speak volumes to the eye, and lighten the labours of the pen. With this reign we bid adieu to monumental effigies and illuminated MSS. Not without gratitude, however, for the services they have rendered us through ages of darkness and difficulty—through scenes of barbaric magnificence, which, however dimly they have been shadowed forth, have yet considerably illustrated the periods of their action, and which must either have remained in " total eclipse—no sun, no moon" existing—no gleam but the imperfect and perplexing one of written description, or rather accidental allusion in obscure and obsolete language, frequently capable of twenty different interpretations.

The portraits of Henry VII. and his family, by Holbein, are too well known to be engraved for this work ; but the kindness of the present possessor of the Sutherland Clarendon enables us to illustrate this chapter with a print from a tracing of a small and beautiful painting of Henry on vellum, of earlier date, and which originally formed part of a most curious collection of authentic cotemporary portraits of the principal sovereigns and nobles of the fifteenth and sixteenth centuries, purchased a few years ago in Paris, by Mr. Dominic Colnaghi. Vide frontispiece to this work.

"At the close of the fifteenth century," says Strutt, " the dress of the English was exceedingly fantastical and absurd, insomuch that it was even difficult to

distinguish one sex from the other." This complaint
is as old as the Conquest; but it is perhaps particularly borne out at this period by the application of
terms to various articles of male apparel which our
ears are accustomed to as indicative of woman's gear.
In a MS. of this date, called the Boke of Curtasye,
the chamberlain is commanded to provide against his
master's uprising "a clene sherte and breche, a *petty-
cotte*, a doublette, a long cotte, a *stomacher*, hys hozen,
hys socks, and hys schoen;" and the author of the Boke
of Kervynge, quoted by Strutt, says to a like personage, "warme your soverayne his petticotte, his doub-
lett, and his stomacher, and then put on hys hozen,
and then hys schone or slyppers, then stryten up his
hozen mannerly, and tye them up, then lace his
doublet hole by hole," &c.

Civil costume of the reign of Henry VII.
Fig. *a*, from Harleian MS. 4939; *b*, from Royal MS. 19, C. 8, dated 1496.

This sort of habit, however, was worn only by the nobility. In Barclay's Ship of Fooles of the Worlde, printed by Pynson A. D. 1508, may be found several notices of the dress of the day. Mention is made of some who had their necks

> " Charged with collars and chaines
> In golden withes, their fingers full of rings,
> Their necks naked almost unto the raines,
> Their sleeves blazing like unto a crane's wings."

And others are called on to " come neare" with their shirts " bordered and displayed in forme of surplois."

Shirts bordered with lace, and curiously adorned with needlework, continued a long time in use amongst the nobility and gentry. A shirt that belonged to Arthur, Prince of Wales, the eldest-born son of Henry VII., made of long lawn, with very full sleeves, and beautifully embroidered with blue silk round the collar and wristbands, is now in the possession of John Gage, Esq., one of the directors of the Society of Antiquaries.

The elegant fashion of slashing makes its appearance about this time, and the opening of the sleeve at the elbow, first observable in the costumes of the reign of Edward IV., has introduced another curious fancy, the complete division of the sleeve into two or more pieces, and their attachment to each other by means of points or laces through which the shirt is seen puffed and protruding[1].

The hood is now rapidly disappearing. Broad felt hats or caps, and bonnets of velvet, fur, and other materials, with a profusion of party-coloured plumes projecting sideways, or drooping in graceful negligence over the shoulder, have become general towards the close of this reign amongst the great and gay. These

---

[1] The upper parts of the hosen are also occasionally slashed and puffed, or embroidered and coloured differently to the lower portions—an indication of their approaching separation.

hats and caps, many of them with embattled or
escalloped edges, are worn so much on one side as
to discover on the other a considerable portion of an
under cap of gold network, or embroidered velvet,
fitting close to the head.   The large plumed cap is
frequently slung behind the back as an ornament,
and the head surmounted, for we cannot say covered,
by one about the size of a blue-coat boy's, or by the
gold net before mentioned.   One cap, peculiar to this
period, is still visible upon the heads of the knaves in
our playing cards ; and a pack of cards in the possession of Francis Douce, Esq., F.S.A., engraved
and printed about this period, probably by Marten
Schoen, a celebrated German artist, who died in

Costume of the reign of Henry VII., Harleian MS. 4425.

1523, exhibits some curious and elegant costume of the close of the fifteenth century.

The shoes were now worn as absurdly broad at the toes as they were previously peaked or pointed. The new fashion is said to have commenced in Flanders about 1470. Paradin says that the two-feet long poulaines were succeeded by shoes denominated duck-bills, the toes being so shaped, but still four or five fingers in length ; and that afterwards they assumed a contrary fashion, wearing slippers so very broad in front as to exceed the measure of a good foot.

The hair was worn enormously long and flowing— a return, in fact, to the fashion of Henry I.'s time. The face was still closely shaved, soldiers and old men only wearing moustaches or beards.

The first mention of a *collar* of the garter occurs in this reign. The mantle, kirtle, hood, and collar, are stated, sub anno twenty-seven of Henry VII., as composing the whole habit of the order sent to Philip, King of Castile; and a collar is seen on the effigy of Sir Giles Daubeny, who died in that year. The whole dress was now of purple velvet, lined with white silk, sarcenet, or taffeta, and no longer embroidered with garters.

THE ARMOUR

of the time of Henry VII. will perhaps be best understood from the engraving in p. 224. The breast-plate is globular, and of one piece, as in the time of Edward IV., but beautifully fluted, as are all the other pieces except the jambs. The sollerets are widened at the toes in accordance with the new fashion of the shoes, the armour invariably taking its general form from the civil costume of the day. The helmet assumes the form of the head, having moveable lames or plates at the back to guard the neck,

Fluted suit of the reign of Henry VII., in the Meyrick collection.

and yet allow the head to be thrown back with ease, as seen in the casquetel of the reigns of Henry VI. and Edward IV. It opened to receive the head by throwing up the mentonnière, or lower part that guarded the chin and throat, as well as the visor which turned upon the same screw. Towards the latter end of this reign the panache, which had first appeared on the apex of the bascinets of Henry V.'s time, was changed for the *plume*, inserted in a pipe affixed for the purpose to the back of the helmet, just above the neck-plates, and instead of consisting of at most but three, was now composed of a profusion of magnificent feathers that streamed down the shoulders almost to the crupper of the horse (vide page 241); and instead of the tassets and tuiles, a new feature in armour called the *lamboys*, from the French *lambeaux*, a sort of petticoat of steel in imitation of the puckered skirts or petticoats of cloth or velvet worn at this time, was introduced, for the better understanding of which we shall refer our readers to the next chapter. The pass guard was introduced during this reign, being plates rising perpendicularly upon the shoulders to ward off the thrust or blow of a weapon at the side of the neck. The tabard was still worn occasionally. Henry VII. is represented on his great seal in an emblazoned one, but it became rarer as the armour was made more splendid; and not only fluted suits, but some that are ribbed and exquisitely engraved, made their appearance during this reign.

The tilting helmet was oval-shaped, but presenting a salient angle in front, and was surmounted, as before, with the orle, or chaplet and crest.

The shield was pentangular, or square and concave, and of various other fantastic shapes.

The sword tapers to a point, and has a ridge down the centre on both sides of the blade.

The halberd, which is first mentioned in the reign of Edward IV., is now a weapon in common use, and halberdiers appear for the first time amongst the English infantry.

As the hand-gun or cannon was first generally known in England during the reign of Edward IV.,

the next improvement in fire-arms, that of placing a
sort of lock to the iron tube with a cock to hold the
match suggested by the cross-bow, and from that
circumstance called the arc-a-bouche or arc-a-bousa,
corrupted into arquebus, was familiarized to the English by Henry VII., who, on establishing the body
of yeomen of the guard in 1485, armed half of them
with bows and arrows, and the other half with arque-
busses. This cock was also called the serpentine,
being in the form of the letter S reversed, and turn-
ing on a pivot in the centre; so that the upper part
which held the match was brought down upon the
pan by pushing back the under. Hans Burgmair's
plates of the triumph of the Emperor Maximilian I.,
represent the appearance and equipment of the harquebussiers at the commencement of the sixteenth
century; suspended from their necks are powder-
flasks of a circular form, or powder-horns. They have
a bullet-bag at the right hip, and a sword at the left,
while they carry the match-cord in their hands.
Their armour consists of a back and breast-plate,
pieces for the arms and thighs, and chain-mail
gorgets for the neck.

THE FEMALE COSTUME

of this period has been in many points familiarized
to the sight of our readers, by the modern French
and English fashions within the last few years. The
large full sleeves confined at intervals from the elbow
to the wrist, or worn " en blouse," as the Parisians
called it, and denominated bishop's sleeves in London: the small waists, the gowns cut square at
the neck, with stomachers, belts, and buckles, or
rich girdles with long pendants in front, and hats
and feathers similar to many still to be seen nightly
at the opera, have all been borrowed from the ladies'

Female costume of the reign of Henry VII.

Figs. *a, b*, and *d*, from Harleian MS. 4425; *c*, from Royal MS. 19, C. 8, dated 1496.

dress of the reigns of Henry VII.[2] Its obsolete characteristics were slashes in the sleeves; the caps and cauls of gold net or embroidery, from beneath which the hair escaping hung down the shoulders half way to the ground[3]; the divided sleeves connected by points like those of the men described in p. 221 ; and a head-dress like a capuchon turned back, of which several varieties are to be seen in paintings

[2] Vide Hans Burgmair's prints, and the portrait of Joan of Arc in the town-house of Orleans, painted about 1490.

[3] Vide figures *b* and *d*. This fashion appears to have been continued from the earliest periods to the reign of Henry VII. at coronations or state nuptials. Elizabeth, the queen of Henry VII. wore her fair yellow hair hanging down plain behind her back with "a calle of pipes over it." Vide Leland's Account of her Splendid Coronation.

and illuminations of this period, particularly in the
portrait of Elizabeth, Queen of Henry VII., by Holbein, and of Margaret, Countess of Richmond, his
mother, who died in 1509 [4].   Elizabeth, the day preceding her coronation, appeared in a state dress,
having a mantle of white cloth of gold damask furred,
with ermines fastened on her breast, with a large
lace curiously wrought with gold and silk, with rich
knoppes of gold at the end tasselled.   Cotton. MS.
Julius, B. xii.

Skelton, the poet laureat of Henry VII., has left
us a humorous description of Eleanor Rumming, a
noted hostess of his time, and her dress may be considered a pretty good model of the attire of females
in humble life.

> " In her furr'd flocket,
> And grey russet rocket,
> Her *duke* of Lincoln green ;
> It had been her's I weene
> More than forty yeare,
> And so it doth appeare.
> And the grene bare threads
> Look like sea-weeds,
> Withered like hay,
> The wool worn away ;
> And yet I dare say,
> She thinks herself gay,

[4] Engraved in Lodge's Illustrious Portraits.   This latter is indeed a similar sort of hood or capuchon to that now worn by the
women of the Pays de Basque ; but the earlier descriptions look
like the lower part of the steeple head-dress, as if the absolute
covering for the head had been preserved, when they threw away
the pinnacle that surmounted it. (Vide fig. *c*.)   On the sides of
it is an ornament also which we take to be the *clog* or *clock*,
afterwards mentioned in describing the mourning dresses.   At the
close of the sixteenth century we find the clog or clock removed
to the stocking which it still adorns.

> Upon a holyday,
> When she doth array,
> And girdeth in her gates,
> Stitched and pranked with plates,
> Her kirtle bristow red,
> With cloths upon her head,
> They weigh a ton of lead.
> She hobbles as she goes,
> With her blanket hose,
> Her shoone (shoes) smeared with tallow [5]."

Speaking of

THE ECCLESIASTICAL COSTUME,

the same writer reproaches the pride and immorality of the clergy. " The bishops," says he,

> " Ryde with gold all trapped,
> In purpall and pall belapped,
> Some hatted and som cappyd,
> Richly and warm wrapped.
> God wotte to their grete paynes
> In rochetts of fyne reynes, (i. e. cloth of Rennes,)
> Whyte as Mary's milk,
> And tabards of fyne sylk,
> And styroppes with gold beglozyd."

He seems almost to have paraphrased the complaints of Pierce Ploughman and Chaucer in the fourteenth century. " The three-cornered caps of popish priests " were after the reformation frequently the objects of derision and reprobation.

---

[5] MS. Harleian, lib. 7333. We confess our ignorance of the article of apparel meant by the word *duke* in the third line of this quotation. Query, *heuke*, a mantle before mentioned.

Mourning habits of the sixteenth century, from Harleian MS. 6064.

MOURNING HABITS.

At the close of the fifteenth century, the superfluous usage of cloth and the vast expenses incurred at the funerals of the nobility and gentry occasioned the promulgation of an edict, by which the habits and liveries, as they were called, were limited to certain quantities.

Dukes and marquises were allowed sixteen yards for their gowns, *slopps* (i. e. mourning cassocks so called), and mantles; an earl only fourteen; a viscount for his gown and mantle twelve; a baron or banneret, being a knight of the Garter, eight yards for his gown and hood; a knight or esquire of the

body six; and all inferior personages five yards for
their gowns; and the liveries for servants decreased
proportionately, from eighteen down to two. An
archbishop was allowed the same as a duke, and to
this edict was added a prohibition to wear hoods to
all persons under the degree of an esquire of the
king's household, except in time of need, that is to
say, bad weather, only tippets of a quarter of a yard
in breadth, and hoods " with a roll sleeve over the
head or otherwise being of that fashion," were forbidden to all persons below the rank of a baron or
an earl's son and heir.

Margaret, Countess of Richmond, the mother of
King Henry VII., issued in the eighth year of his
reign an ordinance for " the reformation of apparell
for great estates of women in the tyme of mourninge :"
wherein it is ordained that the greatest estates " shall
have their surcottes with a trayne before and another
behynde, and their mantles with traynes," " the
greatest estate to wear them longest, with mantles
and tippets," and " that *bekes* be no more used in
any manner of wyse because of the deformetye of the
same[6]." The queen is to wear a surcoat with " the
traynes" as aforesaid, " a playne hoode without
clockes, and a tippet at the hood lying a good length
upon the trayne of the mantell, being in breadth a
nayle and an inche ;" and after the first quarter of a
year the hood may be lined with black satin or furred
with ermine, and all ladies down to the degree of a
baroness are to wear similar mourning, with the
tippets and trains shorter, and to be barbed above
the chin.

---

[6] What these " bekes" may have been we cannot discover by
an examination of the mourning dresses in earlier illuminations.
Throughout the MS. of the fifteenth century, mourners are represented closely enveloped in long black cloaks and cowls, but
nothing like a beak or peak is visible.

Baronesses were to wear surcoats without trains, and mantles "accordinge;" and lords' daughters and knights' wives, surcoats with "meatlye traynes," but no mantles, hoods without clockes, and tippets only a yard and a half long, "to be pynned upon the arme." These estates are to wear the *barbe* under their throats.

The inferior gentry to wear sloppes and coat-hardies, hoods with clockes, and tippets a yard long and an inch broad, pinned upon the side of the hood. All chamberers and other persons, hoods with clockes, and no manner of tippets to be found about them. The barbe too was to be worn by them below the " throat goyll," or gullet, that is, the lowest part of the throat.

The surcoat with the train before and behind, the barbe above the chin, and the hood with the long tippet, all as worn by the highest nobility, are visible enough in the figures given herewith. The front train, it will be perceived, was tucked through and fell over the girdle.

CHAPTER XVI.

REIGNS OF HENRY VIII., EDWARD VI., AND MARY, 1509—1558.

REIGN OF HENRY VIII., 1509—1547.

IT was unnecessary to engrave the portraits of at least the two first of these sovereigns. The images of " Bluff King Hal" and his son Edward are amongst the earliest recollections of our childhood. The first " picture books," illustrative of English history, con· tain their " livelie effigies," handed down from the woodcuts of their own time ; while all the previous monarchs are like the visioned line of Banquo, ima· ginary creations, with so strong a family resemblance even in their dresses, that we may exclaim with Mac· beth, the

> " Other gold-bound brow is like the first,
>   A third is like the former.
>   Why do you show me this ?"

The time is fast arriving, however, when it will be generally acknowledged, that to stamp such false im· pressions upon the pliant but retentive minds of youth is worse than leaving it a blank altogether. To a child a picture is a picture, and it is as easy and much wiser to place the authentic instead of the fic· titious resemblance before it as soon as it is capable of being interested by either.

The ordinary costume of King Henry himself was, of course, that of the nobility and gentry of his time, and we find it to consist of a full-skirted jacket or doublet, with large sleeves to the wrist, over which

is worn a short but equally full coat or cloak, with
loose hanging sleeves, and a broad rolling collar of
fur, a brimmed cap jewelled, and bordered with ostrich
feather ; stockings, and square-toed shoes ; ruffs or
ruffles appear at the wrist. Soon after his accession
the close hose, fitting exactly to the limbs, in fact,
the Norman chaussés, were again revived under the
still older name of *trouses;* and he is described by
Hall as wearing at a grand banquet, given at Westminster in the first year of his reign, a suit of
" shorte garments, little (i. e. reaching but a little)
beneath the pointes, of blew velvet and crymosyne,
with long sleeves, all cut and lyned with cloth
of gold, and the utter (outer) parts of the gar-
mentes powdered with castles and sheafes of arrowes
(the badges of his Queen Catherine) of fyne dokett
(ducat) golde ; the upper part of the hosen of like
sewte and facion ; the nether parts of scarlet, powdered with tymbrelles of fine golde. On his head
was a bonnet of damaske silver, flatte woven in the
stoll, and thereupon wrought with golde and ryche
feathers in it." (Union of the Families of Lancaster
and York ; Life of Henry VIII., fol. 7.) Minuter
fashions were, of course, continually being adopted
or abandoned, and in 1542 we find an Englishman
represented in a frontispiece to Andrew Borde's
Introduction to Knowledge, with a pair of shears in
his hand and a bundle of cloth, as undetermined
which of the prevailing modes to follow.

In the twenty-fourth year of his reign Henry
passed a sumptuary law confining the use of the furs
of black genets to the royal family, and furs of sables
to the nobility above the rank of a viscount. No
person under the degree of a knight of the Garter
might wear crimson or blue velvet or embroidered
apparel, broched or guarded with goldsmith's work,
excepting the sons and heirs of barons and knights,

who were permitted to use crimson velvet and tinsel
in their doublets.

Velvet gowns, jackets, and coats, furs of martens,
mixed, joined, guarded, or broidered, chains, bracelets,
and collars of gold were forbidden to all persons possessing less than two hundred marks per annum, except the sons and heirs of the privileged parties, who
might wear black velvet doublets, coats of black
damask, tawny-coloured russet, and camlet.

Satin and damask gowns were confined to the use
of persons possessing at least one hundred marks per
annum, and the wearing of *pinched* shirts or plain
shirts, garnished with gold, silver, or silk, was forbidden to all persons under the rank of knighthood.
The commonalty and serving men were confined to
the use of cloth of a certain price and lamb's fur
only, and forbidden the wearing of any ornaments or
even buttons of gold, silver, or gilt work, excepting
the badge of their lord or master.

From the above extract and from inventories of the
time we learn that *the shirt* was pinched, i. e. plaited,
plain, and embroidered with gold, silver, or silk.
Amongst Henry's own apparel we find borders of
gold for shirts, and shirts wrought and trimmed with
black and white silk, and shirt bands of silver, with
ruffles to the same, whereof one is " *perled* (studded
or spangled) with gold."

Hose or *stockings* of silk are generally supposed to
have been unknown in this country before the middle
of the sixteenth century; and a pair of long Spanish
silk hose was presented as a gift worthy the accept-
ance of a monarch by Sir Thomas Gresham to Edward VI.; and Howe, the continuator of Stow's
Chronicle, adds, that Henry VIII. never wore any
hose but such as were made of cloth. In an inventory of his apparel, however, preserved in the Harleian Library, we find mention of several pair of

silk hose; one short pair of black silk and gold woven together, one of purple silk and Venice gold, woven like unto a cawl (i. e. of open or network), lined with blue silver sarcenet, edged with a passe-main (lace) of purple silk and gold, wrought at Milan; a pair of white silk and gold hose, knit, and six pair of black silk hose, knit; and in one still earlier, taken in the eighth year of his reign, we find both satin and velvet mentioned as the materials of which his hose were composed. Now at this period it is rather difficult to say whether the expression hose means stockings or breeches, as it was indiffe-rently applied to each by writers of this century. Howe evidently means stockings only, but these richly-embroidered and lined hose, mentioned in this inven-tory, were, we strongly suspect, the *upper* portions of the coverings for the legs, which we now fre-quently find slashed, puffed, and embroidered dis-tinctly from the *lower*; for the same document intro-duces us to the word *stocking* itself, and enlightens us as to its derivation. One of the entries runs thus: "a yarde and a quarter of green velvet for *stocks* to a payr of hose for the king's grace;" ano-ther, the same quantity of " purpul satin to cover the *stocks* of a payr of hose of purpul cloth of gold tissue for the kynge;" and numerous others occur of cer-tain portions of stuff used for " *stockyng* of hose," that is, adding the lower part that covered the legs and feet to that which was fastened by points to the doublet, the ultimate separation of which confounded the hose with the breeches, and left " the stocking" an independent article of apparel, as at the present day. To proceed:—these splendid hose of various coloured and embroidered cloths, velvets, satins, silks, and golden and silver stuffs were attached by points or laces, with tags called *auglettes* or *aglets* (i. e. *aiguillettes*) to the doublet, of equal magnificence.

In the earliest inventory we have quoted, after the enumeration of many splendid doublets, &c. for the king's use, we read of " a doblet of white tylsent, cut upon cloth of gold, embraudered, with hose to the same, and clasps and auglettes of golde, delivered to the Duke of Buckingham."

Over the doublet was worn the jacket, now sometimes called the jerkin, the coat, or the gown, according to fancy or circumstances. A dobelet, jaquet, and hose of blue velvet, cut upon cloth of gold, embroidered, and a dobelet, hose, and jaquet of purple velvet, embroidered and cut upon cloth of gold, and lined with black satin, are entries in the inventory we have just quoted.

In 1535 a jerkin of purple velvet, with purple satin sleeves, embroidered all over with Venice gold, was presented to the king by Sir Richard Cromwell, and another of crimson velvet, with wide sleeves of the like-coloured satin, is mentioned in the inventory before quoted. Of coats we find a great variety in Henry's wardrobe : long coats, short coats, demi-coats, riding coats, coats with bases or skirts, walking coats, tunic coats, and coats of leather, &c. with sleeves, linings, facings, and embroideries of all descriptions[1]. When Henry VIII. met Anne of Cleves he was habited, according to Hall, in a coat of velvet, somewhat made " like a *frocke*, embroidered all over with flatted gold of damaske, with small lace mixed between of the same gold, and other laces of the same going traversewise, that the ground little appeared, and about this garment was a rich guard or border, very curiously embroidered ; the sleeves and

---

[1] Cassaques or cassocke coates, as they were afterwards called, appear at this time ; two of very rich materials occur in this last inventory, and one of them had eleven buttons of gold upon the breast, with loops of the same, " being of little flagonue's cheynes of gold."

the breast were cut and lined with cloth of gold, and
tied together with great buttons of diamonds, rubies,
and orient pearles."

The *frocke* alluded to by Hall is a vestment which
is frequently mentioned about this time. It was, as
Hall says, a sort of coat, jacket, or jerkin, made like
them occasionally with bases or skirts; but Strutt
considers that it had no sleeves: we find it of cloth
of gold, cloth of silver, damaske, black satin, &c. &c.

Gowns, distinguished as long, short, half, strait,
and loose, Turkey and Spanish, with sleeves, collars,
capes, and aglets, and diamond and gold buttons set
upon the sleeves, occur in great quantities; and two
vestments, the *chammer* and *shamen*, described by
Hall as "a gowne cut in the middle," and the
glaudkyn, are spoken of in the earlier inventories of
this reign.

Both the sleeves and the capes to the various vestments were generally separate articles added or taken
from the body of the dress at pleasure, by the means
of points or buttons. "A pair of truncke sleeves of
redde cloth of gold, with cut workes, having twelve
pair of agletes of gold, and a pair of French sleeves
of green velvet, richly embroidered with flowers of
damask gold, pirl of Morisco work, with knops of
Venice gold, cordian raised, either sleeve having six
small buttons of gold, and in every button a pearl,
and the branches of the flowers set with pearles," are
amongst many entries of the same description; the
sleeves were also *ruffed* or *ruffled* at the hand, as we
perceive in the portrait of Henry. An entry occurs
of a pair of sleeves "ruffed at the hande, with straw-
berry leaves and flowers of golde, embroidered with
black silke." They were not added to the shirt till
the next century. Cloaks and mantles of great magnificence are described by Hall; some of the former
worn baldrick or sash-wise, so as not to conceal

the splendour of the other garments. The placard and stomacher have been described in the last chapter; They seem to have been superseded by the *waistcoat*, which is first mentioned in the latest inventories of this reign. It was worn under the doublet, and had sleeves, and being made of rich materials, such as cloth of silver, quilted with black silk, "and tuffed out with fine camerike" (cambric), must have been occasionally visible, perhaps in consequence of the slashing of the upper garments, which fashion was carried to a great excess at this time.

Camden, in his ' Remains,' tells a pleasant story of a shoemaker of Norwich, named John Drakes, who, in the time of Henry VIII., coming to a tailor's, and finding some fine French tawney cloth lying there, which had been sent to be made into a gown for Sir Philip Calthrop, took a fancy to the colour, and ordered the tailor to buy as much of the same stuff for him, and make him a gown of it, precisely of the same fashion as the knight's, whatever that might be. Sir Philip, arriving some time afterwards to be measured, saw the additional cloth, and inquired who it belonged to. "To John Drakes," replied the tailor, "who will have it made in the selfsame fashion as yours is made of." "Well," said the knight, " in good time be it; I will have mine as full of cuts as thy shears can make it :" and both garments were finished according to the order. The shoemaker, on receiving his gown slashed almost to shreds, began to swear at the tailor, but received for answer, " I have done nothing but what you bade me; for as Sir Philip Calthrop's gowne is, even so have I made yours." " By my latchet !" growled the shoemaker, " I will never wear a gentleman's fashion again."

Slashed shoes, and buskins of velvet and satin, with very broad round toes, and caps and bonnets of sundry shapes and materials, some only bordered, others laden with feathers, are characteristic of this reign[2]. The chaperon or hood has quite vanished from the inventory of a gentleman's wardrobe, except those worn by official personages, knights of the Garter, &c. The hair had been worn exceedingly long during the last reign, but Henry VIII. gave peremptory orders for all his attendants and courtiers to poll their heads, and short hair in consequence became fashionable, and continued so for a considerable time. Beards and moustaches were worn at pleasure.

The collar and the great and lesser George, as at present worn, were given to the knights of the Garter by King Henry VIII., who reformed the statutes of the order and altered the dress. The surcoat was made of crimson velvet, and a flat black velvet hat of the fashion of the time superseded the chaperon, which was still however worn for ornament only, hung over the shoulder, and thence called the *humerale*; it was of crimson velvet, the same as the surcoat. The *lesser George* was not worn before the thirteenth of this reign, when it hung in a gold chain or riband upon the breast; and from a memorandum of the thirty-eighth of Henry's reign we find the colour of the riband was *black*[3].

THE ARMOUR

of this period is principally remarkable for its additional decoration. The lamboys, introduced during

---

[2] The chapeau montaubyn is mentioned by Hall as a hat or cap, of this period. Henry VIII. is said to have worn one with a rich coronal; the folde of the chapeau lined with crimson satin, and on that a brooche with the image of St. George. (Chronicle, reprint, p. 598.) "Hattes of crimosyne velvet;" "hattes after dauncers' fashions, with fesaunts' feathers in them;" "bonnettes of white velvet wrapped in flat golde of damask," *cum multis aliis*, may be found recorded in the chronicles of this time.

[3] Ashmole's History of the Order.

Henry VIII. from his great seal.

the reign of Henry VII. and described in the last
chapter, appear throughout this and the following
reign ; but when they are not appended to the breast-
plate, tassets and cuishes, composed of several plates
instead of one, are seen upon the thigh. A magnificent suit of the former fashion is to be seen in the
collection at the Tower. It was presented by the
Emperor Maximilian I. to Henry VIII. on his marriage with Catherine of Arragon, and before the
inspection and arrangement of the horse armoury by
Sir S. Meyrick, was supposed to have belonged to
Henry VII. The complete suit both for horse and
man is beautifully engraved with legendary subjects,
badges, mottoes, &c., and is precisely similar in

shape to a suit preserved in the little Belvidere palace
at Vienna, which belonged to Maximilian himself, and
to that in which Henry is represented on his great
seal. (Vide engraving on the previous page.) Raised
armour, the forerunner of the embossed, was introduced in this reign; the ground is frequently kept
black, and the pattern raised about the tenth of an
inch, polished. Puffed and ribbed armour, in imitation of the slashed dresses of the day, is also occasionally met with; we have engraved a suit here from
a drawing of one in the Meyrick collection, with the
two-handed sword of the time resting on the shoulder.

Suit of puffed and ribbed armour, temp. Henry VIII., in the Meyrick
collection.

The breast-plate was still globose, but towards the

middle of this reign rose to an edge down the centre called the tapul—a revival of an old fashion. Towards the end of the reign the breast-plate presented a salient angle in the centre. The tilting helmet disappeared altogether about this period, and a head-piece called a coursing-hat was worn with a mentonnière. The helmet was adorned with the streaming plumes before mentioned. (Vide engraving from great seal of Henry VIII.) The gauntlets were mostly made of overlapping plates without fingers.

To the list of weapons, we have to add the *pertuisane* or *partizan,* a variety of the pike or spontoon. The Asiatic art of inlaying weapons with gold was introduced about this period into Europe by Benvenuto Celini, and blades so adorned were called *damasquinée*, from the practice originating at Damascus. The hackbut, first mentioned in the reign of Richard III. now became common; and to the match-lock was now added the *wheel-lock*, also invented by the Italians. It was a small machine for producing sparks of fire by the rapid revolution of a wheel against a piece of sulphuret of iron held like the flint in the modern musket, only that the cock was on the side where the pan now is. The spring which turned the wheel was attached to a chain formed like those in watches, and wound up by an instrument called a spanner; a catch was connected with the trigger, which, being pulled, liberated the wheel, and the cock having been previously brought down upon it, the friction of the pyrite produced the fire. This piece was called the fire-lock as well as the wheel-lock, though differing greatly from the later invention so called.

The pistol and its variety, the dag or tacke, are also of this period, the difference consisting only in the shape of the butt-end; that of the former terminating in a knob like the pommel of a sword-hilt, and

that of the latter being merely cut in a slanting
direction [4].

Military costume, temp. Henry VIII., from drawings in the British Museum.
Cotton. MS. Augustus II.

The pike was introduced into France by the Swiss
in the time of Louis XI., and soon became an infantry
weapon throughout Europe. Pikemen composed a
principal part of the English army from the reign of
Henry VIII. to that of William III.

FEMALE COSTUME.

It would be strange indeed if we were at a loss
for an illustration of the female costume of any period
of this reign, considering that Henry married no less
than six wives in the course of thirty-eight years,

---

[4] Vide page 253. The pistol superseded the mace in the hands
of officers during this reign, and a most interesting specimen of
the mace and; pistol *combined* was purchased for the national collection at the sale of Mr. Brocas's armour.

and consequently ensured us so many portraits of noble and princely dames by the best painters of his day. We must beg, however, to refer our readers to Lodge's popular and beautiful work for the prints engraved from them.

In number and name, the principal parts of a lady's dress continued unchanged ; the only novelty in the latter being the mention of the *partlet* and *waistcoat*. The partlet is supposed by Mr. Strutt to have taken the place of the gorget, which had latterly been used only for mourning habiliments, and called the barbe. Our fair readers will perceive in the costumes of this period a covering for the neck and throat, similar to what is now called a habit-shirt ; and this we have reason to believe was called the partlet. It sometimes had sleeves attached to it, and was made of stuffs of the most valuable and delicate kind. In the inventory we have so often quoted, appear "two partelets of Venice gold, knit, two partelets of Venice gold, caul fashion, two partelets of white thread, and two partelets of white lawn wrought with gold about the collars." The partelets are seen in numberless portraits of this period, most beautifully embroidered with gold.

The waistcoat was a similar garment to that of the same name worn by the men. "Two wastcotes for women being of clothe of silver, embroidered, both of them having sleeves," is an entry in the same inventory.

The gowns of the nobility were magnificent, and at this period were open in front to the waist, showing the kirtle, as the inner garment or what we should call the petticoat was then termed. Their fashions were various in detail, though possessing the general character of the costume of the time.

" Gowns of blew velvet, cut and lined with cloth of gold, made after the fashion of Savoy," were worn

by the ladies accompanying Henry at a masque
in the sixth year of his reign; and Anne of Cleves,
the same writer tells us, wore, on her first interview
with Henry VIII., " a ryche gowne of cloth of gold
raised, made round, without any trayne, after the
Dutch fashion [5]."

Seven yards of purple cloth of damask gold are
allowed for a kirtle for Queen Catherine (of Arragon)
in a wardrobe account of the eighth year of Henry's
reign.   The ladies' sleeves were as distinct from their
body vestments as we have already found the men's,
and attached at pleasure to the gown or waistcoat.
Much splendour was lavished on this part of the
dress, and its various fashions were singularly quaint
and elegant.   Amongst the inventories of this reign
we find three pair of purple satin sleeves for women ;
one pair of linen sleeves, paned with gold over the
arm, quilted with black silk, and wrought with
flowers between the panes and at the hands ; one
pair of sleeves of purple gold tissue damask wire,
each sleeve tied with aglets of gold ; one pair of
crimson satin sleeves, four buttons of gold being set
on each sleeve, and in every button nine pearls [6].

[5] A variety of gowns, single and lined, and of the most costly
materials, are enumerated in an inventory taken of the royal
wardrobes at the Tower, as belonging to " her majesty and my lady
the princess."

[6] The dress of Queen Catharine (Parr) is thus described by
Pedro de Gante, secretary to the Spanish Duke de Najera, who
visited Henry VIII. in the year 1543—44.   " She was dressed in
a 'delentera' of cloth of gold, and a 'saya' (i. e. petticoat or
kirtle) of brocade, with sleeves lined with crimson satin, and
trimmed with three-piled crimson velvet; her train was more
than two yards long.   Suspended from her neck were two crosses
and jewel of very rich diamonds, and in her head-dress were many
and beautiful ones.   Her girdle was of gold, with very large pendants."

The same writer describes the Princess Mary, afterwards
queen, as a person of pleasing countenance, and "so much be-

Hall, the chronicler, who revels in the description of the splendid shows and pageants of all ages, and describes with as much minuteness and confidence those which took place in the fourteenth as he does those of which he was an eye-witness in the sixteenth century, may be trusted respecting the latter, at least as far as suits our purpose. At a banquet given in the first year of Henry's reign, upon Shrove-Sunday, in the parliament-chamber at Westminster, he speaks of six ladies who formed part of a show towards the close of the evening, "whereof two were appareyled in crimson satyn and purpull, embrowdered with golde, and by vynettes ran floure de lices, of golde, with marvellous ryche and strange tires on their heads: other two ladies in crimosyn and purpull, made like long slops, embroudered and fretted with golde after the antique fascion, and over the slop was a shorte garment of clothe of golde, scant to the knee, facioued like a tabard, all over with small double rolles, all of flatte golde of damask fret and fringed golde, and on their heads skaynes (scarfs), and wrappers of damaske golde with flatte pypes, that strange it was to beholde: the other two ladies were in kirtles of crymosyne and purpull satyn, em-broudered with a vynet of pomegranattes of golde; all the garments cut compass-wise, having demy sleeves, and naked down from the elbows"—(the first appearance of bare arms since the time of the ancient Britons),—"and over their garments were vochettes of plesaunces rouled with crymsyne velvet and set with letters of golde like caractes (query, characters?). Their heades rouled in pleasauntes and typpets like the Egipicians, embroudered with golde; their faces,

loved throughout the kingdom that she is almost adored!" She was dressed in a saya of cloth of gold, with a gown or loose robe (tropon) of violet coloured three-piled velvet, with a head-dress of many rich stones.

necks, arms, and handes covered in fine pleasaunce black; some call it lumberdynes, which is marveylous thinne, so the same ladies seemed to be nigrost or blackmores." What are the descriptions of the court-newsman in our days to this? What joy for 'the Morning Post' or 'the Court Journal' to have their columns filled with a report of the dresses worn at such a fancy ball as this given at Westminster in 1509, "for all the ambassadours which were here out of diverse realmes and countries."

The various head-dresses of this period will be best understood from the engraving. The cap or coif, familiarized to us as the "Mary Queen of Scots' cap," seems to have been introduced about this pe-riod. Those worn by the ladies at an entertainment given at Greenwich in the third year of Henry's reign were "all of golde." The French hood was another head-dress in fashion at this time (if indeed it were not the name of the cap just mentioned). Hol-lingshed tells us that Anne of Cleves, the day after her arrival in England, wore a French hood after the English fashion, which became her exceeding well. The miniver, or three-cornered caps, were worn throughout this reign. They were white, says Stow, and three-square, and the peaks full three or four inches from the head. The aldermen's wives made themselves bonnets of velvet, after the fashion of miniver caps, but in the time he wrote, A. D. 1631, he adds, they were almost forgotten.

THE DRESSES OF THE MERCHANTS, CITIZENS, AND OTHERS

appear in numberless prints of the time[7]. In the history of John Winchcomb or Witcomb, the famous clothier, called Jack of Newbury, he is described as

[7] Vide in particular "the Great Bible" printed in 1539, with engravings on wood, said to have been designed by Hans Holbein.

going to Henry VIII. dressed in a plain russet coat,
a pair of white kersie slopps, or breeches [8], without
welt or guard (i. e. lace or border), and stockings of
the same piece, sewed to his sloppes; and his widow,
in the same work, is described, after having laid aside
her weeds, as coming out of the kitchen in a fair
train gown stuck full of silver pins, having a white
cap on her head, with cuts of curious needlework
under the same, and an apron before her as white as
driven snow. Her wedding dress is also specified in
the same history in the following manner: the bride
being habited in a gown of sheep's russet and a kirtle
of fine worsted, her head attired with a *billiment*
(habiliment) of gold, and her hair as yellow as gold
hanging down behind her, which was curiously
combed and plaited according to the manner of those
days, was led to church by two boys with bride laces,
and rosemary tied about their silken sleeves. The
maidens employed in spinning are said to have been
dressed

> " In *petticoats* of stamel red,
> And milk-white kerchers on their head,
> Their smock-sleeves like to winter's snow
> That on the western mountains flow,
> And each sleeve with a silken band
> Was fairly tied at the hand."

Here we have the first mention of the petticoat in
the present sense of the word, and henceforward we
find it used synonymously with kirtle.

Articles of dress at this period, even among the
middle ranks, were frequently bequeathed in wills;
William Cheryngton Yeoman, of Water-beche, 14th
August, 1540, leaves " to my mother *my holy-
day gowne.*" Nicholas Dyer, of Teversham, 29th
October, 1540, " to my sister Alice Bichendyke,

[8] The term *"slopp"* is now unceremoniously transferred to the
nether garments—wherefore we cannot pretend to determine.
A dealer in ready clothing is still called a slop-seller.

13*s.* 9*d.*, which she owed me, *two kerchiefs of holland,"* &c.   John Holden, rector of Gamlingay, 29th October, 1544, leaves to Jone Grene " *my clothe frock* lined with sattin of cypress." These entries are from wills in the Ely registry.

Howe, the continuator of Stow's Annals, informs us that many years prior to the reign of Queen Mary (and therefore as early as the time of Henry VIII. at least) all the apprentices of London wore blue cloaks in summer, and in the winter gowns of the same colour, blue coats or gowns being a badge of servitude about this period.   Their breeches and stockings were usually made of white broad-cloth, " that is round slopps or breeches, and their stockings sowed up close thereto, as they were all but of one piece." The " city flat cap," so often mentioned by writers of the time of James and Charles, was probably the cap of Edward VI.'s time, worn by the citizens long after it had gone out of fashion at court.   When apprentices or journeymen attended upon their masters or mistresses at night, they went before them holding a lantern in their hands, and carrying a long club upon their shoulders.   Some apprentices wore daggers in the daytime, behind or at the side.   Sir Walter Scott has drawn an admirable picture of the brawling 'prentices of James's time from these materials, in his ' Fortunes of Nigel.'

THE ECCLESIASTICAL COSTUME

underwent a considerable change at the Reformation ; but we must refer our readers to the portraits in Lodge's work and the Great Bible before mentioned for their pictorial illustration.   Vide also the print after Holbein, of Henry VIII. granting their charter to the barber-surgeons, for the official costume of the reign.

REIGN OF EDWARD VI., 1547—1553; AND MARY, 1553—1558.

General costume of the reigns of Edward VI. and Queen Mary.

Fig. *a*, Sir J. Tyrell in the reign of Edward VI. from Strutt. The rest from Fox's Book of Martyrs, temp. Mary.

The reigns of Edward VI. and Mary introduce us to the small flat round bonnet worn on one side the head, and preserved to this day in the caps of the boys of Christ's Hospital, whose whole dress is indeed the costume of the citizens of London at the time of the foundation of that charity by the young and amiable Edward. Blue coats were the common habit of apprentices and serving-men, and yellow stockings were very generally worn at this period. The jackets of our firemen and watermen are also of this date, the badge being made in metal and placed

on the sleeve in the sixteenth century, instead of embroidered on the breast or back of the garment itself
as previously. Minstrels, players, and all retainers
of the nobility were thus attired. In the year 1556 a
remonstrance from the privy council was presented to
the lord president of the north, stating that certain
lewd persons, to the number of six or seven in a
company, naming themselves to be the servants of
Sir Francis Lake, and wearing his livery or badge
upon their sleeves, have wandered about these north
parts representing certain plays reflecting on her
majesty and King Philip, and the formalities of the
mass.

The preposterously broad or square-toed shoe was
ousted by proclamation during Mary's reign, and the
trunk-hose, as the stuffed upper stocks were now
called, were nearly covered by the long flaps or skirts
of the coats and doublets.

The well-known print, after Holbein, of Edward VI. founding Christ Church Hospital, presents
us with the official and ecclesiastical costume of this
period.

THE ARMOUR

of these two reigns underwent no material alteration.
The projection of the tapul gradually descended from
the centre of the breast-plate till it completely disappeared, and the waist was considerably lengthened. The morion came into general use. Brigan-
dine jackets were worn by the archers, with steel
skull-caps. In Mary's reign the waist again shortened, and by the statute of the 4th and 5th of Philip
and Mary, we learn that the military force of the
kingdom was composed of demi-lancers, who supplied
the place of the men-at-arms; pikemen, who wore
back and breast-plates with tassets, gorgets, gauntlets, and steel hats; archers, with steel skull-caps

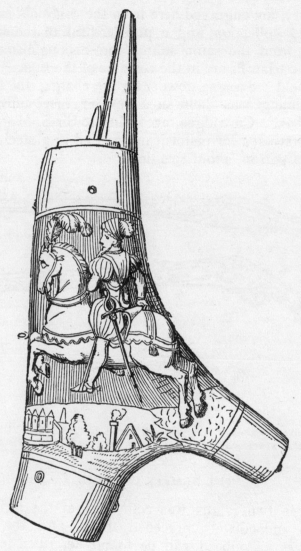

Powder-flask of the reign of Mary, in the Meyrick collection.

and brigandines ; black bill-men or halberdiers, who wore the armour called almain rivet, and moriens or sallets ; and haquebutiers similarly appointed. A long wheel-lock dag and pistol of the reign of Edward VI., and a pocket wheel-lock pistol of the reign

of Mary, are engraved here from the originals in the
Meyrick collection, and a powder-flask of the latter
period, from the same source, presents us also with
an equestrian figure in the costume of the time.   The
flask held the coarse powder for the charge, the finer
for priming was held in a smaller case called a
touch-box.   Cartridges, according to Sir S. Meyrick,
were first used for pistols, and carried in a steel case
called a patron, about this time.

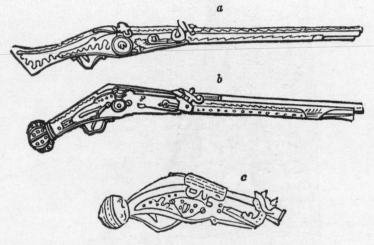

Fig. *a*, wheel-lock dag;   *b*, wheel-lock pistol, temp. Edward VI.;   and
c, pocket wheel-lock pistol, temp. Mary, from the Meyrick collection.

THE FEMALE COSTUME

of these two reigns was composed of the fashions
which immediately preceded them, and the few
novelties introduced will be found described in the
next chapter, under the reign of Elizabeth.

Chapter XVII.

REIGN OF ELIZABETH, 1558—1603.

Early costume of Queen Elizabeth, from a miniature portrait forming part of the collection alluded to, page 219.

WE begin this chapter, as in duty bound, with the costume of the sovereign whose reign we are about to investigate, and shall proceed at once with the dress of the ladies of this period, leaving the habits of the gentlemen, both civil and military, for the conclusion of the chapter. It seems an act of supererogation to attempt to describe the personal costume of "Good Queen Bess." Her great ruff rises up indignantly at the bare idea of being unknown or forgotten. Her jewelled stomacher is piqued to the extreme, and her portentous petticoats strut out with tenfold importance at the slight insinuated against their virgin mistress, who lived but for conquest and display, and thought infinitely less of

bringing a sister-queen to the block than of failing to
make an impression upon a gentleman-usher. But
with all due respect to her ruff and devotion to the
petticoats in general, we must beg to observe, that the
best-known portraits of Elizabeth are those executed
towards the close of her reign, and which belong as
much to the seventeenth as to the sixteenth century.

Through the kindness of Mr. Dominic Colnaghi,
we have the gratification of presenting our readers
with an unpublished portrait of the queen, from a
curious painting executed at the commencement of
her reign, representing her in a dress as similar as
possible to that of her sister and predecessor, in a
portrait painted by the same hand and in the same
collection; the upper dress being a sort of coat of
black velvet and ermine, fastened only on the chest,
and flying open below, disclosing the waistcoat and
kirtle or petticoat of white silk or silver embroidered
with black. She wears a ruff, it is true, but not the
famous one to which she owes at least half her reputation. Her neck is also encircled by a gauze kerchief
or scarf, knotted like that worn by Queen Mary.

Stubbs, who wrote his 'Anatomy of Abuses' in this
reign, notices the peculiar fashion of this masculine
habit and its enormous sleeves. "The women,"
says he, "have doublets and jerkins as the men
have, buttoned up to the breast, and made with
wings, welts, and pinions on the shoulder-points, as
man's apparel in all respects; and although this be
a kind of attire proper only to a man, yet they blush
not to wear it."

About the middle of this reign the great change
took place that gave the female costume of the sixteenth century its remarkable character. The body
was imprisoned in whalebone to the hips; the partelet, which covered the neck to the chin, was removed,
and an enormous ruff, rising gradually from the front

of the shoulders to nearly the height of the head behind, encircled the wearer like the nimbus or glory of a saint. From the bosom, now partially discovered, descended an interminable stomacher, on each side of which jutted out horizontally the enormous *vardingale*, the prototype of that modern-antique, the hoop, which has been so lately banished the court, to the great joy of all classes of his majesty's subjects saving only the metropolitan dressmakers. The cap or coif was occasionally exchanged for a round bonnet like that of the men, or the hair dressed in countless curls, and adorned with ropes and stars of jewels, and at the close of the reign (for the first time) with feathers.

The perfection of this costume is familiar to us, as we have before noticed, in the portrait of Elizabeth taken in the dress in which she went to St. Paul's to return thanks for the defeat of the Spanish armada, A. D. 1588, engraved by Crispin de Passe, from a drawing by Isaac Oliver.

In addition to the ruff, she wears a long mantle of some delicate stuff, with a high-standing collar edged with lace, and expanding like wings on each side of the head. This was probably made of fine lawn or cambric.

In the second year of her reign began the wearing of lawn and cambric ruffs, they having before that time, says Stow, been made of holland, and now, when the queen had them of this new material, no one could starch or stiffen them ; she therefore sent for some Dutch women, and the wife of her coachman Guillan became her majesty's first starcher.

In 1564 Mistress Dingham Vander Plasse, a Fleming, came to London with her husband, and followed the profession of a starcher of ruffs, in which she greatly excelled. She met with much encouragement amongst the nobility and gentry of this country, and was the first who publicly taught the art of starching, her price being four or five pounds for each scholar, and twenty shillings in addition for teaching them how to seeth or make the starch.

Stubbs falls foul of this " liquid matter which they call starch," wherein he says " the devil hath learned them to wash and dive their ruffs, which being dry will then stand stiff and inflexible about their necks." It was made, he tells us, of wheat flour, bran, or other grains, sometimes of roots and other things, and of all colours and hues, as white, red, blue, purple, and the like.   He mentions also "a certain device made of wires, crested for the purpose, and whipped all over either with gold, thread, silver, or silk," for supporting these ruffs, and called " a suppertasse or under-propper."   These " great ruffs or neckerchers, made of hollande, lawne, cambric, and such cloth," so delicate that the greatest thread in them "shall not be so big as the least hair that is," starched, streaked, dried, patted, and underpropped by the suppertasses, " the stately arches of pride," sometimes overshadowed three or four orders of minor ruffs placed gradatim one beneath the other, and all under " the master-devil ruff," which was itself clogged with gold, silver, or silk lace of stately price, wrought all over with needlework, speckled and sparkled here and there with the sun, the moon, the stars, and many other antiques strange to behold : some are wrought with open work down to the midst of the ruff and further ; some with close work ; some with purlid lace and other gewgaws, so clogged, so pestered that the ruff is the least part of itself. Sometimes they are pinned up to their ears, and sometimes they are suffered to hang over the shoulders like flags or windmill sails fluttering in the air.

Their gowns, continues the satirist, be no less famous than the rest, for some are of silk, some of

velvet, some of *grograin*, some of taffata, some of
scarlet, and some of fine cloth, of ten, twenty, or
forty shillings the yard ; but if the whole garment be
not of silk or velvet, then the same must be layed
with lace two or three fingers broad all over the
gown ; or if lace is not fine enough for them, he
says they must be decorated with broad gardes of
velvet edged with costly lace. The fashions too of
the gown were as various as its colours, and " changing with the moon; for some be of the new fashion,
and some of the olde ; some with sleeves hanging
down to the skirts trailing on the ground, and
cast over their shoulders like cow-tails ; some have
sleeves much shorter, cut up the arm, drawn out
with sundry colours, and pointed with silk ribbands,
and very gallantly tied with love-knotts, for so they
call them." Some had capes reaching down to the
middle of their backs faced with velvet or fine taffata,
and "fringed about very bravely;" others were
plaited and crested down the back " wonderfully,
with more knacks" than he can express.

Their petticoats, he says, were of the best cloth and
the finest die, and even of silk, grograin, &c., fringed
about the skirts with silk of a changeable colour.
" But what is more vain," he adds, "of whatever the
petticoat be, yet must they have *kirtles*, for so they
call them, of silk, velvet, grograin, taffata, satin, or
scarlet, bordered with gards, lace, fringe, and I cannot tell what." Here the kirtle is again distinguished
from the gown and petticoat, and is evidently the
garment worn immediately under the gown, and at
this time completely discovered by it, the skirt or
train of the gown or robe being only just visible on
each side of the figure.

The nether stocks or stockings, we are told, were
of silk, jarnsey, worsted, cruel, or the finest yarn,
thread, or cloth that could possibly be had; and

they were " not ashamed to wear hose of all kinds of changeable colours, as green, red, white, russet, tawney, and else what not"—"cunningly knit" too, and " curiously indented in every point with quirks, clocks, open seams, and every thing else accordingly."

As early as the third year of Elizabeth, we read that Mistress Montague, the queen's silk woman, presented to her majesty a pair of black knit silk stockings, made in England, which pleased her so much, that she would never wear any cloth hose afterwards; not only on account of the delicacy of the article itself, but from a laudable desire to encourage this new species of English manufacture by her own example. Soon after this, says Stow, William Rider, then apprentice to Thomas Burdet, at the bridge foot, opposite the church of St. Magnus, seeing a pair of knit worsted stockings at an Italian merchant's, brought from Mantua, borrowed them, and having made a pair like unto them, presented them to the Earl of Pembroke, which was the first pair of worsted stockings knit in this country.

In Stubbs' time we perceive stockings of silk, worsted, and yarn, had become common.

In 1599, William Lee, master of arts, and fellow of St. John's College, Cambridge, invented a stocking-frame. Lee was born at Woodborough, in Nottinghamshire, and is said to have been heir to a good estate. Tradition attributes the origin of his invention to a pique he had taken against a townswoman with whom he was in love, and who, it seems, neglected his passion. She got her livelihood by knitting stockings, and with the ungenerous object of depreciating her employment he constructed this frame, first working at it himself, then teaching his brother and other relations. He practised his new invention some time at Calverton, a village about five miles from Nottingham, and either he or his

brother is said to have worked for Queen Elizabeth.
The other stocking manufacturers used every art to
bring his invention into disrepute ; and it seems they
effected their purpose for that time, as he removed
from Calverton, and settled at Rouen in Normandy,
where he met with great patronage ; but the murder
of Henry IV. of France, and the internal troubles
subsequent to that event, frustrated his success, and
he died at Paris of a broken heart. Stow says that
Lee not only manufactured stockings in his frame,
but " waistcoats and divers other things."

The ladies' shoes were of many fashions. " They
have corked shoes, puisnets, pantoffles, and slippers,"
says Stubbs ; " some of black velvet, some of white,
some of green, and some of yellow, some of Spanish
leather, and some of English, stitched with silk and
embroidered with gold and silver all over the foot,
with other gewgaws innumerable."

The cork shoes here mentioned continued in
fashion amongst the ladies the greater part of the
seventeenth century.

" Then," exclaims the censor, " must they have
their silk scarfs cast about their faces, and fluttering
in the wind, with great lapels at every end, either of
gold, or silver, or silk, which they say they wear to
keep them from sun-burning. When they used to
ride abroad, they have masks and visors made of
velvet, wherewith they cover their faces, having holes
made in them against their eyes whereout they look ;
so that if a man knew not their guise, he would think
that he met a monster or devil."

Again : " their fingers must be decked with gold,
silver, and precious stones ; their wrists with bracelets and annulets of gold and costly jewels; their
hands covered with sweet-washed (i. e. perfumed)
gloves, embroidered with gold and silver ; and they
must have their looking-glasses carried with them

wheresoever they go;" and he is especially indignant against those who " are not ashamed to make holes in their ears, whereat they hang rings and other jewels of gold and precious stones."

A pocket looking-glass was the common companion of the fashionables of both sexes at this time. The ladies carried it either in their pockets or hanging at their sides, and sometimes it was inserted in the fan of ostrich or other feathers—one of the most elegant appendages to the costume of this period, and lately brought again into fashion, though more as an ornament for a room than as a substitute for the folding fan of ivory, which, however beautifully carved, is certainly not comparable to it either for use or elegance.

We have slightly mentioned the fashion of wearing the hair at the commencement of this chapter; we will conclude with the more elaborate account by Stubbs. He says it must be curled, frizzled, crisped, laid out in wreaths and borders from one ear to the other, and, lest it should fall down, must be " underpropped with forkes, weirs," &c., and ornamented with great wreathes of gold or silver curiously wrought, bugles, ouches, rings, glasses, and other such gewgaws, which he being "unskillful in women's tearms," cannot easily recount. " Then upon the toppes of their stately turrets stand their other capital ornaments; a French hood, hatte, cappe, kircher, and such-like, whereof some be of velvet, some of this fashion, and some of that;" cauls made of netwire that the cloth of gold, silver, or tinsel, with which the hair was sometimes covered, might be seen through; and lattice caps [1] with three horns or cor-

---

[1] In an ordinance for the reformation of gentlewomen's head-dress, written in the middle of Elizabeth's reign, it is said that none shall wear an ermine or lattice bonnet unless she be a gentlewoman born, having arms. Harleian MSS. No. 1776.

ners like the forked caps of popish priests: "and every merchant's or artificer's wife or mean gentlewoman indulged in these extravagant fashions."

Fig. *a*, English lady of quality, 1577, from Weigel's wood-cuts; *b*, English lady of quality, 1588, from Caspar Rutz.

In the

MALE COSTUME

an entire change was perfected in this reign. We say perfected, because it had commenced almost invisibly during the reigns of Henry VIII. in England, and still earlier abroad; and during the brief reigns of Edward VI. and Queen Mary had made gradual progress, and apparently in the very opposite direction to fashions in general; that is, from the lowly to the noble; till at the accession of Elizabeth, the peculiar habit which has taken its name from her, viz., the "Elizabethan costume," appeared in all its

beauty, or deformity, as our readers may think best.
The large trunk hose, the long-waisted doublet, the
short cloak or mantle with its standing collar, the
ruff, the hat, band and feather, the shoes and roses,
are all seen in the earliest paintings or prints of this
period, and the positive date of the introduction of
either seems to be a difficult and a debated question
even to those who lived nearest the time.

To begin with the hose, which, since their separation into upper and nether stocks, have had rather
an ambiguous existence. As early as the reign of
Henry VII. we perceive instances of the upper part
being of a different pattern to the lower; and Hall
describes hosen so varied in his account of the banquet at Westminster in the first year of the reign of
Henry VIII. The bases or skirts to the coats and
jackets of that reign descending nearly to the knee,
rendered any alteration in the upper stock invisible,
but occasionally a glimpse is caught of either the
upper stock "bombasted" out, or of independent
breeches, no longer mere drawers, of ample dimensions, descending as low as the border of the bases.
On the abandonment of the latter, these large
breeches or sloppes became an important and splendid part of apparel; and while the long hose were
either supplanted by, or new christened, the *trauses*,
the upper stock, or the breeches worn over them,
received the name of trunk-hose, and were stuffed,
slashed, paned, and ornamented in the most quaint
and extravagant manner, the nether stock settling for
good and all upon the lower part of the leg, under
the modern denomination of stocking.

Strutt quotes the following curious note from a
manuscript in the Harleian library.—"Memorandum:
That over the seats in the parliament-house there
were certain holes, some two inches square, in the
walls, in which were placed posts to uphold a scaf-
fold round about the house within, for them to sit

upon who used the wearing of great breeches stuffed
with hair like wool-sacks, which fashion being left the
eighth year of Elizabeth, the scaffolds were taken
down, and never since put up." " The date on this
memorandum," Strutt adds, " is not very perfect, but
I think it is anno 33 Eliz." The fashion of wearing
that particular sort of large breeches might have
been left in the eighth year of Elizabeth, certainly, as
we have no mode of ascertaining the identical description to which the writer refers, the form varying
in almost every representation; but the fashion of
wearing great, nay, enormous breeches, rather increased than fell off during the reign of Elizabeth,
and they were worn preposterously large by James I.;
and Henry IV. of France, who ascended the throne
in 1589, within two years of the date of the memorandum, is generally painted in precisely the same
costume: and this circumstance gives us faith in the
testimony of Randal Holmes, who says, " About the
fortieth year of Elizabeth the old fashions which men
used at the beginning of her reign were again revived, with some few additions made thereto, such as
guises, double ruffs, &c."

But let us apply to our old friend Stubbs, who has
anatomized these abuses, and afforded us so much
information already respecting the costume of the
ladies.

He begins by assuring us that no people in the
world " are so curious in new fangles" as those of
this country, and first describes their costly shirts of
cambric, holland, lawn, and the finest cloths, wrought
throughout with needlework of silk and curiously
stitched with open seams, and many other knacks
beside, which rendered them so expensive that some
cost " horrible to hear!" ten pounds apiece—a long
price, doubtless, for a shirt at any time—the meanest
worn costing a crown, or a noble at least. The
great ruffs worn by the men, he describes almost in

the same words as those in which he descanted upon
the ruffs of the ladies ; adding, however, that every
body will have them whether they can afford them
or not, and sooner than go without, will sell or
mortgage their land on Shooter's Hill, Stangate
Hole, or Salisbury Plain; or risk the loss of their
lives at Tyburn with a rope : in token whereof, he
says, "they have now newly (1595) found out a
more monstrous kind of ruff, of twelve, yea, sixteen
lengths apiece, set three or four times double ; and
it is of some fitly called 'three steps and an half to
the gallows.'"

And now we come to the trunk-hose or breeches,
which he tells us are of divers fashions and sundry
names : the French hose, the Gallic hosen, and the
Venetian. The French hose are of "two divers
making ; the common sort contain length, breadth,
and sideness sufficient, and they are made very
round ; the other sort contain neither length,
breadth, nor sideness proportionable, being not past
a quarter of a yard on the side whereof some be
paned or striped, cut and drawn out with costly
ornaments, with *canions* adjoined, reaching down
beneath the knees." These closer-fitting hose were
most probably the sort that came into fashion in the
eighth year of Elizabeth, as mentioned by the writer
of the foregoing memorandum, as they are seen upon
the figure of Henry III. of France, A. D. 1574-1589,
(vide Montfaucon's Monarchie Française,) with the
canions, or *canons* attached, which were not tags
or tubes at the ends of ribands or laces, as Mr.
Strutt has conjectured, but one or more rolls terminating the breeches below the knee, as a common French dictionary would have informed him.
"The Gallic hosen," Stubbs continues, "are made
very large and wide, reaching down to the knees
only, with three or four gardes apiece laid down
along the thigh of either hose. The Venetian hosen

reach beneath the knee to the gartering-place of the
leg, where they are tied finely with silken points,
and laid on also with rows or gardes, as the other
before." They were made of silk, velvet, satin,
damask, and other precious stuffs, costing, sometimes,
if we may believe the writer, a hundred pounds a
pair; but in that case we should imagine either
magnificently embroidered or adorned with precious
stones. To these are added boot-hose of the finest
cloth, and also splendidly embroidered from the
gartering-place upward, with "birds, beasts, and
antiques," and made wide enough to draw over all,
and long enough to reach the waist.

Of the doublets worn in these days we find as
great a variety as of the hose. They fitted the body
very closely from the commencement of the reign,
and the waist gradually lengthened to its conclusion.
In Stubbs' time they wore what afterwards obtained
the name of the long peasecod-bellied doublet,
quilted and stuffed with four, five, or six pounds of
bombast, the exterior being of satin, silk, taffata,
grograine, chamlet, gold or silver stuff "slashed,
jagged, cut, carved, pinched and laced with all kind
of costly lace of divers and sundry colours." These
bombasted doublets formed a point in front, hanging
over the girdle, and, allowing for a little caricature,
is to this day the body dress of our old and inestima-
ble friend Punch, whose wardrobe of Italian origin
dates as nearly as possible from this identical period.
Over these were worn coats and jerkins, some with
collars, some without, some close to the body, some
loose, which they called mandillians [2], covering the
whole of the body like sacks or bags, some buttoned

[2] Mandevilles, which Randal Holmes describes "as a loose
hanging garment," and "much like to our jacket or jumps, but
without sleeves, only having holes to put the arms through; yet
some were made with sleeves, but for no other use than to hang
on the back."

down the breast, some under the arm, and some
down the back, some with flaps over the breast, some
without, some with great sleeves, some with small,
and some plaited and crested (striped) behind, and
curiously gathered, some not; one man having as
many sorts of apparel as there are days in the year.
They had cloaks also of white, red, tawney, black,
green, yellow, russet, violet, &c., made of cloth,
silk, velvet, and taffata, and after the Spanish,
French, and Dutch fashions : some short, scarcely
reaching to the girdlestead, or waist ; some to the
knee, and others trailing on the ground, resembling
gowns rather than cloaks, and guarded with velvet
guards, or else faced with costly lace of gold, silver,
or silk, three or four fringes (fingers ?) broad down
the back, about the skirts, and every where else. A
new fashion in the author's time was to guard the
cloaks, round about the skirts, with bugles, and other
kinds of glass, " and all to shine to the eye."

Besides, he tells us these cloaks were so faced and
lined that the inner side cost as much as the outer.
Some had sleeves and some hoods to pull up over
the head ; some were " hanged with points and tassels of gold, silver, and silk:" and, in conclusion, he
asserts that the day had been when a man might have
bought two cloaks for less money than the cost of
one at the time he wrote, they had such store of
workmanship bestowed on them.

The nether stocks or stockings, and shoes and
slippers of the men, he describes as similar to those
of the women. The former with quirks and clogs
about the ancles, and the latter " corked," of all
colours, and richly ornamented. The pantoffles or
slippers he especially ridicules, exemplifying the
difficulty of keeping them on the feet in the street,
and asking how they should be handsome " when
they go flap, flap, up and down in the dirt, casting
up the mire to the knees of the wearer ?"

Of hats and caps he enumerates a vast variety. Some sharp on the crown, pearking up like the spear or shaft of a steeple standing a quarter of a yard above the crown of their heads, some more, some less, to please the fantasies of their inconstant minds. Some flat and broad on the crown, like the battlement of a house, some with round crowns and bands of all colours; others again wore their hats without bands, which Stubbs calls a new fashion, which they father on the Frenchmen; and all these hats or caps of velvet, taffata, or sarcenet, were ornamented with great bunches of feathers, which had latterly become so much the rage that every child wore them, and many got a good living by dyeing and selling of them. To these head-coverings, he adds some made of a certain kind of fine hair, which they call beaver hats, of twenty, thirty, and forty shillings apiece, fetched

Costume of the reign of Elizabeth about 1588, from John Weigel's wood-cuts.

from beyond sea, whence a great sort of other varieties do come.

The flat hat, or cap of estate, worn by the knights of the Garter, was changed for one with a higher crown of the fashion of the time, but no other alteration took place in the dress.

THE ARMOUR

of this reign seldom comes lower than just beneath the hip, complete suits being used only for justing, and not always even for that purpose, knights often appearing in the lists without armour for the legs or thighs. The breast-plates were made much thicker, in order to be bullet proof; the tassets of them began to be made of one plate each, but marked in imitation of several. The point of the tapul reappeared at the bottom of the breast-plate, and projected downwards, in conformity with the shape of the peasecod-bellied doublet described, p. 267. Opposite are engraved the variously-shaped morions of the time of Elizabeth, in chronological order, and a selection from the figures embossed on the last gives the military costume of the close of her reign (about 1590).

Carabines, petronels, and *dragons* are frequently mentioned amongst the fire-arms of this period. The *petronel* was so called from *poitrinal,* being fired with its straight and square butt-end held against the chest. The *dragon* received its name from its muzzle, being generally ornamented with the head of that fabled monster, and the troops who used it subsequently acquired the name of *Dragons* and *Dragoons* from this circumstance. The origin of the appellation of the *carabine* or *carbine* is disputed. One derivation is from the vessels called *Carabs,* on board of which it has been presumed

Morions of the reign of Elizabeth, in the Meyrick collection. The costume from the last of the series, temp. 1590.

1558. 1560. 1570. 1590.

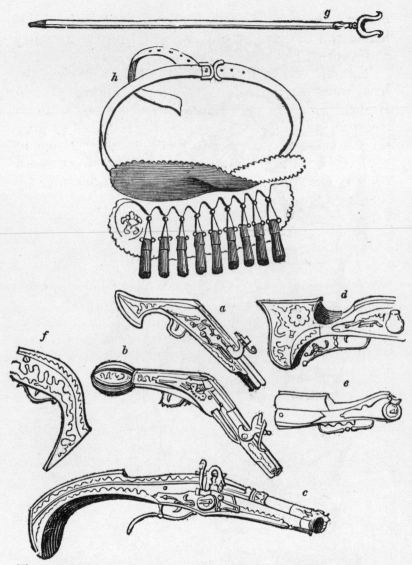

Fire-arms, musket-rest, and bandoliers, temp. Elizabeth, from the Meyrick collection.

they were first used. Troops called *Carabins*, a sort of light cavalry from Spain, are first mentioned A. D. 1559. Our engraving exhibits a dag (fig. *a*), a pistol (fig. *b*), and a dragon (fig. *c*), and the butt-ends of a carabine (fig. *d*), a petronel (fig. *e*), and a *dcmi-haque* or *hack-butt* (fig. *f*), all with wheel-locks, and of the reign of Elizabeth, from the armoury at Goodrich Court.

The rest was introduced for the long heavy match-lock musket, during the reign of Henry III. in France (vide fig. *g*). Bandoliers or sets of leathern cases, in each of which a complete charge of powder for a musket was carried to facilitate the loading of a piece, were used till the close of the seventeenth century (vide fig. *h*), when they were superseded by the cartridge-box.

Chapter XVIII.

REIGN OF JAMES I., 1603—1625.

The costume of the reign of James I. was little more than a continuation of the dress of the latter part of Elizabeth's. The long-waisted or peasecod-bellied doublet remained in vogue, and the conical-crowned hat and large Gallic or Venetian hosen, slashed, quilted, stuffed, and guarded (or laced), were worn as before. The increase in size, from the quantity of stuffing used in the garments, we may partly trace to the pusillanimous character of the new monarch. Dalzel, a cotemporary of James, informs us, in his ' Fragments of Scottish History,' that that monarch had " his cloathing made large, and even the doubletts quilted for (fear of) stellets (stilettoes) ; his breeches in great plaits and full stuffed. He was naturally of a timorous disposition, which was the gretest reason of his quilted doubletts."

The ruff was occasionally exchanged for a wide stiff collar, standing out horizontally and squarely, made of the same stuff, and starched and wired as usual, but plain instead of plaited or pinched, and sometimes edged like the ruff with lace. These collars were called bands [1].

[1] Both the band and the ruff were in this reign stiffened with yellow starch, in preference to all other colours. This fashion is said to have been introduced from France by a Mrs. Turner, who was afterwards executed for poisoning Sir Thomas Overbury. Vide page 292. In the play of Albumazzar, published A.D. 1614, Armelina asks Trincalo, " What price bears wheat and saffron, that your band is so stiff and so yellow?" Bulwer speaks of the " Cobweb-lawn yellow starched ruffs." Pedigree of the English Gallant, p. 536.

Towards the close of James's reign, however, we perceive a slight alteration. Short jackets or doublets, with tabs and false sleeves hanging behind, succeed to the long-waisted doublets, and the hose, instead of being slashed or laced, were covered with loose broad straps, richly embroidered or adorned with buttons, and discovering the silk or velvet trunk at the narrow intervals between them. Vide portrait of Henry, Prince of Wales, page 278. The stockings were gartered beneath the knee, and the garters fastened in a large bow or rosette on one side. The loose Gallic hosen were still worn, and fastened to the doublet or jacket just above the tabs by innumerable points.

In a MS. in the Harleian Library is the following description of the dress of the famous George Villiers, Duke of Buckingham, the favourite of James I. "It was common with him at any ordinary dancing to have his clothes trimmed with great diamond buttons, and to have diamond hatbands, cockades, and earrings; to be yoked with great and manifold knots of pearl, in short, to be manacled, fettered, and imprisoned in jewels : insomuch that, at his going over to Paris in 1625, he had twenty-seven suits of clothes made, the richest that embroidery, lace, silk, velvet, gold and gems could contribute; one of which was a white uncut velvet, set all over, both suit and cloak, with diamonds, valued with fourteen thousand pounds, besides a great feather stuck all over with diamonds, as were also his sword, girdle, hatband, and spurs." The following extract from a letter of James I. to the same nobleman, and to the Prince of Wales, whom Buckingham had accompanied to Madrid in 1623, relates also to the fashion of wearing jewels in the hat :—

"I send you," writes the king to his son, "for youre wearing, the three bretheren that ye knowe

full well, but newlie sette, and the mirroure of
Fraunce, the fellow of the Portugall dyamont,
quiche I wolde wishe you to weare alone in your
hatte, with a little blakke feather;" and to Buckingham he says, " as to thee, my sweete gossippe, I
send thee a faire table dyamont, quiche I wolde once
have gevin thee before if thou wolde have taken it,
and I have hung a faire pearle to it for wearing on
thy hatte, or quhaire thou plaisis, and if my Babie"
(as he always called Charles) " will spaire thee the
two long dyamonts in forme of an anker, with the
pendant dyamont, it were fit for an admiral to weare [2].
. . . . If my Babie will not spaire the anker from
his mistresse, he may well lend thee his rounde
brooche to weare, and yett he shall have jewells to
weare in his hatte for three great dayes."

In Dekker's Horn-book, dated 1609, we read,
" When your noblest gallants consecrate their hours
to their mistresses and to revelling they wear feathers
then chiefly in their hats, being of y[e] fairest ensigns
of their bravery;" and John Taylor, the water poet,
reprobates the spendthrift and the gallant, who

> " Wear a farm in shoe-strings edged with gold,
> And spangled garters worth a copyhold;
> A hose and doublet which a lordship cost;
> A gaudy cloak three mansions' price almost;
> A beaver band and feather for the head,
> Prized at the church's tythe, the poor man's bread."

Silk, worsted, and thread stockings were now
almost universally worn, and cloth or woollen stockings considered unfashionable.

In ' The Hog hath lost its Pearl,' a play by Robert Taylor, printed 1611, one of the characters
remarks, that good parts, without the habiliments

---

[2] The Duke of Buckingham was Lord High Admiral.

of gallantry, are no more set by than a good leg in a woollen stocking.

In the History of Jack of Newbury, a merchant is described in a grave-coloured suit, with a black cloak; and in a comedy by Dekker, published A. D. 1612 [3], a man is told to walk " in treble ruffs like a merchant."

The hat worn by the knights of the Garter at this time was high-crowned, and feathers having been latterly neglected (perhaps in favour of the jewelled hatband, which is frequently seen in this reign unaccompanied by a plume), were re-introduced in the tenth year of James's reign. Some variation appears also in the colour of the mantle of foreign princes; that sent to Frederick, Duke of Wurtemberg, in the fourth year of this reign, is stated to have been " of a mixed colour; to wit, purple and violet."

The riband also, to which the lesser George, or medal, was appended round the neck, was during this reign changed from black to blue. One of blue, or sky colour, is ordered in the twentieth of James I. [4]

The viscount's coronet, composed of an unlimited number of pearls round a circlet of gold, dates from this reign, and was first worn by Viscount Cranbourn, created 20th August, second of James I.

ARMOUR AND WEAPONS.

James I. is stated to have remarked of armour, that it was an excellent invention, for it not only saved the life of the wearer but hindered him from doing hurt to any body else. The increasing use and improvements in fire-arms combined with other causes to bring it into disrepute, and before the close of this reign the armour of the heaviest cavalry terminated at the knees. Henry, Prince of Wales,

---

[3] Entitled ' If this be not a good Play the Devil's in it.'
[4] Ashmole's History of the Order.

Henry, Prince of Wales, from Drayton's Polyolbion, 1613.

appears only armed to the waist in the above engraving, copied from Drayton's Polyolbion.

Amongst the cavalry, the intercourse with Spain changed the name of lancer into cavalier. The infantry consisted of pikemen and musketeers; and during this reign the caliver, a matchlock that could be fired without a rest, came greatly into use, and ultimately superseded the long fire-arm altogether. A military treatise, published in 1619, by Edward Davis, gentleman, tells us, that "a soldier must either accustom himself to bear a piece or a pike. If he bear a piece, then must he first learn to hold the same; to accommodate his match between the two

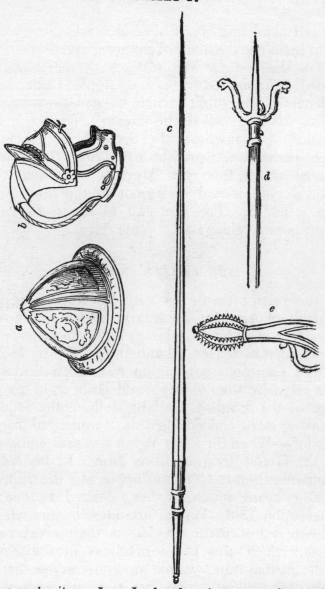

Fig. *a*, a morion, temp. James I.; *b*, a bourginot; *c*; a swine's feather; *d*, a linstock; *e*, the butt of a pistol; all from the Meyrick collection.

foremost fingers and his thombe, and to plant the great end on his breast with a gallant souldier-like grace......His flaske and touch-box must keep his powder, his purse and mouth his bullets; in skirmish

his left hand must hold his match and piece, and the
right hand use the office of charging and discharging."

To the rest for the musket or matchlock was
added in James's time a long rapier blade, for the
defence of the soldier when he had discharged his
piece.   It was called the sweyne's feather, " hog's
bristle," and sometimes the Swedish feather, having
been perhaps a Swedish invention.   See one engraved above from the Meyrick collection, fig. c,
with a morion and bourginot of the same period,
figs. a and b.   The butt-end of the pistol in this
reign became elongated.   Vide fig. e.

THE FEMALE COSTUME

of this reign presents us with few variations.   The
portrait of Anne of Denmark, queen of James I.,
exactly resembles, in the general character of the
dress, that of Queen Elizabeth, painted by Holbein.

The enormous vardingale was worn throughout
this reign by the nobility ; and Bulwer, in his pedigree of the English Gallant, tells us the following
amusing story concerning this " unnatural disguise-
ment :"—When Sir Peter Wych was sent ambassador
to the Grand Seignor from James I., his lady accompanied him to Constantinople, and the Sultaness,
having heard much of her, desired to see her;
whereupon Lady Wych, attended by her waiting-
women, all of them dressed in their great vardingales, which was the court-dress of the English
ladies at that time, waited upon her highness.   The
Sultaness received her visitor with great respect, but,
struck with the extraordinary extension of the hips of
the whole party, seriously inquired if that shape was
peculiar to the natural formation of English women,
and Lady Wych was obliged to explain the whole
mystery of the dress, in order to convince her that

she and her companions were not really so deformed as they appeared to be.

The ruffs and bands or collars worn at this time by the ladies were generally stiffened with yellow starch like those of the gentlemen. In the old play called ' Lingua, or the Combat of the Tongue and the Five Senses for superiority,' published A. D. 1607, we have a curious list of the articles of a fashionable lady's wardrobe. " Five hours ago," says one of the characters, " I set a dozen maids to attire a boy like a nice gentlewoman, but there is such doing with their looking-glasses; pinning, unpinning; setting, unsetting; formings and conformings; painting of blue veins and cheeks. Such a stir with sticks, combs, cascanets, dressings, purls, fall squares, busks, bodices, scarfs, necklaces, carcanets, rabatoes, borders, tires, fans, palisadoes, puffs, ruffs, cuffs, muffs, pusles, fusles, partlets, friglets, bandlets, fillets, corslets, pendulets, amulets, annulets, bracelets, and so many *lets* (i. e. stops or hindrances), that she is scarce dressed to the girdle; and now there is such calling for fardingales, kirtles, busk-points, shoe-ties, and the like, that seven pedlars' shops, nay, all Stourbridge fair, will scarcely furnish her. A ship is sooner rigged by far than a gentlewoman made ready !"

In ' the London Prodigal,' published A. D. 1605, Civit says to his sweetheart,—" Frances, I'll have thee go like a citizen, in a guarded gown and a French hood :" and in ' Eastward Hoe,' a comedy of the same date, Girtred says to her sister,—" Do you wear your quoif with a London licket, your stamen petticoat with two guards, the buffen gown with tuftaffetie cap and the velvet lace." And grogram gowns, lined throughout with velvet, durance petticoats, and silver bodkins are mentioned by her as other parts of the apparel and ornaments of citizens' wives and daughters.

CHAPTER XIX.

REIGN OF CHARLES I. AND COMMONWEALTH, 1625—1660.

THE reign of Charles I., 1625—1648, introduces us to the most elegant and picturesque costume ever worn in England, and from the circumstance of its being the habit of the time in which Vandyke painted, it has acquired the appellation of the Vandyke dress. It has been familiarized to us not only by the numberless prints from the works of that great master, but through the medium of theatrical representations, being, of all costumes, perhaps the best adapted for the stage, and therefore generally selected for such plays as are not fixed by their subject to some other particular era. For the same reason, with pardonable licence, plays founded on incidents of the reign of Charles II. are acted in costumes of the reign of Charles I.; but the point was rather strained by the late Mr. Kemble, who formed out of the habits of the three reigns of Elizabeth, James, and Charles a conventional costume for the whole of Shakspeare's historical plays, from King John to Henry VIII. The intention was, however, a laudable one. Mr. Garrick had broken ground, by assuming a fancy dress for the part of Richard III., but he played Macbeth to the last in a court suit of sky-blue and scarlet laced with gold. Mr. Kemble's good sense and determined spirit induced him to reform this altogether; and though, to the antiquary, it was as ridiculous to see the " gracious Duncan" in trunk-hose as in velvet breeches and silk stockings, the

absurdity was not so striking to the million, and
stage effect was infinitely heightened by the change.
Of late years the taste for spectacle has at least had
the good effect of inducing managers and actors to
pay stricter attention to these matters, and two or
three of Shakspeare's plays were revived a few sea-
sons back at Covent Garden theatre, with their costume corrected by the writer of this work, under the
sanction of Mr. Charles Kemble. Much, however,
remains to be done. Richard III. still wears the
trunks of James I., with the plumed hat of Charles
II., and the "majesty of Denmark," supposed to
have been buried before the Conquest, revisits "the
glimpses of the moon" in armour of the seventeenth
century. The French are far before us in this matter, as they are indeed in nearly every thing else
connected with dramatic entertainments. But to
return to the time of Charles I. The picturesque
habit of which we have spoken was introduced about
the middle of his reign. At the commencement, the
fashions of the later years of his father's reign seem
to have been preserved, and there was scarcely a
nation in Europe that had not contributed its share
to them. In Ben Jonson's comedy of the ' New
Inn,' first acted in 1629, a beau observes—

> " I would put on
> The Savoy chain about my neck, the ruff,
> The cuffs of Flanders ; then the Naples hat
> With the Rome hatband, and the Florentine agate,
> The Milan sword, the cloak of Geneva set
> With Brabant buttons ; all my given pieces,
> My gloves, the natives of Madrid," &c.

And in his ' Tale of a Tub,' a later performance, mention is made of " long sawsedge hose, and breeches
pinned up like pudding-bags ;" and long breeches,
in imitation of the Dutch fashion, are said to have

been worn in this reign, and by Charles I. These
latter we take to be the breeches resembling short
trousers, descending almost to the boot-top, and
either fringed or adorned with a row of points or
ribands.

At the commencement of the civil war, when the roy-
alist party began to be denominated Cavaliers, and the
republican, Round-Heads, the costume of England
was as divided as its opinions ; but the dress of the
Cavalier was gallant and picturesque in the extreme.
It consisted of a doublet of silk, satin, or velvet, with
large loose sleeves, slashed up the front; the collar
covered by a falling band of the richest point lace,
with that peculiar edging now called Vandyke; a
short cloak was worn carelessly on one shoulder.
The long breeches, fringed or pointed, as we have
already mentioned, met the tops of the wide boots,
which were also ruffled with lace or lawn. A broad-
leafed Flemish beaver hat, with a rich hatband and
plume of feathers, was set on one side the head, and a
Spanish rapier, hung from a most magnificent baldrick
or sword-belt, worn sashwise over the right shoulder.
The doublet of silk or velvet was frequently exchanged in these troublous times for a buff coat,
which was richly laced, and sometimes embroidered
with gold or silver, and encircled by a broad silk or
satin scarf tied in a large bow, either behind or over
the hip, in which case the short cloak was perhaps
dispensed with[1]. In some instances a buff jerkin,
without sleeves, was worn over the doublet. Allusions are frequent in the old plays of this period to
these defensive garments[2]. Charles I., in the twelfth

[1] The artist is particularly referred to Bleau's Atlas for authorities for nearly all the varieties of costume, both civil and
military, of this reign.

[2] The Duke of Albemarle, who compiled his observations on
military affairs in 1646, recommends instead of the taces or tassets,

year of his reign, determined to restore the mantle of the order of the Garter to its original colour, and it was accordingly worn, on the installation of the Prince of Wales, of a rich celestial blue ; the surcoat and humerale remained crimson; the hat was of black velvet as before. As early as the second year of his reign he had ordered the badge of the order (the cross surrounded by the garter) to be worn by the knights on their daily dresses, and in 1629 it was formed into a star by surrounding it with rays as it is at present.

The beard was worn very peaked, with small upturned moustaches; the hair long in the neck, and sometimes, it should seem, powdered. John Owen, Dean of Christchurch and Vice-Chancellor of Oxford, appears, in 1652, " in querpo like a young scholar, with powdered hair, snake-bone bandstrings, a lawn band, a large set of ribands pointed (i. e. tagged) at the knees, Spanish leather boots with large lawn tops, and his hat most curiously cocked" (i. e. the flap turned up) : a dress well enough for a young gallant, but, as Strutt truly observes, " improper enough for a clergyman." In the treble portrait of Charles I., by Vandyke, the king wears a jewel in one ear only.

Although it does not furnish us with any particular information, we cannot refrain from quoting in this place the description of the dress of Oliver Cromwell, as given by an eye-witness, Sir Philip Warwick. " The first time that I ever took notice of him," says that gentleman, " was in the beginning of the Parliament held in November 1640, when I vainly thought myself a courtly young gentleman, for we courtiers valued ourselves much upon our good

" a girdle of double buff, eight inches broad, to be worn under the skirts of the doublet, to which it is hooked." He also advises the use " of a good long buff glove for the left hand."

clothes. I came one morning into the house well clad, and perceived a gentleman speaking whom I knew not, very ordinarily apparelled; for it was a plain cloth suit, which seemed to have been made by an ill country tailor; his linen was plain, and not very clean; and I remember a speck or two of blood upon his little band, which was not much larger than his collar; his hat was without a hatband; his stature was of a good size; his sword stuck close to his side."

Helmets or head-pieces of the time of Charles I. and Cromwell.

THE ARMOUR

at this period, being still considered very cumbrous, was, with the exception of helmets, back and breastpieces with tassets, which were worn by the pikemen and musketeers, confined to the pistoliers and heavy horse. Many noblemen and officers contented themselves with a cuirass over a buff coat; and some entire regiments of cavalry were thus armed, and acquired from thence the name of Cuirassiers. Dragoons, first raised in France in the year 1600 by the Marshal de Brisac, were now part of our English army, and wore at this time " a buff coat with deep skirts and an open head-piece with cheeks."

According to a treatise published at Cambridge, called ' Militarie Instructions for the Cavalrie,' dated 1632, we find that force divided into four classes: " the lancier, the cuirassier, the harquebouse and carbine, and the dragone."

The lancier was to wear a close casque or head-piece, gorget, breast and back (pistol and culiver-proof[3]), pauldrons, vambraces, two gauntlets, tassets, culessets, culets or guarde de reins, a good sword (stiff, cutting, and sharp-pointed), with a girdle and hanger so fastened that he might easily draw it; a buff coat with long skirts to wear between his armour and his clothes; his lance either of the usual or pike-shape, only thicker at the butt-end, eighteen feet long, with a thong of leather to fasten it round the right arm; one, if not two pistols of sufficient bore and length; a flask, cartouch-box, and all appur-tenances fitting.

The cuirassier, armed as we have described, with pistols hanging at his saddle, and a good sword, stiff and sharp-pointed like the lancier; he is also to wear a scarf, the only sign of company or uniform at this time, when the buff coat and cuirass concealed the clothes, though scarlet had been long the prevail-ing colour of the royal troops, and was retained by Cromwell.

The harquebusier, "by the late orders rendered in by the council of war," is to wear, besides a good buff coat, a back and breast like the cuirassier, more than pistol-proof, a head-piece, &c. ; a harquebuss, two feet and a half long, hung on a belt by a swivel; a flask, touch-box, and pistols.

The carbineer is to have a good buff coat, a car-

[3] Culiver or caliver, corrupted from calibre, a fire-arm of the particular bore ordered by government, and lighter than usual match or wheel-lock. "Put me a caliver into Wart's hand.' Henry IV. p. 2.

bine or petronel hanging as the harquebuss, a sword, girdle, and hangers, a flask and a touch-box.

" The dragone," we are told, " is of two kinds, pike and musket: the pike is to have a thong of leather about the middle of it for convenience of carrying. The musketeer is to have a strap fastened to the stock of his piece almost from the one end to the other, by which, being on horseback, he hangeth it at his back, keeping his burning match and the bridle in the left hand."

In 1645 the harquebussiers were accounted the second sort of cavalry, and wore triple-barred helmets, cuirasses with guard de reins, pauldrons and vambraces; at the same time the dragoons changed their muskets for the shorter piece called a dragon, from whence they had derived their name abroad, and in 1649 they carried the caliver.

The pot-helmet or open head-piece with cheeks (fig. *a*), the single and triple-barred helmets worn by the dragoons and harquebussiers of this period (figs. *b* and *c*), are engraved above from the originals at Goodrich Court.

The modern fire-lock was invented about this period, and the improvement was suggested by a peculiar fire-arm called the *snaphaunce*, from its being invented and used by a set of Dutch marauders called *snaphans* or poultry-stealers: the light of the match betrayed them, and they could not afford to purchase the expensive wheel-lock, they therefore substituted a flint for the pyrite, and an upright moveable furrowed piece of steel in lieu of the wheel; the cover of the pan being pushed back, the piece of steel was brought to stand over it and the spark elicited as at present. The snaphaunce was known as early as Elizabeth's time; but the fire-lock dates from about 1635. Before this invention the wheel-lock was frequently called the fire-lock; but that term was afterwards used for the modern piece alone. The musket-rests and sweyne's feather were abandoned during the civil wars.

THE FEMALE COSTUME

at the commencement of the reign underwent no change. The French hood and the vardingale were still worn, and the high-crowned hat was adopted by citizens' wives and country-women, particularly of the puritanical party.

Gentlewoman.   Citizen's Wife.   Countrywoman.
From Speed's Map of England.

The following is "a catalogue" of the apparel and ornaments of a fantastical lady of fashion, by the anonymous author of the dramatic pastoral called 'Rhodon and Iris,' said in the title-page to have been first acted **May 3, 1631**, at the florists' feast at

Norwich. The speaker acknowledges it to be " as tedious as a tailor's bill ;" but it is interesting to us for the names it contains of " all the devices" he is " commanded to provide, videlicet :"—

" Chains, coronets, pendans, bracelets, and ear-rings ;
　Pins, girdles, spangles, embroyderies, and rings ;
　Shadowes, rebatoes, ribbands, ruffs, cuffs , falls,
　Scarfes, feathers, fans, maskes, muffs, laces, cauls,
　Thin tiffanies, cobweb lawn, and fardingals,
　Sweet fals, vayles, wimples, glasses, crisping-pins,
　Pots of ointment, combes, with poking-sticks and bodkines,
　Coyfes, gorgets, fringes, rowles, fillets, and hair-laces,
　Silks, damasks, velvets, tinsels, cloth of gold,
　Of tissues with colours of a hundred fold ;
　But in her tyres, so new-fangled is she,
　That which doth with her humour now agree,
　To-morrow she dislikes ; now doth she sweare
　That a loose body is the neatest weare ;
　But ere an houre be gone she will protest,
　A strait gowne graces her proportion best ;
　Now calls she for a boisterous fardingall,
　Then to her hips she'll have her garments fall ;
　Now doth she praise a sleeve that's long and wide,
　Yet, by and by that fashion doth deride ;
　Sometimes she applauds a pavement-sweeping traine,
　And presently dispraiseth it againe ;
　Now she commends a shallow bande so small,
　That it may seem scarce any bande at all ;
　But soon to a new fancy doth she reele,
　And calls for one as big as a coach-wheele :
　She'll wear a flowing coronet to-day,
　The symball of her beauty's sad decay ;
　To-morrow she a waving plume will try,
　The emblem of all female levitie :
　Now in her hat, then in her hair is drest ;
　Now, of all fashions, she thinks change the best :
　Nor in her weeds alone is she so nice,
　But rich perfumes she buys at any price ;

Storax and spikenard she burns in her chamber,
And daubs herself with civet, musk, and amber ;
        *   *   *   *   *   *
Waters she hath to make her face to shine,
Confections eke to clarify her skin ;
Lip-salves, and clothes of a rich scarlet dye
She hath, which to her cheeks she doth apply ;
Ointment, wherewith she pargets o'er her face,
And lustrifies her beauty's dying grace," &c. &c.

Massinger, in his 'City Madam,' printed A. D.
1659, gives us to understand that the French hood,
and the buffin gown mentioned in the previous reign,
were at that time out of fashion. "My young ladies
in buffin gowns and green aprons—tear them off!—
and a French hood too—now 'tis out of fashion—a
fool's-cap would be better!" In the same play Luke
describes the dress of a rich merchant's wife in the
speech he makes to the city madam :—

"You wore
Sattin on solemn days ; a chain of gold,
A velvet hood, rich borders, and sometimes
A dainty minever cap ; a silver pin
Headed with a pearl, worth three-pence, and thus far
You were priviledged—no one envied it—
It being for the citie's honour that
There should be a distinction made between
The wife of a patrician and a plebeian.
        *   *   *   *   *   *
Since your husband was knighted, as I said,
The reverend hood cast off, your borrow'd hair
Powdered and curled, was, by your dresser's art,
Formed like a coronet, hanged with diamonds
And richest orient pearls ; your carkanets
That did adorn your neck, of equal value ;
Your Hungerland bands and Spanish quellio ruffs,
Great lords and ladies feasted to survey

> Embroidered petticoats; and sickness fain'd
> That your night-rails, at forty pounds apiece,
> Might be seen with envy of the visitants;
> Rich pantables (slippers) in ostentation shown,
> And roses worth a family."

And at this time accordingly we find a change in the female costume, which renders it equally elegant with that of the other sex. The hood and vardingale disappear, and with them the yellow starched ruffs and bands. In Killigrew's Parson's Wedding, published in the next reign, he alludes to the time when " yellow starch and wheel vardingales were cried down [4]." The wearing of yellow starched ruffs had indeed declined from the time that Mrs. Turner, a physician's widow, who had a principal hand in the poisoning of Sir Thomas Overbury, was executed [5] : she went to the gallows with a yellow ruff round her neck, and it consequently became unfashionable. Bulwer says, " it is well that the fashion died at the gallows with her that was the supposed inventrix of it." But she was not the inventrix : it originated in France. Mrs. Turner is said to have introduced it into England. The habit of a lady of the close of Charles's reign is given on the facing page, from a print after Hollar ; it is distinguished by its rich full sleeves and elegant falling collar edged with lace. The hair too is dressed after the fashion revived in our days, and the approach to the costume of Charles II.'s reign generally indicated. The mask was much worn in this reign.

The ladies of the republican party were chiefly

---

[4] A. D. 1615. But in a play, printed as late as 1661, called ' the Blind Lady,' a serving-man says to a chamber-maid, " You had once better opinions of me, though now you wash every day your best handkerchief in yellow starch."

[5] Howel's Letters.

English lady of quality, A.D. 1640, from Hollar's 'Ornatus Muliebris.'

distinguished by the plainness of their attire and their
adherence to some of the more staid and sober articles
of the old dress, such as the hood, the high-crowned
hat, &c.

CHAPTER XX.

REIGN OF CHARLES II., 1660—1685.

Charles II. and his Queen, from Heath's Chronicle, 1662.

WITH the restoration of the house of Stuart, Fashion also regained the throne, from which she had been driven by the stern and puritanical republicans, and, like the " merry monarch" with whom she returned, many were the mad pranks she played in the delirium of her joy; many the excesses she committed. Taste and elegance were abandoned for extravagance and folly; and the male costume, which in the time of Charles I. had reached the highest point of picturesque splendour, degenerated and declined from this moment, and expired in the square coat, cocked hat, full-bottomed wig, and jack-boots of the following century.

The birth of these odious articles may be traced to Charles II.'s reign; at the commencement of which a few fantastical additions to the Vandyke costume injured but did not totally destroy it. The doublet was made exceedingly short, open in front, without any under waistcoat, and displaying a rich shirt, which bulged out from it over the waistband of the loose breeches, which, as well as the large full sleeves, were exceedingly ornamented with points and ribands. Beneath the knee hung long drooping lace ruffles, and the falling collar of lace, with a high-crowned hat and plume of feathers, still preserved some of its old gallant cavalier character; but the fashions of the court of Louis XIV. of France soon found their way across the water " to Whitehall Stairs," and the servile imitation of the courtiers of the Grande Monarque gave rise to that absurd and detestable monstrosity, a periwig. His majesty, it appears, when a little boy, had remarkably beautiful hair, which hung in long waving curls upon his shoulders, and the courtiers, out of compliment to their young sovereign, had heads of false hair made to imitate his natural locks, which obtained the name of perukes. When the king grew up, he returned the compliment by adopting the article himself, and the perruque or peruke speedily lodged upon the heads and shoulders of all the gentlemen of England, under the corrupted appellation of a periwig [1].

[1] Holme spells it " perawicke." A letter was written by Charles II. to the University of Cambridge forbidding the members to wear periwigs, smoke tobacco, and read their sermons!

"Misfortunes never come single," says the proverb. So extraordinary a head-dress as the periwig demanded a different covering to the high-crowned hat or broad-leafed Spanish sombrero. Down went the crown and up went the brims at the side ; a row of feathers was placed round it in lieu of the chivalric plume, and the first approach was made to the cocked hats of the eighteenth century.

As early as the year 1658 the petticoat-breeches had made their appearance in England ; and the fashion of wearing large stirop hose or stockings, two yards wide at the top, with points through several eyeletholes, by which they were made fast to the petticoat-breeches by a single row of pointed ribands hanging at the bottom, was brought to Chester from France in that year by one William Ravenscraft, whose name has from this circumstance been rescued from oblivion by Randal Holmes, the Cheshire herald, whose notes on dress, in the Harleian

and when he was at Newmarket, Nathaniel Vincent, doctor of divinity, fellow of Clare Hall, and chaplain to his majesty, preached before him in a long periwig and holland sleeves, according to the fashion in use amongst gentlemen at that time. This foppery displeased the king, who commanded the Duke of Monmouth, then chancellor of the university, to cause the statutes concerning decency of apparel among the clergy to be put in execution ; which was accordingly done. Strutt's Dress and Habits, vol. ii. ; Hone's Every Day Book, vol. i. ; Ath. Oxon. vol. ii. col. 1033.

It must be remembered, however, that false hair was worn by both sexes and in great profusion during the reigns of Elizabeth and James I. ; and the expression " a robustious *periwig* pated fellow," is used by Shakspeare in his Hamlet, written about 1600. In that passage, however, he most probably alludes to the character wig worn by a tragic actor, and not to a general fashion.

When the Marquis of Buckingham and Prince Charles went to Paris in 1623, in their way to Spain, "for the better veiling of their visages his highness and the marquis bought each of them a periwig somewhat to overshadow their foreheads," See Reliq. Wottonianæ, p. 85

Library, were written about 1660. Under the date of 1659 Holmes gives the following description of a gentleman's dress: " A short-waisted doublet and petticoat-breeches, the lining being lower than the breeches, is tied above the knees; the breeches are ornamented with ribands up to the pocket, and half their breadth upon the thigh; the waistband is set about with ribands, and the shirt hanging out over them." These petticoat-breeches at length assumed the shape of the skirts or bases to the doublets and jerkins in Henry VIII.'s time; and, with the usual caprice of fashion, the doublet or jacket, which was so short at the beginning of this reign that it scarcely came below the breast, was, towards the conclusion of it, elongated to the middle of the thigh, with sleeves to the elbows, terminated by rows and bunches of ribands, from under which bulged forth the sleeves of the shirt, ruffed and adorned also pro-

Charles II. and a courtier, from a scarce print by Faithorne,

fusely with ribands; in this shape, with buttons and button-holes all down the front, it became in fact a coat, and accordingly, in an inventory of apparel provided for Charles II. in 1679, we find a complete suit of one material, under the familiar designation of coat, waistcoat, and breeches. Pantaloons are mentioned in the same inventory, and a yard and a half of lutestring allowed for them. Holland drawers, and flannel and cotton trousers, are also amongst the items.

Long and short kersey stockings are reckoned amongst the exports in the Book of Rates, as it stood in the twelfth of Charles II.; and we also find there stockings of leather, of silk, of woollen, and of worsted, for men and children; Irish stockings, and

Costume of the close of Charles II.'s reign, from the print of the funeral of
General Monk, 1670.

the lower end of stockings, which, Mr. Strutt observes, are probably what are now called socks; and among the imports, hose of *crewel*, called mantua hose, and stockings of *wadmol*.

Neckcloths or *cravats* of Brussels and Flanders lace were worn towards the close of this reign, and tied in a knot under the chin, the ends hanging down square.

The costume of the knights of the Garter became in this reign exactly what it is at present. The cap of estate, with its ostrich and heron plume, and the broad blue riband worn over the left shoulder and brought under the right arm, where the jewel or lesser George hangs, being introduced in their present form shortly before the publication of Ashmole's History of the Order.

The baron's coronet, composed of six pearls set at equal distances round a circlet of gold (four of which only are seen in engravings), dates from this reign.

THE MILITARY COSTUME

was nearly that of the Civil Wars and the Commonwealth; but armour was gradually falling into disuse. Vambraces were abandoned by hargobussier s in the first year of the Restoration; and the helmet and corslet or cuirass, or the gorget alone, worn over a buff coat, formed the total defence of steel at this period worn by the officers.

" The arms, offensive and defensive," says the statute of the thirteenth and fourteenth of Charles II., " are to be as follows: the defensive arms (of the cavalry), a back, breast, and pot, and the breast and pot to be pistol-proof. The offensive arms, a sword and a case of pistols, the barrels whereof are not to be under fourteen inches in length. For the foot, a musketeer is ordered to have a musket, the barrel not under three feet in length; a collar of bandeliers,

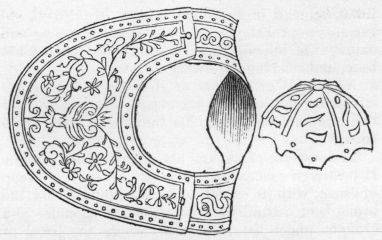

Gorget and steel skull-cap, from the Meyrick collection.

with a sword. Pikemen are to be armed with a pike made of ash, not under sixteen feet in length, with a back, breast, head-piece, and sword."

The present familiar names of the regiments comprising the British army commence from this reign. The Life Guards were raised in 1661; composed and treated, however, like the Gardes du Corps of the French, being formed principally of gentlemen of family and distinction, who, themselves or their fathers, had fought in the civil wars. In the same year the Blues were also embodied, and called the Oxford Blues, from their first commander, Aubrey, Earl of Oxford. The Coldstream Foot-guards date their formation from 1660, when two regiments were added to the one raised about ten years previously by General Monk at Coldstream, on the borders of Scotland. To these were added the 1st Royal Scots, brought over from France at the Restoration; the 2d, or Queen's, raised in 1661; the 3d, or Old Buffs, from their accoutrements being composed of buffalo leather, embodied in 1665; the Scotch Fusiliers (now the 21st foot), raised in 1678, and so called from their carrying the *fusil*, invented in France in

1630, being a firelock lighter than the musket, but about the same length ; and the 4th, or King's Own, raised in 1680. During this reign the *bayonet* was invented at Bayonne, whence its name ; it was some-times three-edged, sometimes flat, with a wooden hilt like a dagger, and was screwed or merely stuck into the muzzle of the gun. Bandoliers were still worn in 1670, but had been gradually growing into dis-esteem, according to Sir James Turner, for the last thirty years. *Cartridge-boxes* of tin, upon the prin-ciple of the old *patron* of Elizabeth's time, are strongly recommended by Lord Orrery.

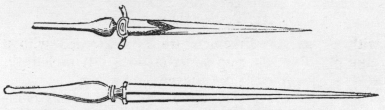

Bayonets of the earliest form, from the Meyrick collection.

THE FEMALE COSTUME

of the days of Charles II. ! What a bevy of beauties does the mere mention of it conjure up to our recol-lection. The lovely Hamilton, the blushing Bagot, the bewitching Stewart, the tender-eyed Temple, La triste Heretiere, Nell Gwyn. Who has not doated on them in the Memoirs of Grammont, or on the walls of Hampton Court. Charles II.'s beauties were the very reverse of their mothers in dress as in demeanour. The starched ruff, the steeple-crowned hat, the rigid stomacher, and the stately fardingale, were banished with the gravity and morality of their wearers. A studied negligence, an elegant déshabille, is the prevailing character of the costume in which they are nearly all represented ; their glossy ring-lets escaping from a simple bandeau of pearls, or adorned by a single rose, fall in graceful profusion upon snowy necks, unveiled by even the transparent lawn of the band or the partelet, and the fair round arm, bare to the elbow, reclines upon the voluptuous satin petticoat, while the gown, of the same rich material, piles up its voluminous train in the background.

The numerous and splendid engravings from paintings of this period, to be met with in every printseller's window or private portfolio, render engravings of this costume perfectly unnecessary.

CHAPTER XXI.

REIGNS OF JAMES II. AND WILLIAM AND MARY, 1685—1702.

Portraits of William III., from prints of the time; the first after a painting by Visscher.

THE two brief reigns of James II. and William III. are distinguished by scarcely any novelty in the civil costume. The petticoat-breeches were again exchanged for those which tied beneath the knee; but the latter were made to sit closer than of yore, and the stockings drawn over them to the middle of the thigh. The periwig became more monstrous, and it was the fashion for the beaus to comb their perukes publicly, for which purpose large combs of ivory or tortoise-shell, curiously chased and ornamented, were carried in the pocket as constantly as the snuff-box, which had latterly also become an indispensable appendage to a fine gentleman. At court, in the mall, and in the boxes of the theatre, a gallant of these days combed his peruke during a conversation or flirtation with the same air that a modern exquisite would twirl his moustaches. The full-bottomed wig was worn by the learned professions and those who affected particular gravity. Farquhar, in his comedy of 'Love and a Bottle,' written in 1698, remarks that "a full wig" is imagined as "infalliable a token of wit as the laurel."

The broad brims of the hats were now frequently turned up on two sides; they were ornamented by several feathers placed round them, or by bows of ribands. To turn up the brim or flap of the hat was, in the language of that day, to cock it, and each gallant cocked his hat according to his own fancy, or after the style of some leader of fashion.

William III., from a print dated 1694.

One mode was called after the unfortunate Duke of Monmouth, the Monmouth cock.

To the broad-falling bands had now succeeded the small Geneva bands, like those worn by our modern clergymen and councillors [1], and the rich neckcloth or cravat of Brussels or Flanders lace was worn by the nobility and men of fashion exceedingly long, and the ends passed through the button-holes of the waistcoat. *Shoe-buckles* began to displace the rosettes; some difficulty exists in assigning an exact date to their introduction: buckles for shoes are mentioned as early as the reign of Edward IV., but they were most likely used to fasten the strap that crossed the instep on one side of the shoe, and must have been exceeding small, as they do not appear in any illumination or effigy. The earliest date we have heard assigned to the shoe-buckle, properly so called, is 1680. They became general in the reign of Queen Anne.

THE MILITARY COSTUME.

The helmet is now seldom worn, and the full flowing wig contrasts itself most ridiculously with the steel cuirass.

Carabineers, so called from the fire-arm they carried, began to be embodied in James II.'s time, and were formed into regiments in the reign of William III. They wore breast and back plates, and iron skull-caps sewn in the crowns of their hats (vide engraving, page 300). They were armed with swords, and carried pistols in holsters; the carbine slung behind by a belt and swivel.

James II. added to the British cavalry the 1st, or King's regiment of Dragoon Guards, 6th of June, 1685; and the 2d, or Queen's Dragoon Guards, in

---

[1] Except that instead of being two small pieces worn for distinction merely, they were bonâ fide collars, the ends of which hung negligently out over the waistcoat.

the same year. They were trained to act either on foot
or on horseback, the men being armed with firelocks
and bayonets in addition to their swords and pistols.

To the infantry were added the fifth and seventh
regiments (the latter called the Royal Fusiliers), both
embodied in 1685, and the Welsh Fusiliers, or
twenty-third regiment, in 1688.

The bayonet was still a dagger, but the ring, added

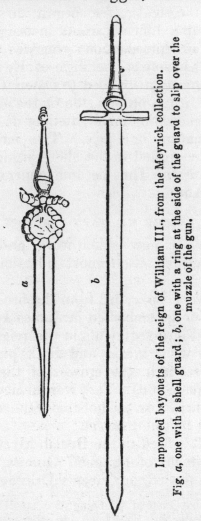

Improved bayonets of the reign of William III., from the Meyrick collection.

Fig. a, one with a shell guard; b, one with a ring at the side of the guard to slip over the muzzle of the gun.

to the guard at first for defence, was brought into great use at this time on the Continent. In one of William III.'s campaigns in Flanders a French regiment advanced against the British twenty-fifth, with bayonets fixed by a ring over the muzzle. Lieutenant-Colonel Maxwell ordered his men to screw their bayonets into the muzzles of their muskets to receive the French, who he expected were coming to the charge, when the latter suddenly threw in a heavy fire, to the astonishment of the British, who could not understand how it was possible to fire with fixed bayonets. They, however, recovered themselves, charged, and drove the enemy out of the line. This improvement suggested the socket bayonet, which was shortly afterwards invented and displaced entirely the pike. Two bayonets are engraved here of the time of William III.; the improved one, with the ring at the side of the guard, has a blade two feet long.

THE FEMALE COSTUME

remained unaltered during the reign of James II.; but some Dutch fashions appear to have followed the court of William and Mary. The bosom, which had been for some years past indelicately exposed, was again consigned to the guardianship of the jealous and formal stomacher. The elegant full sleeve of the gown was replaced by a tight one, with a cuff above the elbow, in imitation of the coats of the gentlemen, from beneath which fell a profusion of lace in the shape of ruffles or lappets; and a long glove, in the portrait of Queen Mary by Visscher, (vide second engraving, p. 308,) completes the envelopment of the arm in satin, lace, and leather. The hair, which had latterly been permitted to fall in natural ringlets upon the shoulders, and seldom

Costume of Queen Mary, from two prints of the time.

burthened with more ornaments than a jewel or a
flower, was now combed up from the forehead like a
rising billow, and surmounted by piles of ribands
and lace, disposed in regular and alternate tiers[2], or
the ribands were formed into high stiffened bows, like
the lately fashionable coiffure à la Giraffe, and covered
or not, as it might happen, by a lace scarf or veil,
that streamed down each side of the pinnacle.   Farquhar, in his comedy of ‘Love and a Bottle,’ mentions “ the high top-knots;” and Swift, the “ pin-
ners edged with colberteen,” as the lace streamers
were called.   The fan in its modern, or what would
now be termed “old fashioned” shape, is seen in the
hands of the Duchess of Portsmouth and Queen
Mary, having superseded its picturesque predecessor
during the reign of Charles II.

---

[2] This head-dress was sometimes called a *tower,* but is more
generally known under the extraordinary, we should almost
think satirical, denomination of a *commode!*

In the

ECCLESIASTICAL COSTUME

the only novelty is the peruke. Archbishop Tillotson is the first prelate represented in a wig. It is however of moderate dimensions, and not much unlike a natural head of hair. In one of his sermons the pious primate alludes to this innovation : " I can remember," says he, " since the wearing the hair below the ears was looked upon as a sin of the first magnitude ; and when ministers generally, whatever their text was, did either find or make occasion to reprove the great sin of long hair, and if they saw any one in the congregation guilty in that kind, they would point him out particularly, and *let fly at him* with great zeal."

Chapter XXII.

COSTUME OF THE EIGHTEENTH CENTURY, FROM THE ACCESSION OF ANNE, AND TO THE PRESENT PERIOD.

Gentlemen of the reigns of Queen Anne, George I. and II., from Jeffrey's collection, published in 1757.

a, 1700-15; *b,* 1735; *c,* 1745; *d,* 1755.

We have at length arrived at the last period the fashions of which can be a subject of interest or inquiry to our readers.   With

THE REIGN OF QUEEN ANNE (1702—14)

vanished every relic of our chivalric costume except the sword, which still completes the full dress of the court of St. James's.

Square-cut coats and long-flapped waistcoats with pockets in them, the latter meeting the stockings, still drawn up over the knee so high as to entirely conceal the breeches, but gartered below it ; large hanging cuffs and lace ruffles ; the skirts of the coats stiffened out with wire or buckram, from between which peeped the hilt of the sword, deprived of the broad and splendid belt in which it swung in the preceding reigns ; blue or scarlet silk stockings with gold or silver clocks ; lace neckcloths ; square-toed short-quartered shoes, with high red heels and small buckles ; very long and formally-curled perukes, black riding-wigs, bag-wigs, and nightcap-wigs ; small three-cornered hats laced with gold or silver galloon, and sometimes trimmed with feathers, composed the habit of the noblemen and gentlemen during the reigns of Queen Anne and

GEORGE I. (1714—27.)

Minuter fashions were of course continually arising and disappearing, adopted and named after some leader of the ton, or in commemoration of some public event. The famous battle of Ramilies, for, instance, introduced the Ramilie cock of the hat, and a long gradually-diminishing plaited tail to the wig, with a great bow at the top, and a smaller one at the bottom called a *Ramilie tail*, and the peruke itself a *Ramilie wig*, which was worn as late as the reign of George III. Tying the hair is said to have been first introduced by the noted Lord Bolingbroke. (See Nash's Collect. for Worcestershire, i. 561.) The cocked hat had a variety of shapes in the reign of Queen Anne. In No. 526 of the Spectator, "John Sly, a haberdasher of hats and tobacconist," is directed to take down the names of such country gentlemen as have left the hunting for the military cock of the hat upon the approach of peace ; and in No. 532 is a letter written in the name of the said John Sly, in which he states that he is preparing hats for the several kinds of heads that make figures in the realms of Great Britain, with cocks significant of their powers and faculties. His hats for men of the faculties of law and physic do but just turn up to give a little life to their sagacity; his military hats glare full in the face; and he has prepared a familiar easy cock for all good companions between the above-mentioned extremes [1].

THE REIGN OF GEORGE II. (1727—60)

produced no alteration in the general character of the dress; but to the catalogue of wigs we find added the tye-wig and the bob-wig, the latter sometimes worn without powder. The Ramilie tail was followed by the pigtail, which appears in prints of this reign as early as 1745, and some young men wore their own hair dressed and profusely powdered. In the Rambler, No. 109, dated 1751, is a letter from a young gentleman, who says his mother " would rather follow him to the grave than see him sneak about with dirty shoes and blotted fingers, hair unpowdered, and a hat uncocked;" and, in 1753, the Adventurer, No. 101, contains a description of the gradual metamorphosis of a greenhorn into a blood. " I cut off my hair and procured a brown bob periwig of Wilding, of the same colour, with a single row of curls just round the bottom, which I wore very nicely combed and without powder. My hat, which had been cocked with great exactness in an equilateral triangle, I discarded, and purchased one of a more fashionable size, the fore

[1] November 25, 1712, John Sly writes to say he has seen of late French hats of a prodigious magnitude pass by his observatory.

corner of which projected near two inches further than those on each side, and was moulded into the shape of a spout." The fashion, however, soon changed, for we find he afterwards altered his hat by considerably elevating and shortening the fore corner of it till "it no longer resembled a spout, but the corner of a minced pye."

This latter fashion was succeeded by a larger cocked hat imported from Germany, and distinguished by the name of the Kevenhuller; and, at the commencement of the reign of

GEORGE III. (1760)

we are told "hats are now worn upon an average six inches and three-fifths broad in the brim, and cocked between Quaker and Kevenhuller. Some have their hats open before like a church spout, or the scales they weigh flour in; some wear them rather sharper, like the nose of a greyhound, and we can distinguish, by the look of the hat, the mode of the wearer's mind. There is the military cock, and the mercantile cock; and while the beaux of St. James's wear their hats under their arms, the beaux of Moorfields Mall wear them diagonally over their left or right eye. Some wear their hats with the corners, which should come over their foreheads, in a direct line pointed into the air. Those are the Gawkies. Others do not above half cover their heads, which is indeed owing to the shallowness of their crowns." The hat edged with a gold binding, the same informant tells us, was at that time the distinguishing badge of "the brothers of the turf." In 1770 the Nivernois hat was the rage. It was exceedingly small, and the flaps fastened up to the shallow crown, which was seen above them, by hooks and eyes. The corner worn in front was of the old spout or shovel-shape, and stiffened out by a wire. Gold-laced hats were again general in 75; and in 78 were adopted by many to give them a military or distinguished air, and to escape the press-gangs that were remarkably busy in that year[2].

Round hats began to be worn in the morning shortly after this date, and the French revolution, in 1789, completed the downfal of the three-cornered cocked hat on both sides of the channel. It was insulted in its decay by the nick-name of " an Egham, Staines, and Windsor," from the triangular direction-post to those places which it was said to resemble ; but a flat, folding, crescent-shaped beaver still called a cocked hat, but more correctly an opera-hat, distinguished the beaux at the theatre, from whence it derived its name, and at full-dress evening parties till within the last few years, and the chapeau-de-bras, a small triangular silk article, the shadow of its gold-laced prototype, slipped under the arm of the courtier. The old original three-cornered cocked hat, banished from the fashionable world, has found a temporary refuge on the heads of the state coachmen of our royal and noble families, and enjoys a sort of life-interest in the pegs of Greenwich and Chelsea Hospitals, dropping to the earth with its veteran wearer. The opera-hat has given way to the crush-hat, and the chapeau-de-bras is but just tolerated within the privileged precincts of the court.

The wig was likewise doomed to feel the influence of the French revolution. During the latter half of the eighteenth century it had gradually diminished in size, and the practice of frizzing, plastering, and powdering the hair till it was at least as ugly as a wig,

---

[2] For this and several other interesting facts concerning the fashions of the long reign of George III., we are indebted to the notes and conversation of a highly esteemed Octagenarian, whose veracity is as unquestionable as his memory is extraordinary.

has even now some faithful followers. In 1772 a most macaw-like *toupée* and a portentous tail distinguished *a maccaroni* (vide print, entitled Maccaroni's Courtship, published February 1, 1772); but the republican spirit of the Parisians revived the classical coiffure of Rome, and a "tête à la Brutus" put to flight the " ailes de pigeon" of the ancient regime. The bag still clings to the collar of the courtier, though the wig, and even the powder, has been gradually dispensed with, and a solitary pigtail is now and then seen reclining on an elderly gentleman's shoulder, as if only to remind us

> " That such things were
> And were most dear to us."

The square-cut coat and long-flapped waistcoat of the reign of Queen Anne and the first two Georges underwent an alteration about the middle of the reign of their successor. The skirts were unstiffened, the waists shortened, and the cut of the present court suit introduced. Cloth became the general material for the coat, and velvet, silk, satin, and embroidery were reserved for court dresses, or waistcoats and breeches only. The latter were, from the close of George II.'s reign, worn over the stocking as at present, and fastened first by buckles and afterwards by strings. The shoes were worn with longer quarters and larger buckles[3]. The lace cravat was abandoned about 1735, and a black riband worn round the neck tied in a large bow in front[4]. To this succeeded

[3] In 1777 the buttons of the coat and the buckles on the shoes were worn of an enormous size, and occasioned the production of a caricature called ' Buckles and Buttons, or I'm the thing, deme !' A beau with *steel buttons* dazzling a lady, is the subject of another caricature of the same year.

[4] This must not be confounded with the solitaire, which was a black riband worn loosely round the neck almost like an order of knighthood. Vide portraits of Buffon, published by the Society.

white cambric stocks, buckled behind; and to them
(about 1789) the modern muslin cravat, in which it
was, at one time, the fashion to bury the chin.
About the same period the shirt-collar appeared and
the ruffle vanished. The coat was made with lapels
and a tail, being cut square in front above the hips
as well as the waistcoat, which, deprived of its flaps,
was soon made as ridiculously short as it had previously been unnecessarily long[5]. Pantaloons and
Hessian boots were introduced about the same period[6]: but from this time the fashions are in the
recollection of most of our readers. Short boots and
loose trousers, the result of the visit of the Cossacks
to London, have, together with frock-coats, rendered
our costume more convenient and less formal, and
could we exchange the heavy and tasteless beaver
hat for some light and more elegant head-covering,
the dress of the present day, if not so picturesque as
that of Charles I.'s time, would at least have com-
fort and durability to recommend it; and an Englishman, instead of being caricatured, as of yore,
with a pair of shears in his hand as uncertain what
fashion to adopt, might remain contented, and described as

> " An honest man close buttoned to the chin,
> Broad-cloth without, and a warm heart within."

Three orders of knighthood were added to that of
the Garter during this century:—

1st. The order of St. Andrew, or the Thistle, instituted by Queen Anne, who signed the statutes on
the 31st of December, 1703. The knights wear a
green riband over their *left* shoulders, appendant to
which is the image of St. Andrew, with his cross

---

[5] The short waistcoat is seen in prints as early as 1786.
[6] Hessian boots are caricatured in 1799.

before him, in a circle of gold enamelled green, with
the motto of the order, "Nemo me impune lacessit;"
a collar composed of thistles and sprigs of rue linked
together, enamelled green, with the figure of St.
Andrew irradiated, appendant to it, encircled by the
motto; and on the left breast a star, composed of St.
Andrew's cross, with four silver rays issuing between
the points of the cross, upon a field Vert, a thistle of
gold and green encircled by the motto.

2d. The order of the Bath, instituted by George I.
1725. Its insignia being a star of eight points
Argent; in the centre, three imperial crowns Or, encircled by the motto "Tria juncta in uno;" a broad
riband of a scarlet colour worn over the *right* shoulder
with the badge appended to it, viz.—Azure, three
crowns Or, surrounded by the motto.

3d. The order of St. Patrick, instituted by
George III., February 5, 1783 [7].

In attempting to describe the

COSTUME OF THE LADIES OF THE EIGHTEENTH CENTURY,

we fling ourselves upon the generosity of those of
the nineteenth, as a mere catalogue of the various
articles introduced by fashion in our later days would,
to make it complete, occupy more space than our
limits can afford; and the very contemplation of
them in the innumerable prints of the time has
nearly bewildered us. An intelligent writer on this
subject has remarked, that Fashion, from the time of
George I., "has been such a varying goddess, that
neither history, tradition, nor painting has been able
to preserve all her mimic forms ; like Proteus strug-
gling in the arms of Telemachus, on the Phanaic

[7] The Guelphic or Hanoverian order was added by his late
Most Gracious Majesty, George IV.

coasts, she passed from shape to shape with the rapidity of thought." And Addison tells us that there is not so variable a thing in nature as a lady's headdress, which rose and fell in his own memory above thirty degrees.

It is probable, however, that the inconstancy of fashion is not very much greater now than it was shortly after the Norman invasion, and in almost every succeeding century have we quoted the lamentations of some poet or historian over the caprices and extravagance of his cotemporaries, male and female, lay and ecclesiastic. It is the multiplication of authorities that increases our difficulty with our information, but, on the other hand, (and we call the attention of our readers most particularly to this fact,) the costume of a nation is not disturbed by the introduction or abandonment of minute alterations and ephemeral fashions. Although we may scarcely find two figures dressed or armed precisely alike in a dozen coeval monuments or paintings, the general character of the time is stamped upon *all*, and to that we have, at first from necessity, and now upon principle, confined ourselves.

THE REIGN OF QUEEN ANNE, 1702—1714,

was brief as it was " happy and glorious." The dress of the ladies during the greater part of her short and gentle sway resembled, in its general features, that of the time of James II. and William III. The tower or commode was still worn, and the gowns and petticoats flounced and furbelowed so that every part of the garment was " in curl," and a lady of fashion " looked like one of those animals," says the Spectator, " which in the country we call a Friezland hen." But, in 1711, we find Mr. Addison remarking, that " the whole sex is now dwarfed and shrunk into a race of beauties that seems almost another species. I remember several ladies who were once very near seven foot high, that at present want some inches of five. How they came to be thus curtailed I cannot learn ; whether the whole sex be at present under any penance which we know nothing of, or whether they have cast their head-dresses in order to surprise us with something in that kind which shall be entirely new, though I find most are of opinion they are at present like trees lopped and pruned that will certainly sprout up and flourish with greater heads than before." He confesses himself, however, highly pleased with the coiffure then in fashion, which, as may be seen by the later portraits of Queen Anne, was of a natural, and consequently elegant description ; the hair clustering in curls down the back of the neck, and though hair-powder was worn by some, her majesty's chesnut ringlets are unsullied by that abominable composition.

The praise the essayist lavishes upon the ladies' heads he is shortly, however, obliged to qualify by his reprobation of a new fashion that sprung up a few months later. This was the introduction of the true heiress and successor of the fardingale—the enormous, inconvenient, and ridiculous hoop. In Sir Roger De Coverley's picture gallery, his great-great-grandmother is said to have on " *the new-fashioned petticoat, except that the modern is gathered at the waist.*" The old lady was evidently in the wheel fardingale, which projected all round, for the knight adds—" My grandmother appears as if she stood in a large drum, whereas the ladies now walk as if they were in a go-cart ;" the whalebone petticoat, on its first introduction, presenting a triangular rather than a hooped appearance. In the month of July in that year, we find it was swollen out to an enormous size, so that what the ladies had lost in height they made up in breadth; and a correspondent, speaking of the unfashionable country ladies at sixty miles distance from London, says they can absolutely walk in their hooped petticoats without inconvenience.

Hoods of various colours were worn by ladies at the opera in 1711-12, and cherry colour was the prevailing fashion of the latter year. Scarlet stockings were worn by fashionable belles, and the practice of taking snuff is mentioned in No. 344 of the Spectator as one that fine ladies had lately fallen into. The practice of wearing black patches on various parts of the face is amusingly ridiculed in several papers, and its application to party politics satirized in the 81st number.

The affectation of a male costume by ladies for riding-suits is repeatedly noticed and censured by the Spectator. In No. 104 is a description of a lady in a coat and waistcoat of blue camlet, trimmed and embroidered with silver, with a petticoat of the same stuff, by which alone her sex was recognized, as she wore a smartly-cocked beaver hat edged with silver, and rendered more sprightly by a feather; and her hair, curled and powdered, hung to a considerable length down her shoulders, tied like that of a rakish young gentleman's, with a long streaming scarlet riband. They also assumed the male periwig on those occasions, in addition to the coat, hat, and feather. An exceedingly little muff was in fashion in 1710-11, and a black silk mantua is mentioned in the pleasant story of Brunetta and Phillis, No. 80.

Ladies of the reign of George II., from Jeffrey's collection.
a, 1735; *b*, 1745; *c*, 1755.

THE REIGNS OF GEORGE I. 1714-27, AND GEORGE II. 1727-60,

boast of Hogarth for their illustrator, and introduce small frilled or puffed caps, loose gowns called sacques, and cloaks with hoods, termed cardinals. The hoop maintained its post, though it frequently changed its fashion. In 1735 we perceive it projecting all round like the wheel fardingale; the petticoat short and the gown without a train. In 1745 the hoop has increased at the sides and diminished in front, and a pamphlet was published in that year, entitled 'The enormous abomination of the Hoop-petticoat, as the fashion now is.' Ten years later it is scarcely discernible in some figures, and in 1757 it re-appears expanding right and left into the shape which the court-dress of George III.'s reign has rendered familiar to us. In 1735 we find the heads

still low and covered by small frilled caps, and flat
gipsy-looking straw hats of moderate dimensions. In
1745-6 the caps are still smaller, but the hats larger;
and a little bonnet, tied under the chin, appears almost
of the last modern fashion.   Aprons had become
part of the dress of a fashionable belle during the
early part of this century, and in 1744 they reached
to the ground.   They were next shortened, and
lengthened again before 1752, as a lady is made to
exclaim in the Gray's Inn Journal, No. 7, that "short
aprons are coming into fashion again."   In the same
year we find a successor to the hood in the *capuchin,*
or a new name for the old head-covering.   " Mr.
Needlework! bid John come round with the coach
to the door, and bring me my fan, gloves, and capuchin in an instant."   And in the 8th number of the
same work is an advertisement of the sale by auc-
tion of "the whole stock of a coquette leaving off
trade, consisting of several valuable curiosities," &c.,
amongst which are mentioned "a transparent capuchin," "an elegant snuff-box with a looking-glass
within it, being a very good pocket companion for a
beauty," directions for painting and the use of cos-
metics, and "the secret of putting on patches in an
artful manner, showing the effect of their different
arrangement, with instructions how to place them
about the eye in such a manner as to give disdain,
an amorous languish, or a cunning glance; translated from the French."

With regard to ornaments, the *watch* and *etui*
adorned the waist; the jewelled necklace sparkled
on the bosom, and bracelets were worn over the
long gloves.   Shortly after the accession of

GEORGE III., A. D. 1760,

a necklace, composed of several rows of gold chains,
beads, or jewels, the first close round the throat, and

the others falling in festoons one under the other so
as to cover the whole neck, was highly fashionable,
and called "an esclavage," from the collar and chains
with which the wearer seemed laden. In 1772, the
print, called a Maccaroni Courtship, exhibits the same
ridiculous toupée and curls by which the gentleman's
head-dress of the same day was made hideous. (Vide
engraving, fig. *a*.) A pretty cap, called the wing or fly-
cap, and resembling one still worn in Holland, concealed in some instances the deformity of the hair,
revealing only the club in which it was worn behind
(fig. *b*); the cap was again surmounted by a bonnet
laden with bows and bunches of ribands, and the gown
was tucked up behind as country girls frequently wear
it at this day. The maccaroni head-dress was followed
by those mountains of curls, powder, flowers, and feathers, which rose "alp above alp" upon the foreheads
of our stately grand-mammas, fufilling the prophetic
fears of Addison, and which, notwithstanding every
body wore them, were as much laughed at and caricatured then as they would be at present. Several
prints, published in the years 1776-7, represent these
head-dresses composed like the figures in some of our
recent pantomimes constructed by the clown from the
contents of the nearest green-grocer or butter-man.
In one called 'the Green Stall' the long side curls
are imitated by carrots similarly disposed, and in
another the slanting summit of the mountain is laid
out as a parterre, and a gardener is seen at work in it!
'The maiden Aunt,' published July 4, 1776, exhibits
a paroquet perched upon the powdered precipice, and
completing with its wings and tail the ludicrous effect
of the picture (fig. *c*). In 1778 and 1783 we still
meet with varieties of this fashion, which certainly is
not exceeded in absurdity and ugliness by the horned
and heart-shaped head-dresses of the fifteenth century.   In 1783 a change appears to have taken

place, and a flat-crowned broad-brimmed straw or silk hat, surrounded with ribands, is worn upon the hair, which lowered atop, bulges out at the sides like a bishop's wig profusely powdered, while two or three immense curls fall from beneath it upon the shoulders (fig. *i*). In 1786-9 an improvement appears, which a modern writer attributes, in a great measure, to the taste of Sir Joshua Reynolds, Angelica Kauffman, Hopner, and the other painters of that day. The hair was worn full and flowing, we may almost say dishevelled; but powder maintained its ground till 1793, when it was discarded by her Majesty Queen Charlotte and the Princesses, and at length disappeared, we trust for ever, from the toilets of a British beauty. Ladies wore white stockings even in mourning as late as the year 78. Mrs. Damer, the eccentric and celebrated sculptor, is said to have been the first female who wore black silk stockings in England; which circumstance, combined with other peculiar habits, obtained for her the epithet of " Epicinean" in the newspaper epigrams of the day. Though the large hoop was, towards the close of the eighteenth century, only worn at court or in full dress, the pocket hoop is ridiculed in 1780 by a print in which a girl so attired is placed beside a donkey laden with a pair of panniers (fig. *h*). For the abolition of the court hoop we are indebted to the taste of George IV. The other excrescence lingered in fashion more or less till the French revolution in 89, which affected the female as powerfully as the male costume of Europe. Fashion, ever in extremes, rushed from high-peaked stays and figured satins, yard-long waists and hooped petticoats, into the lightest and slightest products of the loom, which clung round the form, whether graceful or ungainly, and were girdled absolutely under the armpits. Let those who have laughed at the habits of our ancestors—let the Lady Patroness

Costume of the reign of George III., from various prints.

Fig. *a*, 'Maccaroni Courtship,' 1772; *b*, 1773; *c*, 'Maiden Aunt,' 1776; *d* and *e*, 1777; *f*, 'Trip to Scarborough,' 1778; *g*, 'Good Advice,' 1783; *h*, 'The Modern Hoop,' 1780; *i*, *k*, and *l*, 1783, 1786, 1789, from prints after Hopner.

of Almack's, who would start back with a scream of horror at the idea of figuring in the wimple and gorget of the thirteenth, or the coat-hardie and monstrous head-dresses of the fourteenth, fifteenth, or even eighteenth century, peep into a lady's pocket-book or fashionable magazine, of which the cover is scarcely old—let her recall by such a glance the costume in which she paraded Bond-street and the Park as lately as 1815 or 20, (remembering at the same time that the fashions of the reign of Rufus or Henry V. have been rudely copied by monkish illuminators ignorant of the first principle of design, and their natural deformities made still more hideous by a total absence of taste and skill in the delineator, while those of the reigns of George III. and IV. have been displayed by creditable and even first-rate artists[8], to the best advantage,) and then favour us with her honest opinion of the difference between the periods in ugliness and absurdity.

THE UNIFORM OF THE BRITISH ARMY

dates from the commencement of the eighteenth century. Scarlet and blue had long been the two principal colours of the cloth ordered for the array of the king's troops, in accordance with the blazon of the royal standard ; the guide from the commencement of heraldry for the liveries of retainers and domestics having been the armorial bearings of their lord or leader. But the men-at-arms were, during the early periods of our history, covered with mail or plate, and of the lighter armed troops the smallest number

---

[8] Many of the numbers of the Parisian work on fashions, from whence Mrs. Bell's were taken, bear the initials of the admirable Horace Vernet, now president of the French Royal Academy of Painting.

perchance was brought into the field by the sovereign himself, the host comprising the contingents
of the barons, and the followers of every knight
in it wearing the colours of the particular banners
they served and fought under. A white cross was
the general badge of the English troops in the time
of the crusades, and was worn as late as the reign
of Edward IV. In Henry VIII.'s time we find
soldiers in white coats with a red cross, but these
were most probably furnished by the city of London.
And Stow speaks of the marching watch wherein
the archers wore coats of white fustian, signed on
the breast and back with the arms of the city (the
red cross aforesaid). In the sixteenth and seventeenth centuries scarfs of the royal colours, or family
colours, were worn by officers either over the shoulder
or round the waist, and sometimes round the arm.
As armour became abandoned, the necessity for uniform became more apparent, and scarlet with blue
facings was definitively established as that of the
British army during the reign of Queen Anne, at
which time also the pike ceased to be carried, and
the musket and socket bayonet became the general
weapons of the infantry. The cartouch-box supplied
the place of the bandelier; every species of body
armour was discarded, the gorget dwindling into the
ornamental trifle now known by that name. The
red and white feather was worn in the reign of Queen
Anne; the black cockade appeared about the time
of George II.; but we have not been able to trace
its origin, or fix the exact period of its introduction:
it was perhaps assumed in opposition to the white
cockade, the well-known badge of the Jacobite
party. Italy furnished Europe with its harness of
plate, and Germany seems to have contracted for the
supply of its uniform. The Prussian sugar-loaf cap
was adopted with the Prussian tactics; and the uni-

form of the grenadiers of 1745 has been handed down to posterity by Hogarth, in his ' March to Finchley.' At that time the officer's sash, which had succeeded to the scarf, was still worn like its prototype over the shoulder, and as in the Dutch army to this day.

In the London Chronicle for 1762, vol. xi., a writer says, " I hope no person will think us disaffected, but when we meet any of the new-raised infantry wearing the buttons of their hats bluff before, and the trefoil white worsted shaking as they step, we cannot help thinking of French figure dancers."

In the reign of George III. the sugar-loaf cap of the grenadiers was exchanged for the present mountain or muff of bear-skin, and the abolition of flowered and pomatumed heads, three-cornered cocked hats and pigtails took place during the last war; the hat being first superseded by a cap with a shade and high brass plate in front (1800), and finally by the present shako (1816).

The coat and waistcoat followed the fashion of the time. The large skirts of the former were first doubled back to a button in the centre, a fashion preserved in the jacket that succeeded it (1813) and the coatee (1820) of the present day, when the necessity no longer exists. The white breeches and black gaiters were, during the last reign (1823), exchanged for trousers, and the long white gaiters with black buttons and garters, worn as state dress by the foot guards, were at the same time exchanged for white trousers and gaiters.

The three-cornered gold-lace cocked hat was retained by the life guards as late as their first campaign in the Peninsula, and their cropping and docking have been commemorated by the waggish authors of the Rejected Addresses in their imitation of the ultra-loyal Fitzgerald :—

"Though humbled Gallia scoff,
God bless their pigtails though they're now cut off."

The said pigtails having been shortened to seven inches in 1804, and taken off entirely in 1808. The cocked hat was succeeded by a helmet with a horse-tail flowing down the back (1812), after the fashion of the French dragoons and cuirassiers, and as if to make "assurance double sure," our gallant fellows were armed with the breast-plate immediately after the battle of Waterloo, in which they had proved themselves more than a match for cavalry so defended. The bear-skin crest was substituted for the horse-tail (1817), and the grenadier fur cap was tried upon the heads of the life guards during the last reign, but speedily abandoned, being found too cumbrous and oppressive, and the helmet with its bear-skin crest returned to [9]. The Blues exchanged their buff belts for their present white appointments in 1821. The principal change in the light cavalry was the revival of the lance and the equipment of the regiments so armed in the Polish uniform, and the last important alteration is that just made by his present Majesty, who has been pleased to command that scarlet shall be the uniform of every regiment in the service, with the exceptions of the rifle brigade and the life guards blue.

THE NAVY OF ENGLAND

was distinguished by no particular costume from that of the army till the time of George II. Naval commanders wore scarlet in the reign of Elizabeth by her majesty's order, and that order was confirmed by James I. as we have stated in the proper place. During the subsequent reigns that regulation was

[9] While this work is passing through the press, the grenadier fur caps have been again ordered for the life guards.

neglected, and naval officers appear to have been habited according to their own fancy, and armed like the military, while their ships' companies were sometimes clothed like the land forces in the colours of their captain.   Our tars are too gallant to feel annoyed by the information that their long-cherished uniform was first worn by a lady. In 1748 George II. accidentally met the Duchess of Bedford on horseback in a riding-habit of blue faced with white, and was so pleased with the effect of it that, a question having been just raised as to the propriety of deciding upon some general dress for the royal navy, he immediately commanded the adoption of those colours[10] ; a regulation which appears never to have been gazetted, nor does it exist in the records of the Admiralty office, although a subsequent one, in 1757, refers to it.   Epaulettes are a recent addition to the uniform, and were at first considered a species of dandyism.   The heroic Nelson, who was in after-life so proud of his well-won stars and orders that he made himself a mark for the fatal bullet in his last action by an unnecessary display of them, declared in a letter, the extract of which was lately read at the Society of Antiquaries[11], that he should certainly "*cut the acquaintance*" of two officers (one of them the late gallant Sir Alexander Ball), in consequence of their mounting epaulettes in imitation of military foppery.   The three-cornered cocked hat was worn by the common sailors as late as the reign of George III.   In the London Chronicle, 1762, we are told that sailors wear the sides of their hats uniformly

[10] This traditionary, but certainly authentic information was communicated by Mr. Locker, one of the commissioners of Greenwich Hospital, to Mr. Ellis, and formed part of an interesting paper on the subject of the Naval Uniforms, read by the latter gentleman at the Society of Antiquaries, Thursday, March 18th, 1830.

[11] Thursday, March 18th, 1830.

tacked down to the crown, and look as if they carried a triangular apple-pasty upon their heads.   An
enormous pigtail is still worn by some of our
" jolly jack tars," and has occasionally, we have been
told, offered an effectual resistance to the edge of an
enemy's cutlass.

His present Majesty, King William IV., himself a
sailor, has changed the facings to scarlet, which,
together with the gold-laced blue trousers introduced
by King George IV. have given, in our humble
opinion, much too military a character to the uniform.
The costume consecrated by the victories of St. Vincent, Aboukir, and Trafalgar; the glorious badge of
the hundred triumphs which have established our
supremacy on the ocean, that was never seen upon
a sauntering midshipman in the streets of London
without awaking a glow of pride and gratitude in
the hearts of those " who live at home at ease," has
been confounded with the old artillery uniform,—a
livery equally honourable we admit, and as highly
distinguished, but certainly not so truly national as
that of the service which England may be said to
have created—which has grown with her growth
and strengthened with her strength, and the decay of
which will be the first melancholy signal of her own
destruction.

> " Britannia needs no bulwarks,
>   No towers along the steep :
>   Her march is on the mountain wave,
>   Her home is on the deep !"

Chapter XXIII.

NATIONAL COSTUME OF SCOTLAND.

Scotch brooch of silver, from Mr. Logan's work.

No rational doubt can exist of the great antiquity of the national costume of Scotland; that the chequered stuff which still forms it is the variously-coloured garment of the Gauls described by Diodorus, at one time the common habit of every Celtic tribe, but now abandoned by all their descendants except the hardy unsophisticated Gaelic mountaineer, is admitted, we believe, by every antiquary who has made public his opinion on the subject. But to the same extent that our credence is given to the fact is our wonder awakened that the existence of so peculiar a habit should have been passed unnoticed by every chronicler and traveller, whether native or foreign, for upwards of a thousand years! Yet such is the case, as far as we have been able to discover. The Scots are first mentioned by Porphyry towards the end of the third century; they are noticed again by Ammianus Marcellinus in 360, and by Claudian in 390. Under the name of Caledonians, however, we have an account of them by Tacitus as early as the close of the first century; but he merely describes them in general terms as in a state of great barbarity.

Herodian, Xiphilin, and Isidore speak of them as naked savages, with stained or punctured bodies, wearing iron rings round their middles. Gildas describes the Scots and Picts of his time as having only a piece of cloth tied round the loins; and the whole host of Saxon, Norman, English, French, aye, and Scotch chroniclers, down to the fifteenth century, are silent respecting a costume which must have excited the curiosity of foreigners by its singularity, and constituted the pride of the natives from its antiquity.

Fordun, the historian of Scotland, who wrote in 1350, contents himself with describing the Highlanders as " of goodly person, but mis-shapen attire;" and Froissart, the minute and pictorial Froissart, in his account of Edward III.'s expedition in 1326, merely tells us, that ten thousand pairs of old worn-out shoes, made of undressed leather, with the hair on, were left behind by the Scotch on that midnight retreat which baffled the English, and terminated the inglorious campaign.

The seals and monuments of the early kings and nobles of Scotland represent them armed and attired in the same fashion as their Anglo-Norman cotemporaries. Illuminated MSS. afford us no assistance; and Lesly, Buchannan, and Beague, all writers of the sixteenth century, bear the first unequivocal testimony to the existence and prevalence of a party-coloured garment in Scotland. To these three au-

thors may be added the writer of a chronicle of the
same date, preserved in Lord Somers's Tracts, who
tells us, "the inhabitants of the Western Isles de-
lighted to wear marled cloths, specially that have
long stripes of sundry colours. Their predecessors
used short mantles or plaids of various colours, sundry
ways divided, and amongst some the custom is observed to this day; but for the most part now they
are brown, most near to the colour of the hadder
(heather), to the effect when they lie among the
hadder the bright colours of their plaids shall not
betray them."

At the same time John Major, who wrote the
history of his native country in Latin, merely remarks
their being without stockings or covering for the legs,
and wearing a cloak for an upper garment; and
Lindsay of Piscottie, whose chronicle of Scotland,
from 1437 to 1542, is in the vulgar tongue, says,
"the other pairts northerne are full of mountaines,
and very rude and homelie kynd of people doth in-
habite, which is called the Reid-Shankis or Wyld
Scotes. They be clothed with ane mantle, with ane
schirt, faschioned after the Irisch manner, going
bair-legged to the knee;" but not a word of the
chequered pattern of these garments. Indeed, unless
"faschioned after the Irisch manner" relates to their
cut alone ; he implies by that expression that the
shirt or body-dress was the *leni-croich*, or large
saffron-coloured shirt worn by the Irish of that day,
and which Mr. Logan, in his ' History of the Gael,'
informs us, but without quoting his authority, was
actually worn by the Scotch Highlanders [1].

The authentic portraits of royal and noble personages of Scotland engraved in Mr. Lodge's beautiful
work, comprising those of the Regent Murray; George
Gordon, Marquis of Huntley; Henry, Lord Darnley,

[1] History of the Gael, 2 vols. 8vo. London.

King of Scotland; David Leslie, first Lord of
Newark; James Hamilton, Earl of Arran; James
Graham, Marquis of Montrose; Archibald Campbell,
Marquis of Argyll; William Kerr, Earl of Lothian.;
John Leslie, Duke of Rothes, &c. &c. exhibit no
trace of a national costume, and the painting of the
Surrender of Mary, Queen of Scots, at Carberry Hill,
engraved by Vertu, and representing the royal and
confederated Scotch forces in battle array, appears
equally destitute of any distinction of dress, though
the banners of the respective leaders are scrupulously
emblazoned, and the artist, one should suppose,
could not have been ignorant of the existence of
a national habit at that time in Scotland [2].

There appears to us but one way of accounting
for so strange a discrepancy. The striped and chequered "garb of old Gaul" must have fallen into
disuse throughout the southern and most civilized
portions of Scotland at a very early period, and its
manufacture and wear have been confined to the
Western Isles and the remotest retreats of the ancient
Celtic population, from whence it may have been
gradually re-adopted by the Highland clans during
the seventeenth century, and its popularity increased
by its assumption by Charles Edward, "the young
chevalier," and the subsequent prohibitory statutes
which the rebellion gave rise to.

But it is time for us to retrace our steps and
examine more narrowly into the texture, form, and
manner of wearing this ancient and singular habit,

---

[2] One of the earliest representations of a Highlander is to be
found in Speed's maps of Scotland, published at the commencement of the seventeenth century. The figure has merely a chequered mantle flung over its shoulders, being, with that exception,
perfectly naked. The Highland woman is wrapped in a similar
cloth, which is drawn over her head as well. No great dependence
can be placed upon their fidelity.

which is identified throughout modern Europe with the name Scotland.

With all our aversion from speculation and jealousy of tradition we find ourselves in this instance without other guides, and must consequently either lay down our pen at once or follow them with it to the verge of probability. We have already stated that the earliest known authorities who allude to the chequered dress are of the sixteenth century. Heron, however, in his History of Scotland, says, that in Argyle and the Hebridæ, before the middle of the fifteenth century, tartan was manufactured of one or two colours for the poor, more varied for the rich.

Now the word tartan is derived by Mr. Logan from the Gaelic *tarstin* or *tarsuin*, " across ;" but the French had the word *tiretaine* for a woollen cloth as early as the thirteenth century (vide p. 118), which generally appears to have been dyed of a whole colour, and originally scarlet; while the true Gaelic term for the Highland plaid or mantle is *breacan-feile*, literally the " chequered, striped, or spotted covering," and, as we have already mentioned in the first chapter of this work, the party-coloured cloth woven by the Gauls and Britons was by them called *breach* and *brycan*, from *breac*, speckled or spotted. The word tartan therefore, whatever may be its origin, is, we are inclined to believe, the name of the material itself, and not of the pattern it may be worked in [3]. In a wardrobe account of the time of James III. of Scotland, A. D. 1471, quoted by Mr. Logan, occurs an entry of " an elne and ane halve of blue tartane to

[3] *Tarsa, tarsin,* and *tarsna* is used for across, athwart, over, through, past, and would apply to the crossing of threads in the weaving of any sort of cloth, and, with the exception of *tarsnan,* which signifies a cross-beam, the root *tars* or *tart,* in all its combinations, expresses things which cross so minutely as to deceive the sense, as the spokes of a wheel in motion, light shining through glass, &c.

lyne his gowne of cloth of gold," and of "halve au elne of doble tartane to lyne collars to her lady the quene;" and in 1485 our own Henry VII. displayed in Bosworth Field a banner of "yellow tarterne," on which was painted a dun cow. That it was a stuff much used for banners as well as dresses in the fifteenth century appears evident from the order of Richard III. (in the document quoted page 215 of this work) for the furnishing of "350 pensills (small streamers) of tarteryn," as well as the same number " of buckram," gonfanons " of fustian," standards and trumpet banners of sarcenet, &c.,[and it seems to have been superseded in modern days by the "bunt-ing," of which our ship-colours and other flags are now made[4].

Mr. Logan informs us that woollen cloths " were first woven of one colour, or an intermixture of the natural black and white, so often seen in Scotland to the present day." And we may add, that it will be recognized by our readers as the stuff lately rendered fashionable for trousers, under the name of " shep-herd's plaid." The introduction of several colours we have seen, however, dates from the earliest period of its manufacture, and it is asserted, both in Ireland and in Scotland, that the rank of the wearer was indi-cated by the number of colours in his dress, which were limited by law to seven for a king or chief, and four for the inferior nobility[5]; while, as we have already quoted from Heron, it was " made of one or

[4] As these tartans are charged at the rate of nearly sixteen shillings per yard, they must have been of a superior texture to the common breachan worn by the Western Islanders and the peasantry of Argyleshire; the latter was the coarse homespun woollen cloth, and it is most probable that the former was that mixture of linen and woollen called linsey woolsey by the English and *tiretaine* by the French to this day.

[5] In the law of colours, the Ilbreachta of Tigheirnmas, men-tioned in page 354 of this work.

two colours" (that is to say plain, or merely chequered
with another colour) "for the poor." Of the superior breachans, Mr. Logan informs us, that green and
black, with a red stripe, seems to have predominated;
and in an Italian MS. of the close of the fourteenth
century, in the library of his Royal Highness the
Duke of Sussex, containing a multitude of illuminations illustrative of scripture history, the curtains
of the tabernacle are repeatedly depicted of those
identical colours disposed in the exact pattern of the
modern tartan.

This variegated stuff was also called by the Highlanders *cath-dath*, commonly translated, as Mr.
Logan informs us, " war colour," but ingeniously
rendered by a friend of that gentleman, " the strife of
colours," an etymology which has certainly the high
merit of being as probable as it is poetical and characteristic. The epithet is exactly such as a Highland
senachie would have applied to the splendid breachan
of his chieftain.

The breachan or plaid, we are told by the same
writer, was originally a large mantle of one piece,
belted round the body, and thence called "the belted
plaid;" and he seems to consider that it was also
called the *triughas* or *truis*, the word being derived
from the root *trus*, gather, *truss* or tuck up; that it
formed of itself the entire ancient dress, and that the
latter appellation was transferred to the pantaloons
and stockings joined, which were adopted on the prohibition of the ancient dress. But not only have we
positive evidence of the truis forming a remarkable
portion of the original Gaulish, British, and Irish
dress, but Mr. Logan himself almost immediately
afterwards proceeds to describe them as either knit
like stockings, or, *according to the ancient manner*,
formed of tartan cloth, nicely fitted to the shape, and
fringed down the leg; adding that "there is pre-

served a Gaelic saying respecting this garment," by
which the quantity of stuff required for its making
may be ascertained. We must surely, therefore, be
under some error in understanding him to deny the
antiquity of the truis.

In support of his assertion, however, he quotes the
historians Major and Lindsay, who describe the
Highlanders as bare-legged from the knee, and instances the many curious expedients resorted to in the
rebellion to evade wearing breeches according to the
royal order, with the declaration of an old Highland
farmer, that " he would never lippen to a bodach that
wore the breeks." But their disuse by the lower
classes, in the seventeenth and eighteenth centuries,
is no proof of their non-existence at a much earlier
period ; and if the truis were so much the object of
their aversion and contempt, and not acknowledged a
portion of their ancient national costume, how comes
it that the young Pretender, who, during his romantic
expedition into England, marched on foot from Car-
lisle to Derby in the Highland garb at the head of his
forces, and had assumed that garb undoubtedly for
the sake of flattering the prejudices of his Gaelic followers, should have worn the obnoxious articles, as
he certainly did ? Vide engraving given herewith,
from a portrait of him in that identical costume.

Nay, more! If the truis are not parts of the
ancient Highland dress, why are they named amongst
the prohibited articles of apparel in the Act of 1747,
quoted by Mr. Logan himself, and ordaining that
" neither man nor boy, except such as should be employed as officers and soldiers, should, on any pre-
tence, wear or put on the clothes commonly called
Highland clothes, viz. the plaid, phillibeg or little
kilt, *trouze,* shoulder-belts, or any part whatsoever of
what peculiarly belongs to the Highland garb, and
that no tartan or party-coloured plaid should be used
for great coats or upper coats?" We copy the para-

graph from Mr. Logan's own pages. The "breeks,"
attempted to be forced upon the nether limbs of the
brawny Highlanders, were the Lowland and English
knee-breeches of George II.'s reign, with all the
buttons and buckles thereunto belonging.

Prince Charles Edward Stuart, from a portrait in the possession of
Mr. G. A. Williams, Cheltenham.

The *phillibeg* or *kilt*, in Gaelic, *feile-beag*, i. e. the
" little covering," is another bone of contention
amongst the writers on Celtic antiquities. At present it is a petticoat in the modern sense of the word,
being a separate article of attire and put on like a
woman's petticoat; but originally, we have no doubt,
it signified literally a " little coat," being the corresponding habit to the Irish *cota*, *filleadth* or *fallings*[6],
and the British *pais*, which, with the mantle and the

  [6] *Fillead*, in Irish, is used to express a garment folded or
plaited round the person, and *fillead-beg* would signify the
" lesser plaited dress."

trousers, formed the complete Gaulish or Celtic costume. *Kilt* is a lowland Scotch or Saxon appellation, and also signifies a shortened or tucked-up garment. "To kilt" is to truss or tuck up. The lassie says, in the well-known song,—

> " I'll kilt my coats aboon my knee,
> And follow my laddie through the water."

The period of the separation of the ancient *feile-beag* into a waistcoat and kilt is at present unknown, but we imagine it to have been a comparatively recent arrangement.

The *sporan* or pouch is a distinguishing feature of the Highland costume; but its first adoption, in its present peculiar and ornamented form, is equally involved in mystery. That of Simon Frazer, Lord Lovat, executed in 1746, is said, by Mr. Logan, to have been smaller and less decorated. A wallet, or *dorlach*, carried on the right side, was worn as early as the fourteenth century, as we have evidence, in the effigy of a knight in the cathedral church of Iona or Ilcolmkill[7]; and some such appendage to the girdle is of very early occurrence in the costume of most nations. The tasselled sporan is however more like the pouch of a North American Indian, than the European gypsire or aulmoniere of the middle ages, and its position in front is an additional peculiarity.

Coverings for the head were little cared for by the hardy Celtic and Teutonic tribes; but a cap or bonnet (*cappan* and *boined*), answering the double purpose of a hat and a helmet, was occasionally worn by their chiefs, as much perhaps for distiction as for defence. Its material was originally leather, and its shape, amongst the Britons and the Irish, conical. The flat cloth bonnet, now worn in Scotland, we do not consider to have formed part of the primitive costume. If ancient, it is of Saxon, Norman, or

[7] Vide Hamilton Smith's Ancient Costume of England, &c. pl. 21,

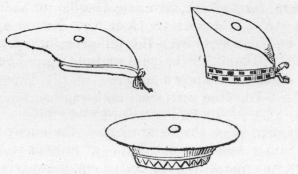

Scotch bonnets from Mr. Logan's work.

Danish introduction. A cap, not very dissimilar, occurs in English costume as early as the reign of Henry III.; and one shape, though not the best known of the Scotch bonnet, bears a curious affinity to the still earlier Phrygian cap worn by the Saxon, the Anglo-Norman, and most probably the Dane. Its colour, blue, was very early distinguished as the favourite colour of the Caledonians, but the chequered band, which now generally surrounds it, according to General Stewart, originated as lately as Montrose's struggle, when it was assumed as a badge of the fallen family of the Stewarts; the arms of their house being a fess, checquy azure and argent in a field, Or; in which case we must presume it was originally white and blue. The general colours are now white and red, or red and blue, alterations likely enough to have been made by the victorious party, either then, in the time of Cromwell, when the cross of St. George (gules in a field argent) displaced the royal arms, or in the rebellions of 1716 and 1745, when red and blue had become the colours of the reigning family.

A much older decoration of the bonnet is undoubtedly to be found in the eagle feather, the peculiar mark of a chief, and the sprigs of holly, broom, and other plants assumed by the various clans; a sort of natural heraldry which supplied the place of the emblazoned shield or embroidered badge, and preceded, it is most probable, the distinction of the family Tartans.   Mr. Logan gives a curious list of the badges of this description appropriated by the different clans; and some of the Frazers and Mackensies were subjected to penalties for wearing them after the disarming act of 1745.

The chequered stockings, gartered round the calf of the leg, are assuredly not of Celtic origin.   To the Saxon or the Dane, whose cross garterings and half stockings or soccas, we have described in the second and third chapters of this work, the North Britons must surely have been indebted for this portion of their attire.   The garter, as worn at present with a rose, is altogether a modern innovation.

The primitive shoes have been described by Froissart from ten thousand specimens.   Like the *brogue* of the Irish and the British *esgid*, they were made of untanned leather with the hair on.   With the modern shoe came the shoe-buckle : its introduction is dated by Mr. Logan about 1680.

The principal ornaments of the Celtic Gaël were the *brooch* and the *belt*; the first of silver, and sometimes of exceeding magnitude, embellished with cairn gorums, and other gems both native and foreign.   Bruce's brooch was long, and may be still in the possession of the MacDougles, of Lorn.   Another similar relic is in the custody of the Campells, of Glenlyon, and is engraved in Pennant.   The belt was also highly ornamented, principally with silver, from the earliest periods.   Ferash or Fergus, a Scottish knight, is described in the Norse account of Haco's expedition as being despoiled of his beautiful belt by the victor[8].

To sum up our account of the ancient Highland dress in a few words, we see no reason for doubting that it consisted of the mantle, close vest, and

[8] Johnston's translation, p. 99.

trousers, worn by the ancient British and Irish, and Belgic Gauls, with scarcely any variation, with the brooch, bodkin, or fibula, the hairy shoes, the belt, and, in the earliest periods, perchance the torque.

The Saxon and Danish fashions by degrees obtained in the Lowlands, and the intermarriages of the English and Scottish royal families, and the long and close alliance between Scotland and France, contributed to assimilate the costume of the court and the larger burghs and cities to that which prevailed at the moment throughout Europe. The Gaël or Wild Scots, as they were termed, kept aloof from the despised and detested Sassenaghs or Saxons, as they contemptuously termed their lowland countrymen who had associated with, imitated the fashions, and adopted the language of the English colonists, and by the imperfect medium of oral tradition alone are we enabled to arrive at the little knowledge we possess of this singular and primitive people. The precise periods, therefore, when slight alterations took place in their national attire, if recorded at all, must be so in their national ballads, or in the retentive memories of their bards and elders, which are as remarkable as the excessive longevity of the Highlanders in general.

THE FEMALE HABIT

seems to have resembled to a very late period the dress in which Boadicea has been described by Dion Cassius. A tunic or robe gathered and girdled round the waist, and a large mantle fastened by a brooch upon the breast.

The former called the airisard appears from the poems of Alexander MacDonald to have been worn as late as 1740.

White twilled cloth made from fine wool, and called cuirtan [9], was used for interior garments and

[9] " Cuirt" signifies trade or manufacture, and " an" is a Gaelic

hose, by those who indulged in such superfluities.
The latter, denominated *ossan*, evidently from *hosen*,
were of different dimensions, and the larger sort was
called *ossan-preasach.*

The hair before marriage was uncoverd, the head
bound by a simple fillet or snood, sometimes a lock
of considerable length hanging down on each side of
the face, and ornamented with a knot of ribands—a
teutonic fashion. When privileged to cover it, the
curch, curaichd or *breid* of linen, was put on the
head and fastened under the chin, falling in a tapering form on the shoulders. The female costume,
especially of the higher orders, varied in the Lowlands according to the fashionable barometers of
London or Paris ; but an " English gentleman who
visited Edinburgh in 1598, says, the citizens' wives,
and women of the country, did weare cloaks made
of a coarse cloth of two or three colours in chequer-
work, vulgarly called ploddan ;" and " plaiding" is
still the term for the chequered tartans in the Lowlands. The large or full plaid is now worn only by
elderly females ; but during the last century Bird
tells us it was the undress of ladies in Edinburgh,
who denoted their political principles by the manner
of wearing it.

For the

ARMOUR AND WEAPONS

of the Scottish nation we have store of authorities.

Commencing with the Roman invasion, we find
the Scots, like their southern kindred, stripping themselves naked for fight. Stained from head to foot
with their war-paint, and wielding long heavy swords
and round targets [10]. The inhabitants of the coast of

diminutive: hence in the Celtic manner of compounding words
chirtan would mean the lesser or finer manufacture,
[10] Tacitus in Vita. Agricola. Herodian,

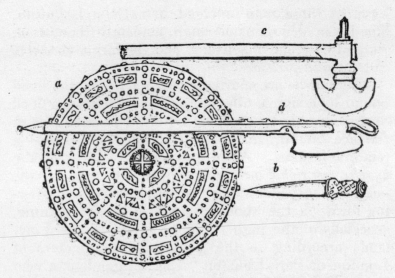

Fig. *a*, Highland target; *b*, a dirk or bidag; *c*, a Jedburgh axe; *d*, a
Lochaber axe : all in the Meyrick collection.

Strathmavern were called Catini, from their use of
the cat, a four-sided or four-spiked club, which they
darted forward at their enemy and recovered by a,
leather thong attached to it.   The Caledonians used
also a spear, furnished with a similar thong, for the
like purpose, and at the butt-end of the shaft it had
a ball of brass filled with pieces of metal to startle the
horses by the noise when engaged with cavalry.

The ringed byrn of the Saxon, and the improved
hauberk of the Norman, soon found their way across
the border, but were adopted by the sovereign and his
lowland chiefs alone ; for though the early monarchs
of Scotland appear upon their seals in the nasal
helmet, and the mascled, ringed, or scaly armour of
the Anglo-Normans, we find the Earl of Strathearne,
at the battle of the Standard, in 1138, exclaiming
" I wear no armour, yet they who do will not ad-
vance beyond me this day."

In the next century Matthew Paris describes the
Scottish cavalry as a fine body of men, well mounted,

though their horses were neither of the Italian or Spanish breed ; the horsemen clothed in armour of iron network [11], and from this period we find the seals, monuments, and chronicles of Scotland agreeing as nearly as possible with those of England, the Scotch being only later in their adoption of the improvements in armour, which generally originated in the south of Europe, and gradually travelled northward.

The Highlanders, however, evinced their wonted contempt for the inventions of the Sassenach, and adhered to their ancient weapons and mode of warfare. Body armour would they none; as the old song says, they

> " Had only got the belted plaid,
> While they (the Lowlanders) were mail-clad men."

Those who encountered Haco at Largs, A. D. 1263, were armed with bows and spears ; the former being a true Highland weapon, though the Gael could never cope with the English archers, who were proverbially said to bear each of them " under his girdle twenty-four Scots," in allusion to the twenty-four arrows with which each man was provided. Winton and Fordun both mention the clan Kay and the clan Quhale, in 1390, armed in the fashion of their country with bows and arrows, sword and target, short knives and battle-axes; and twelve years afterwards Donald, Lord of the Isles, broke in upon the earldom of Ross, at the head of his fierce multitudes, who were armed after the fashion of their country with swords fitted to cut and thrust[12], pole-axes, bows and arrows, short knives, and round bucklers formed of wood or strong hide, with bosses of brass or iron. The short knife was the *bidag* or *dirk* of the Scotch,

---

[11] Sub anno 1244, p. 436, 37.

[12] The cut and thrust sword was the *claidheamh-more.* or claymore,

the *skiene* of the Irish. Although most probably it
is far more highly ornamented at present than it was
in those rude ages, the ancient style of decoration and
pattern is preserved. The intricate tracery on the
hilt is also seen upon the target or targaid—

> " Whose brazen studs and tough bull's hide
> Has dashed so often death aside."

The target here engraved is preserved in the armoury at Goodrich Court.

The dirk or bidag from the same collection is of
the time of Henry VIII.

In 1318, every layman possessed of land, who had
ten pounds' worth of moveable property, was commanded to provide himself with an acton (or haqueton), and basnet (bascinet), together with gloves of
plate, a sword, and a spear. Those who were not
so provided were to have an iron jack, or back and
breast-plate of iron, an iron head-piece or knapiskay,
with gloves of plate ; and every man possessing the
value of a cow, was commanded to arm himself with
a bow and sheaf of twenty-four arrows, or with a
spear[13]. By the iron jack is meant the jacques de
maille, which was worn as late as the sixteenth century, at which period it is described by a French
author, and the person who furnished Holinshed
with his account of Scotland.

In 1385 an order was issued for every French and
Scottish soldier to wear a white St. Andrew's cross
on his breast and back, which if his surcoat or jacket
was white, was to be broidered on a division of black
cloth[14].

In 1388 the Scotch army at the siege of Berwicke

---

[13] Statutes of Robert I.; vide Cartulary of Uberbrothock, p. 233,
M'Farlane's trans.

[14] Acts of the Parliament of Scotland, vol. i.

was astonished by two novelties—the appearance of
artillery, and the heraldic crests upon the English
helmets; an ornament which had not been adopted
in Scotland, though worn for nearly a hundred years
in England.

> " Twa noweltyes that day they saw,
>   That forwith Scotland had been nane:
>   Tymmeris (timbres) for helmetys war the tane,
>   The tothyr crakys were of war."

During the reign of James I. of Scotland, archery
was particularly encouraged, and an order was issued
that all men aged upwards of twelve years " should
busk them to be archers." James III. is said to
have had ten thousand Highlanders with bows and
arrows in the van of his army; and the army of
James V. at Fala, immediately previous to the defeat
at Solway in 1542, consisted of sixty thousand men,
" twenty thousand of whom carried pikes and
spears, and twenty thousand were armed with bows,
habergions, and two-handled swords, " which was
the armour," says Lindsay, " of our Highlandmen."
By this it would appear that in the sixteenth century
the Highlanders, in the royal service at least, had
been induced to wear the same body armour; the
word habergeon at this period meaning indifferently
a breast-plate or a short coat of mail. A French
author in 1574 describes the Scotch as armed with
a sword that was very large and marvellously cutting; and at this period the blades made by Andrea
Ferara became highly prized in Scotland, and whenever procured were fitted into *basket hilts,* which
first appear about this time. An Andrea Ferara,
with its original mounting, is here engraved from
one in the Meyrick collection.

The introduction of hand fire-arms added first the

pistol[15] and afterwards the musket to
the weapons of the Highlander, who
decorated them with silver as liberally
as he had previously done his belt
and his bidag; but the bow continued to be used by him throughout
the seventeenth century, and the last
time it appeared as a British military
weapon was in 1700, when the regiment of Royal Scots, commanded by
the Earl of Orkney, was " armed in
the old Highland fashion, with bows
and arrows, swords and targets, and
wore steel bonnets."

In the unfortunate rebellions of
1714 and 1745, the Highland bidags
and broadswords upon several occasions put the royal forces, cavalry
and infantry, to the rout in less than
seven minutes. The charge of the
Highlanders is described by all writers
as almost irresistible. Firing their
pistols as they advanced, they flung
the discharged weapons at the heads
of their foes, and if bullet and blow
failed to bring down their opponent,

[15] The pistol was sometimes called *dag*, from
the peculiar shape of its butt. The Highlanders
called it *tack*. A Highland fire-lock *tack*, of the
time of George II., the stock of iron and inlaid
with silver, is engraved here from one in the
armoury at Goodrich Court. A brace of snaphaunce Highland tacks are in the same collection, dated 1626, with slender barrels,
which, as well as the stocks, are wholly of
brass.

An Andrea Ferara, with its original hilt, in the Meyrick collection.

they received the point of his bayonet on the target, and dirk or claymore was instantly through his body. Their muskets were invariably thrown away after the first volley, and as late as the battle of Killicranky they flung off their plaids on rushing into action, as their Celtic ancestors had done seventeen hundred years before them.

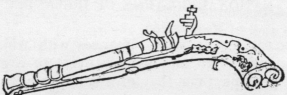

Highland fire-lock tack, time of George II.]

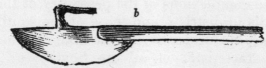

Fig. *a*, battle-axe of the town-guard of Edinburgh; *b*, battle-axe of the town-guard of Aberdeen, from Mr. Logan's work.

Chapter XXIV.

NATIONAL COSTUME OF IRELAND.

CASTING aside the wild romances with which the
early history of Ireland is interwoven, to a greater
degree perhaps than that of any other nation, we
shall proceed at once, upon the authority of Tacitus,
to state that the manners of the Irish differed little
in his time from those of their ancient British
brethren ; and to add, that from every evidence, historical or traditional, the difference was occasioned
by the introduction at some very remote period, either
by conquest or colonization, of a distinct race to its
original inhabitants ;—a fact which is substantiated
by the marked distinction still existing in the persons and complexions of the peasantry of the eastern
and midland districts, and those of the south-western
counties ; the former having the blue eyes and flaxon
hair, characteristic of all the Scythic or German
tribes, and the latter the swarthy cheeks and raven
locks, that bespeak a more southern origin, and point
to Spain as the country from which they had ultimately past, and Asia-Minor, or Egypt, as the land
of their fathers.

In every part of Ireland, weapons and ornaments
have been found precisely similar to those discovered
in England, and proved to have been worn by the
ancient Britons ; and the description of the Irish
dress as late as the twelfth century, by Giraldus
Cambrensis, perfectly corresponds with that of the
Belgic-Gauls and southern Britons, transmitted to

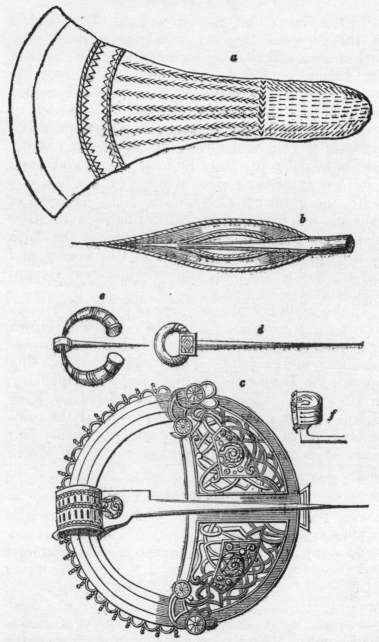

Ancient Irish weapons and ornaments: *a*, engraved battle-axe of bronze, in the possession of Crofton Croker, Esq.; *b*, spear-head of bronze; *c, d, e,* and *f*, brooches, bodkins, &c., from Walker's History of the Irish Bards.

us by the Greek and Roman writers. Undisturbed
by the Imperial Legions, the Irish retained their
ancient arms and clothing for centuries after England
had become a Roman province, and adopted the
costume of its conquerors, and the truis or bracchæ,
the cota and the mantle fastened by a brooch or
bodkin on the breast or shoulder, the torques and
bracelets of gold and silver, the swords and battle-
axes of mixed copper and tin, and spears and darts
headed with the same metal that had gradually superseded the garments of skins, and the weapons of
bone and flint of the original colonists, as in the sister
island, composed the habits and arms of the Irish
chieftains during the early ages of Christianity, and
to the period at which the authentic history of Ireland
commences.

In the ninth century we hear of the Irish princes
wearing pearls behind their ears ; a golden crown
or helmet, of a form resembling the cap of a Chinese
mandarin, and evidently of great antiquity, was dug
up near the Devil's Bit, in the county of Tipperary,
in 1692[1]. A collar of gold was offered by King
Brian on the great altar at Armagh, at the commencement of the eleventh century[2], twenty-four
years subsequent to the period when, as Moore
sings,

" Malachy wore the collar of gold
He won from the proud invader."

From these proud invaders, it appears that the
Irish received, however, some of their first lessons

[1] Engraved in Keating's History of Ireland.
[2] According to the annals of Innisfallen, one of the few unsus-
picious documents relative to the early history of Ireland. The
book of Glen Daloch, popularly attributed to Benin, the disciple
and successor of St. Patrick, commences in the eleventh century ;
and the Brehon laws and the law of colours (Ilbreachta of
Tigheirnmas) are of very uncertain though considerable antiquity.

in warfare, and adopted, in imitation of them, the terrible steel battle-axe, and the round red shield bound with iron.   But these circumstances are gathered from the pages of Giraldus Cambrensis, who has given us a very interesting account of the costume of the Irish in the

TWELFTH CENTURY.

Irish costume of the 12th century, from an illuminated copy of Giraldus Cambrensis, in the possession of Sir T. Phillips, Bart.

" The Irish wear thin woollen clothes, mostly black, because the sheep of Ireland are in general of that colour; the dress itself is of a barbarous fashion. The cochla or cocula, to which was sometimes added the larger mantle worn in Elizabeth's time, was called the canabhas or fillead : they wear moderate close-

cowled or hooded mantles (caputiis), which spread
over their shoulders and reach down to the elbow,
composed of small pieces of cloths of different kinds
and colours, for the most part sewed together[3]; beneath which, woollen fallins (phalinges) instead of a
cloak, or breeches and stockings in one piece, and
these generally dyed of some colour. In riding they
use no saddles, nor do they wear boots or spurs,
carrying only a rod or stick hooked at the upper end,
as well to excite their horses to mend their pace, as
to set forward in full speed ; they use indeed bridles
and bits, but so contrived as not to hinder the horses
of their pasture in a land where these animals feed
only on green grass."

Through the kindness of Sir Thomas Phillips, Bart.,
we are enabled to present our readers with some cotemporary drawings of the Irish costume from an
invaluable manuscript in that gentleman's collection,
which was fortunately preserved from destruction by
being sent from Bristol one day previous to the late
lamentable disturbances and conflagration: it is a
copy of Giraldus Cambrensis, illuminated about the
termination of the twelfth century, and the Irish costume is particularly (and we have no doubt faithfully)
distinguished from the Norman-English ; Dermod
MacMurchard, king of Leinster, and the rest of his
countrymen, being portrayed in the short tunic,
fallings or cota, and the truis, with long beards and
hair, and the Danish axe, and the Normans with long
tunics, gartered legs, shaven faces, and the great broad-
sword of the period. Vide figure of MacMurchard
(the largest) and others of the Irish, at the head

[3] Such at least is our version of the words "variisque colorum
generibus panniculorumque plerumque consutis," which certainly
describes, in rather a roundabout way, what we should now
call patchwork.

of this section. The Irish mantle appears on the shoulders of many of the figures, but the mode of fastening it is not visible ; there are authorities enough, however, to prove that it was by a brooch or bodkin upon the breast[4]. It is singular that it is not party-coloured, as described in the text, nor is the hood attached to it.

About the same period we learn, that when Prince, afterwards King John landed at Waterford, the Irish chieftains came to pay their respects to the son of their monarch, habited in their national costume, wearing linen vests, flowing mantles, long hair, and bushy beards, and approached the prince to offer him, the kiss of peace, which the young Norman courtiers attendant on John considering a familiarity, pre-vented ; and not content with merely repulsing them, pulled the beards which had excited their derision, mimicked their gestures, and finally thrust them with violence from their presence.

THE WEAPONS

used by the Irish in the bloody combats to which this unprovoked insult and aggression gave birth are thus described by Giraldus :—" The Irish use three kinds of arms—short lances, and two darts, as also broad axes excellently well steeled, the use of which they borrowed from Norwegians and Ostmen. They make use of but one hand to the axe when they strike, and extend their thumb along the handle to guide the blow, from which neither the crested hel-

---

[4] See engravings at page 353. The value of silver brooches or bodkins is decided in the Brehon laws. These instruments are known in Ireland by various names ; and are frequently alluded to in the old Irish poems and romances.

met can defend the head, nor the iron folds of the armour the body; whence it has happened in our time that the whole thigh of a soldier, though cased in well-tempered armour, hath been lopped off by a single blow of the axe, the whole limb falling on one side of the horse, and the expiring body on the other." This latter weapon was called by the Irish the tuagh-catha, or battle-axe. There is a hill in the county of Galway called Knock-Tuagha, the hill of axes, from the circumstance of the Irish having gained a victory over the English there by means of their axes. To these "three sorts of arms" Giraldus himself adds another, the sling. "They are also very dexterous and ready, beyond all other nations, in slinging stones in battle, when other weapons fail them, to the great detriment of their enemies;" and in a description of a battle in the annals of Innisfallen, it is related, that the stones came in such rapid showers, that they blunted the arrows in their flight!

Of the ladies' dress, we know nothing further than that it may be inferred from a passage in the annals of Innisfallen, they wore a variety of ornaments, as when the wife of King O'Roorke was taken prisoner, in the year 1152, her jewels became the spoil of the enemy.

The only female figures in the illuminated copy of Giraldus, above mentioned, are attired in long tunics after the Anglo-Norman fashion. There can be little doubt, however, that they wore the mantle fastened on the breast by a bodkin or brooch; and in an Irish romance, quoted by Mr. Walker, we hear of the fair Findalve's spacious veil hanging down from her lovely head, where it was fastened by a golden bodkin. Vol. ii. p. 23. The wearing of bodkins in the hair is so common to this day in Spain, that we can scarcely question the fashion having been derived from that country.

THE ECCLESIASTIC COSTUME

was of course that of the Romish church throughout Europe; and our readers are therefore referred to the corresponding era in England.

In the

FOURTEENTH CENTURY

we find that scarlet cloaks were worn by the Irish chieftains. Amongst the spoils left by the sons of Brian Rae, when they fled from Mortogh, A. D. 1313, were shining scarlet cloaks [5], and the barbaric splendour or quaintness of the Irish chiefs seems to have caught the fancy of the English settlers in the reign of Edward III., as we find the use of it prohibited to them in the celebrated statute of Kilkenny, passed during the administration of Edward's son, the Duke of Clarence. One clause in this act ordains that the English here shall conform in garb and in the cut of their hair to the fashion of their countrymen in England. Whoever affected that of the Irish should be treated as an Irishman; and we need not point out to our readers that the statute evidently meant "ill-treated," so early had the woes and wrongs of that unhappy country begun !

Irish frieze was at this time, however, an esteemed article in England, for a statute passed in the twenty-eighth year of Edward III.'s reign exempts it from

---

[5] Scarlet cloaks were made for the Irish chiefs, by command of King John, who addressed an order to the archbishop of Dublin to that effect. Rymer's Fœdera.

duty under the description of " draps appellez frize-
ware queux sont faitz en Ireland."

In the reign of Richard II. we have first a description, by Froissart, of the four Irish kings who
swore allegiance to that monarch, by which it appears
that the truis had been abandoned, or at this time
was not a part of the regal habit : for Henry Christall, who gave Froissart the information, complains
that they wore no breeches [6], and that consequently
he ordered some of linen cloth to be made for them,
taking from them at the same time many rude and
ill-made things, "tous d'habits comme d'autres
chose," and dressing them in houpelands of silk
furred with miniver and gris : " for," he adds,
" formerly these kings were well dressed if wrapped
up in an Irish mantle." They rode without saddles
or stirrups, the old Irish fashion.

On Richard's first visit to Ireland, in 1394, all the
Leinster chieftains laid aside their caps, skeins, and
girdles, and did homage, and swore fealty on their
knees to the Earl Marshal of England ; and the
same ceremony was performed by the principal chiefs
of Ulster to Richard himself at Drogheda.

The author of the metrical chronicle of the deposition of Richard II., who accompanied him on
his Irish expedition, went with the Earl of Gloucester
to see MacMorough, king of Leinster, and describes
him as riding full speed down hill on a horse without
a saddle, bearing in his hand a long dart, which he

---

[6] But by breeches or brayes may be meant *drawers*, always so
called at that time, and to go without which was esteemed both
in England and France at this period a penance and a shame,
and Christall's ordering them to be made of "linen cloth" is
in favour of our supposition, as to supply the place of truis he
would have ordered garments of woollen cloth, and by the name
of hose or chaussés.

cast from him with much dexterity. To this description is appended an illumination pourtraying Mac Morough in the act of performing this feat, and attended by some of his toparchs. We have engraved it here as an illustration of the

MacMorough, King of Leinster, and his toparchs, from MS. Harleian, marked 1319.

IRISH ARMOUR AND WEAPONS OF THE FOURTEENTH CENTURY.

MacMorough, it will be perceived, wears a bascinet, but without visor or camail, and a long coat of mail, over which is thrown the mantle, and a capuchon like that worn by the English from the time of the Conquest, and which may be indeed the ancient Irish caputium, hangs behind him down his shoulders. His followers wear the capuchon, and no bascinet. The king is bare-footed, and apparently bare-legged, and rides without stirrups. Froissart tells us, on the

authority of Christall, the Irish have pointed knives
with broad blades, sharp on both sides; they cut
their enemy's throat and take out his heart, which
they carry away[7].

THE FIFTEENTH CENTURY

furnishes us with very little direct information. But
by an act passed in the reign of Henry VI. it seems
to be intimated that either the English affected the
Irish, or the Irish the English costume, as it is set
forth that " now there is no diversity in array
betwixt the English marchours and the Irish enemies, and so by colour of the English marchours,
the Irish enemies do come from day to day to other
into the English counties, as English marchours,
and do rob and pill by the highways, and destroy
the common people by lodging upon them in the
nights, and also do kill the husbands in the nights,
and do take their goods to the Irishmen : wherefore
it is ordained and agreed that no manner of man
that will be taken for an Englishman shall have no
beard above his mouth, that is to say, that he have
no hairs on his upper lip, so that the said lip be once
at least shaven every fortnight, or of equal growth
with the nether lip ; and if any man be found
amongst the English contrary hereunto, that then it
shall be lawful to every man to take them and their
goods, as Irish enemies, and to ransom them as Irish
enemies." Whether this similarity of dress was

[7] C. 24. In the army of Henry V., at the siege of Rouen, 1417,
were several bodies of Irish, of whom the greater part had one leg
and foot quite naked; the arms of these were targets, short javelins,
and *a strange kind* of *knives.* Monstrelet's Chron. chap. v. The
"skein" was the strange kind of knife. The " one leg and foot
naked" was a curious uniform.

assumed by the Irish enemies for the purpose of facilitating their inroads and depredations, or the consequence of long neighbourhood and intercommunication, does not appear. The long moustaches worn at this period must certainly have been retained by the English in imitation of the Irish, as beards were not worn in England during the reign of Henry VI. except by aged or official personages. The faces of military men even are seen closely shaved. Another act was passed in this reign forbidding the use of " gilt bridles and peytrals, and other gilt harness."

The military and female costume of persons of distinction appears, from the few monuments preserved of this period, to have resembled the corresponding cotemporary habits in England ; but it is probable, as we shall shortly show, that the ancient national Irish dress was still worn by the generality of the people, and, oddly enough, on the heels of the statute of Henry VI. above quoted, forbidding the English to dress like the Irish, because their was no diversity, comes an act passed by Edward IV., ordaining that " the Irishmen dwelling in the counties of Dublin, Myeth, Wrial, and Kildare, shall go apparelled like Englishmen, and wear beards after the English manner, swear allegiance, and take English surnames," proving that a diversity did exist even in the English pale.

In the reign of Henry VII., Sir Edward Poynings, in order that the parliaments of Ireland might want no decent or honourable form that was used in England, caused a particular act to pass that the lords of Ireland should appear in the like parliament robes as the lords are wont to wear in the parliaments of England. This act is entitled " a statute for the lords of the parliament to wear robes," and the penalty for offending against it was a hundred shillings, to be levied off the offender's lands and goods.

In the sixth year of the same monarch's reign a warm dispute appears to have existed between the glovers and shoemakers about "the right of making girdles, and all manner of girdles." Fine cloth, silk, taffeta, and cloth of gold, are mentioned as worn by the nobility at this time, and worsted and canvas linen for phallangs and mantles, by the poorer classes. Felt caps are also recorded.

THE SIXTEENTH CENTURY

enlightens us considerably, not only as to the dress of its own particular period, bu respecting the ancient Irish costume, of which we have hitherto caught but brief and imperfect glimpses. Pursuing our original determination to set down under each date such documents only as of right belonged to it, we have not interpolated the descriptions of writers of the twelfth century with those of writers of the sixteenth ; but having given these early evidences in their integrity, we may without fear of confusion refer to them occasionally, when the elaborate accounts of such authors as Holinshed, Spenser, and Camden appear to illustrate the obscure allusions of their predecessors.

In the reign of Henry VIII. an act was passed ordaining " that no person or persons, the king's subjects, within this land (Ireland), being or hereafter to be, from and after the first day of May, which shall be in the yeare of our Lord God 1539, shall be shorn or shaven above the ears, or use the wearing of haire upon their heads like unto long lockes, called *glibbes*,

or have or use any haire growing on their upper
lippes, called or named a *crommeal* [8], or use or weare
any shirt, smock, kurchor, bendel, neckerchour,
mocket or linen cappe coloured or dyed with safron,
ne yet use or weare in any of their shirts or smocks
above seven yardes of cloth, to be measured according
to the king's standard, and that also no woman use
or wear any kyrtell or ,cote tucked up or imbroydered
or garnished with silke or couched ne laid with usker,
after the Irish fashion, and that no person or persons
of what estate, condition or degree they be, shall
use or weare any mantles, cote, or hood, made after
the Irish fashion ;" and any person so offending was
liable not only to forfeit the garment worn against
the statute, but certain sums of money limited and
appointed by the act.

In this act, and in the order quoted in the note,
we find mention made of the custom of dyeing the
shirts and tunics with saffron, said by many writers
to have existed in Ireland from the earliest period,
but without their quoting any ancient authority in
support of their statement. Henceforth we find frequent allusions to it; but it is certainly not men-

---

[8] Amongst the unpublished MS. in the State Paper Office, is
another earlier order of Henry VIII., dated April 28, 1563, for
the government of the town of Galway, in which these moustaches
are called *crompeanlis*. The inhabitants are also ordered " not
to suffer the hair of their heads to grow till it covers their ears,
and that every of them wear English caps. That no man or
man-child do wear no mantles in the streets, but cloaks or gowns,
coats, doublets, and hose shapen after the English fashion, but
made of the country cloth, or any other cloth that shall please
them to buy."
" Crom" signifies in the Celtic any thing crooked, also the nose ;
" pean" is the beard of a goat ; and " lis," wicked or mischievous.
" Crompeanlis" is therefore one of those curious compounds
continually met with in this ancient language, and resembling
Greek in the condensed force of expression.

tioned by Giraldus [9], Froissart, or the author of the Natural History before quoted.

In the reign of Elizabeth we find Spenser strongly recommending the abolition of " the antient dress." The mantle he calls " a fit house for an outlaw, a meet bed for a rebel, and an apt cloke for a thief." He speaks of the hood " as a house against all weathers ;" and remarks that while the mantle enables him to go " privilie armed," the being close-hooded over the head conceals his person from knowledge on any to whom he is endangered. He also alludes to a custom of wrapping the mantle hastily about the left arm when attacked, which serves them instead of a target: a common practice in Spain to this day, and probably derived from thence. His objections to the use of mantles by females are as strongly and more grossly urged ; and of the long platted or matted locks, called glibbs, he speaks in terms of equal reprobation: " they are as fit masks as a mantle is for a thief, for wheresoever he hath run himself into that peril of the law that he will not be known, he either cutteth off his glibb by which he becometh nothing like himself, or pulleth it so low down over his eyes that it is very hard to discern his thiefish countenance [10]." He concludes, however, by

[9] Unless by "some colour" and "various colours" we are at liberty to conclude that saffron or yellow was amongst them. Had it been the prevailing colour he would surely have particularized it ; and yet, on the other hand, the shirt and truis in the illuminated copy before mentioned are both frequently painted a light yellow or tawney.

[10] Hooker, who translated Giraldus in 1587, adds this note upon the Irish manner of wearing the hair: "The Irish nation and people, even from the beginning, have beene alwaies of a hard bringing up, and are not only rude in apparell but also rough and ouglie in their bodies. Their beards and heads they never wash, cleanse, nor cut, especiallie their heads ; the haire whereof they suffer to grow, saving that some do use to round it, and by reason the same is never combed it groweth fast together,

admitting that there is much to be said in favour of the fitness of the ancient dress to the state of the country, "as, namely, the mantle in travelling, because there be no inns where meet bedding may be had, so that his mantle serves him then for a bed ; the leather-quilted jack in journeying and in camping, for that it is fittest to be under his shirt of mail, and for any occasion of sudden service, as there happen many, to cover his trouse on horseback ; the great linen roll which the women wear to keep their heads warm after cutting their hair, which they use in any sickness ; besides their thick-folded linen shirts, their *long-sleeved smocks*, their *half-sleeved coats*, their silken fillets, and all the rest, they will devise some colour for, either of necessity, of antiquity, or of comeliness."

Stanihurst, who wrote in the reign of Elizabeth, and whose account of Ireland is published in Holinshed's Chronicles, speaking of Waterford, says, " As they distill the best aqua vitæ, so they spin the choicest rug in Ireland. A friend of mine being of late demurrant in London, and the weather, by reason of a hard hoare frost, being somewhat nipping, repaired to Paris Garden clad in one of these Waterford rugs. The mastifs had no sooner espied him, but deeming he had beene a beare would faine have baited him ; and were it not that the dogs were partly muzzled and partly chained, he doubted not but that he should have beene well tugd in this Irish rug ; whereupon he solemnlie vowed never to see beare baiting in any such weed."

In 1562, O'Neal, Prince of Ulster, appeared at the court of Elizabeth with his guards of Galloglacks,

and in process of time it matteth so thick and fast together that it is instead of a hat, and keepeth the head verie warme, and also will beare off a great blowe or stroke, and this head of haire they call a gliba, and therein they have a great pleasure."

bare-headed, armed with hatchets, their hair flowing
in locks on their shoulders, attired in shirts dyed with
saffron (vel humana urina infectis) ; their sleeves
large, their tunics short, and their cloaks shagged[11].

This passage has been very loosely translated by
several writers, and the expression "thrum jackets"
introduced, which is not at all borne out by the
original, "tuniculis brevioribus et lacernis villosis."
Amongst the rare prints collected by the late Mr.
Douce is one presenting us with the Irish dress of
this day, precisely as described by Camden, Spenser,
and Derricke, with whose poetical and picturesque
account of the Kerns or common soldiers we shall
close our account of the Irish in the sixteenth century :—

> "With skulls upon their powles
>   Instead of civill cappes,
> With speare in hand and sword by sides
>   To beare off afterclappes ;
> With jackettes long and large,
>   Which shroud simplicitie,
> Though spiteful dartes which they do beare,
>   Importe iniquitie ;
> Their shirtes be very strange
>   Not reaching past the thigh,
> With pleates on pleates they pleated are
>   As thick as pleates may lie ;
> Whose sleives hang trailing downe
>   Almost unto the shoe[12],
> And with a mantle commonlie
>   The Irish kerne doe goe ;

[11] Camden, Hist. Eliz. p. 69.

[12] The long sleeve to the shirt or tunic " trailing down almost
unto the shoe," while the body of the garment was so short and
fully plaited, was a European fashion of the close of the fourteenth
century, and if not adopted from the English in Richard II.'s time,
reached Ireland from Spain. The old Celtic tunic had sleeves
tight to the wrists.

Irish of the reign of Elizabeth, from a rare print in the collection of the late Mr. Douce.

DRAVN AFTER THE QVICKE

> And some amongst the rest
> Do use another wede,
> A coate I wene of strange device,
> Which fancie first did breed;
> His skirtes be very shorte,
> With pleates set thick about,
> And Irish trouzes more to put
> Their straunge protractours out."

Now on referring to the print we have mentioned, and which is superinscribed, "Draun after the quicke," (that is) from the life, we find the full-plaited shirts with *long trailing* sleeves; the short coat or jacket with *half sleeves*, very short waisted, *embroidered*, and "with pleates set thick about" the middle; the iron gauntlet, on the left hand, mentioned by Stanihurst[18]; the skull-cap, the mantle, the skein or long dagger, and a peculiarly-shaped sword in as strange a sheath, which corresponds exactly with those upon the tombs of the Irish kings, engraved in Walker's History. The only variation from the descriptions quoted is in their being all bare-legged and bare-footed.

From these accounts we find the Irish of the fourteenth and sixteenth centuries wearing the mantle and hood or capuchium, the tunic, shirt or "phallings," and occasionally the truis or breeches and stockings in one piece, exactly as described by Giraldus in the twelfth century; still armed with the terrible hatchet received from the Ostmen, and the coat of mail adopted from them or their Norman kindred; while England with the rest of Europe had exchanged the hauberk for harness of plate, and ran through every variety of habit which the ingenuity or folly of man had devised during four hundred years.

THE SEVENTEENTH CENTURY

brings the pencil once more to the aid of the pen.
[13] 41, 42, sub anno 1584.

Archer, a Jesuit, and O'More, an Irish Chief, from Walker's Hist.

Mr. Walker has engraved what he terms "a rude but faithful delineation of O'More, a turbulent Irish chieftain, and Archer, a Jesuit retained by him, both copied from a map of the taking of the Earl of Ormond in 1600." O'More, he tells us, is dressed in the barrad, or Irish conical cap, and a scarlet mantle. Archer's mantle is black, and he wears the high-crowned hat of the time. Both appear to be in the strait truis.

Morryson, a writer of the reign of the James I., describes elaborately but coarsely the dress of the Irish in his time. The English fashions, it would appear from him, had amalgamated with the Irish amongst the higher orders, and produced a costume differing not very widely from that of similar classes in England; but "touching the meare or wild Irish

it may truly be said of them, which of old was
spoken of the Germans, namely, that they wander
slovenly and naked, and lodge in the same house (if
it may be called a house) with their beasts.   Amongst
them the gentlemen or lords of counties wear close
breeches and stockings of the same piece of cloth, of
red or such light colour, and a loose coat and a cloak
or three-cornered mantle, commonly of coarse light
stuffe made at home, and their linen is coarse and
slovenly, because they seldom put off a shirt till it be
worn ; and those shirts in our memory, before the
last rebellion, were made of some twenty or thirty
elles, folded in wrinkles and coloured with safron.   .
. . . Their wives, living among the English,
are attired in a sluttish gown to be fastened at the
breast with a lace, and in a more sluttish mantle and
more sluttish linen, and their] heads be covered after
the Turkish manner with many elles of linen, only
the Turkish heads or turbans are round at the top;
but the attire of the Irish women's heads is more flat
in the top and broader in the sides, not much unlike
a cheese mot if it had a hole to put in the head. For
the rest in the remote parts, where the English lawes
and manners are unknown, the very chiefs of the
Irish, as well men as women, goe naked in winter
time."

Speed, who wrote in the same reign, and confirms
the account of Spenser and Morryson respecting the
large wide-sleeved linen shirts, stained with saffron,
their mantles, skeins, &c., adds, " that the women wore
their haire plaited in a curious manner, hanging
down their backs and shoulders from under the
folden wreathes of fine linen rolled about their heads:
a custom in England as ancient as the Conquest, and
though not mentioned by Giraldus, a fashion we have
little doubt of equal antiquity in Ireland."   Engravings of a wild Irish man and woman, of a civil Irish

man and woman, and of an Irish gentleman and
gentlewoman, are here given from the figures round
Speed's map of Ireland[14].

Wild Irish man and woman ; civil Irish man and woman, from Speed's
Map of Ireland.

It was in the reign of James I., says Mr. Walker,
that the Irish dress was to feel the influence of fashion,
and to assume a new form. The circuits of the
judges being now no longer confined within the narrow limits of the pale, but embracing the whole kingdom, the civil assemblies at the assizes and sessions
reclaimed the Irish from their wildness, caused them

[14] Like the Highland figures in the Scotch map, they may be
but the fanciful representations of an artist, or carelessly drawn
from the description only of the writers of the time. The long-
hanging shirt sleeves are certainly not visible.

Irish gentleman and woman, from Speed's Map of Ireland.

to cut off their glibbs and long hair, to convert their mantles into cloaks (as then worn in England), and to conform themselves to the manner of England in all their behaviour and outward forms. The order from the Lord Deputy Chichester, in his instructions to the Lord President and Council of Munster, to punish by fine and imprisonment all such as shall appear before them in mantles and robes, and also to expel and cut all glibbs, is dated May 20th, 1615.

For some years this statute was rigorously enforced, but Charles I. in the tenth year of his reign caused an act to be passed at Dublin, "for repeale of divers statutes heretofore enacted in this kingdom of Ireland," and once more permitted the beard to flourish on the upper lip, allowed the use of gilt bridles, peytrels, and other harness, and left the

Irish generally at liberty to wear either their own national apparel, or the English dress of the day, as might suit their fancy or convenience.

The periwig found its way to Ireland in Cromwell's time, and the first person who wore it is said to have been a Mr. Edmund O'Dwyer, who lost his estate by joining in the opposition to the parliamentary forces. He was known amongst the vulgar by the appellation of " Edmund of the wig."

During the Commonwealth an order was issued by the Deputy Governor of Galway, grounded on the old statute of Henry VIII. and prohibiting the wearing of the mantle to all people whatsoever, which was executed with great rigour; and Harris says, " from that time the mantle and trouze were disused for the most part."

Sir Henry Piers also, in his description of the county of Westmeath, about this period, says, " there is now no more appearance of the Irish cap, mantle, and trouzes, at least in these countries."

That they were worn, however, to a much later period in some provinces, we gather from the letter of Richard Geoghegan, Esq., of Connaught, to Mr. Walker, who has published an extract from it in a note to his work. " I have heard my father say," writes Mr. Geoghegan, " that he remembered some male peasants to wear a truis, or piece of knit apparel, that served for breeches and stockings; a barraid or skull-cap, made of ordinary rags, was the ornament of the head ; a *hatted* man was deemed a Sassanagh (Saxon) *beau*. Brogue-uirleaker, that is, flats made of untanned leather, graced their feet, and stockings were deemed a foppery;" and in an earlier part of his letter, speaking of the dress of the female peasantry of Connaught, he says, " long blue mantles in the Spanish style, bare feet, awkward binnogues or kerchiefs on their heads (generally spotted with soot), and madder-red petticoats, were and *are* the prevalent taste of the *ladies*."

It will be obvious from the above extracts that from the earliest notice of Ireland to a late period in the last century, the national dress was handed down from generation to generation amongst the peasantry; and that many noblemen and gentlemen wore it within the last two hundred years. Persecution, as usual, but attached them more strongly to the prohibited garb, and it is probable that the free exercise of their fancy granted to them by Charles I. conduced more to the ultimate neglect of the long-cherished costume of their ancestors than the peremptory order to abandon it, issued by the officer of Cromwell, or even the exhortations of the Romish clergy to that effect, which are acknowledged to have been of little avail. Certain it is that the Lord Deputy's court at Dublin was in Charles's reign distinguished for its magnificence; the peers of the realm, the clergy, and the nobility and gentry attending it being arrayed of their own free will in robes of scarlet and purple velvet, and other rich habiliments, after the English fashion.

THE END.